*Higher Education Policy Series 39*

# European Dimensions
## Education, Training and the European Union

John Field

Jessica Kingsley Publishers
London and Philadelphia

First published in the United Kingdom in 1998 by
Jessica Kingsley Publishers Ltd
116 Pentonville Road
London N1 9JB, England
and
1900 Frost Road, Suite 101
Bristol, PA 19007, U S A

**Library of Congress Cataloging in Publication Data**

A CIP catalogue record for this book is available from the Library of Congress

**British Library Cataloguing in Publication Data**

A CIP catalogue record for this book is available from the British Library

ISBN 1 85302 432 5

Printed and Bound in Great Britain by
Athenaeum Press, Gateshead, Tyne and Wear

# Contents

# Acknowledgements

Many people have helped me complete this book. I benefited from the comments of students on the Master in Education at the University of Ulster and undergraduates in the Faculty of Education at the Friedrich-Schiller-Universität Jena. There was much constructive advice from participants in the 1995 conference of the Society for Research in Higher Education and a 1996 seminar arranged as part of the Economic and Social Research Council's Learning Society Programme. Many people freely gave interviews; although they must remain anonymous, I am enormously grateful to them. The staff of the European Commission's Belfast office were unfailingly both happy and helpful. As always, I am indebted to Jane Field, who read the manuscript and made numerous critical, helpful comments. Others whom I would like to thank for sharing their understanding of the European Union and its human resources policies are Kevin Fearon, Martha Friedenthal-Haase, Tracey Griffin, Miezyslaw Malewski, Colin Mellors, Jill Preston, Rosalind Pritchard and Peader Shanahan.

John Field
Carrickfergus
February 1997

# Foreword

European integration is influencing the daily lives of Europeans to an extent barely dreamed of when the Common Market was created. This book's main concern is with the nature and impact of the European Union's policies on education and training – an area that was not originally regarded as any of the Common Market's business but which is now repeatedly said by Europe's leading policy makers to be of central and urgent interest. As an actor in the field of education and training policy, the European Union (EU) is a relative newcomer. It is not yet a powerful one, but by the mid-1990s it possessed an agenda for education and training which was radical and far-reaching and which stretched way beyond the formal limits to its powers. How did this come about and how has it affected the world of teaching and learning? Above all, why has it happened – and where are the forces which have taken us this far leading?

A growing literature is addressing these questions, but much of it is highly specialised. Most of it can be found in scholarly journals or professional publications of various kinds. Ronald Sultana estimates that in the decade up to 1994 something like one hundred papers on the theme of education and the EU had appeared in refereed journals in English, French and Italian together. He also claims that much of it 'has been marked by an uncritical acceptance of the goals and processes of European unification, and an approbation of the presumed implications of these for educational practice' (Sultana 1995, p.116). We might add that there are also plenty of European policy briefings aimed at busy educational managers and others who want practical advice or background to help inform funding applications. Naturally, I think that the best of these are my own (Field 1994; Field 1995a). The present book is, though, rather different. It does not merely summarise, though I hope that readers still find it useful; it is certainly not uncritical, though I hope that it is constructive.

The purpose of this book is to examine critically the formation of the Union's policies, assess their impact and place them in a wider analytical context – that of globalisation. As a supra-national agent, the EU represents an attempt to maintain (western) Europe's relative position at a time of intensified world competition. As globalisation threatens the established position of the advanced capitalist nations – leading to a massive restructuring of the economy and bringing about unprecedented juxtapositions of local and national cultures – so the issue of competitiveness rises to the top of the agenda, pulling after it a series of linked policy issues – including that of human resources. The fast-moving, turbulent and unpredictable nature of late modern societies has, in turn, required the EU repeatedly to encroach upon the sovereignty of its member states – a tendency which is well represented in the field of education and training policy.

Any reader who concludes from this that I am sympathetic to the English 'Eurosceptics' is wrong. While I share the Eurosceptics' belief that the Union's institutions seek generally to increase their sovereignty at the expense of the member states, I hope that this book neither endorses nor expresses nationalism of any variety; nor do I share the Eurosceptics' fears over social cohesion and environmental regulation. If anything, I believe that the EU is too modest in both respects, its preference for the lowest common denominator reflecting the member states' anxieties about their vulnerability in the face of more ruthless and less ecologically-minded competitors. Nevertheless, I do not share the assumption that the European Union, and, more particularly, its involvement in education and training, is essentially and invariably benign. If some form of supra-national co-ordination is probably inevitable in a Europe which is visibly disoriented and worried by its future, then we must study the EU every bit as critically as we would examine our own government's performance.

Finally, a word on terminology and language. As a supra-national actor, the EU has a bit of a language problem, starting with its own name. My preference throughout this book has been to use the term 'European Union', other than in direct quotes when an earlier expression was used. On its creation in 1957 it was called the European Economic Community (or, more colloquially, the Common Market). From 1967, when the EEC's Commission merged with the executives of the European Coal and Steel Community and the European Atomic Energy Authority, it was frequently known as the EC. With the

Treaty on European Union (ratified in 1993), it formally became the European Union. Somewhat confusingly, the Union's own institutions still use the term 'the Community' for many purposes. I have opted for consistency, in the hope that this will suit most readers.

Other language difficulties include the heavy layer of acronyms which cover much Union business and the use of specialised terminology. The acronyms may be annoying but the full (and often convoluted) names of the EU's many programmes are even worse. I have explained each acronym on its first use; they are also explained in a glossary at the end of the book. One specialist term that recurs throughout the book is 'competence', which is used in a legal sense to denote a power, or area of decision making, which has been specifically given to the Union or specifically reserved to the member states. It is related, in turn, to the notion of 'subsidiarity', described in 1993 as a 'key concept for the process of European integration' (Hrbek 1994, p.11). A general principle which is enshrined in the Treaty on European Union with the express intention of underpinning the rights of the member states, subsidiarity is best summarised as the desire that decisions should be taken at the lowest level of government at which the desired goals may be best achieved. Like many other pieces of Eurospeak, these terms belong to a class of English expressions which, as one Commission official told me, 'sound better in French' (Interview November 1996). Native English-speakers, who have never worried too much about imposing their own language on others, should not become too excited over this process.

Chapter One

# The European Dimension
# and the Global Context

The wider world is bursting in on education and training as never before. This book deals primarily with recent developments within the European Union. The precise functions and powers of the Union are hotly debated and, as the Union represents an uneasy balance between national sovereignty and shared powers, its influence is likely to remain controversial for the foreseeable future. However, from the outset its chief goal has always been to secure western European prosperity by creating a common market for goods, services, capital and labour, culminating in the creation of a single currency. Inevitably, the Union's remit has strayed well beyond these relatively narrow economic boundaries, and encompassed a broad field of social, cultural and even security policies. Education and training are among those areas where the Union now claims an important degree of competence; judging by its public statements on education and training, the Union's leaders believe that this is an area of considerable importance to Europe's future. The central questions that this book tries to tackle are, therefore, how the EU has acquired its powers in the fields of education and training, how it makes use of those powers to develop its policies and programmes and what, on balance, appears to have happened as a result.

I see the Union's growth as closely related to the wider process of globalisation. On the one hand, the Union has itself become a globalising influence, requiring individual nation states to cede decision-making powers to executive and legislative bodies that can override national sovereignty and creating an environment where there is a tangible pay-off to local or national actors such as schools or colleges or professional institutes who join transnational coalitions and institutions. At the same time, the Union coexists with, sometimes supports and may even reinforce local and national networks and policy making institutions. Some argue, for instance, that the EU provides a framework within which the smaller nations – including those that lack the trappings of statehood, like Scotland – can survive, and perhaps flourish, at the expense of their larger, and traditionally dominant, neighbours (W.E. Paterson 1994). Anthony Giddens (1994) argues persuasively that globalisation can be compatible with powerful local cultures and institutions; what counts is that globalising influences mean that we no longer look at our local habits and relationships in the same old unquestioning way as before. One way of illustrating this point is to consider the way in which we are now much more aware than before of the differences between our own education and training system and that of other countries. International research into schools' effectiveness hits the headlines. Quite a few people have now heard of the 'dual system' of vocational training combined with work-based learning or know of the Japanese expression 'Kaizen' as shorthand for permanent learning in the workplace or have some notion of the American 'Headstart' programmes for early-years children in disadvantaged areas.

Often our knowledge of other systems is extremely selective. Of course, this might be because we are usually interested in finding something that provides a standard against which we can re-examine our own arrangements for teaching and learning. Or it might just arise from ignorance, caused, perhaps, by the difficulty of obtaining reliable information in a language we understand (a gap that EU publications and networks have done a great deal to overcome in the last two decades). As will be confirmed in Chapter Four, education and training have achieved a great deal in recent years in integrating and promoting a European dimension in the curriculum. But this does not in itself necessarily imply that education and training systems across Europe will converge. Any globalising tendencies are always subjected to local circumstances, reworked in the light of local practices and realised by men and women who already have an established complex of relationships and belief systems in place. Clearly, this applies to the EU's interests in education and training. European societies all possess existing systems with their roots deep in their national histories; national governments often find it difficult to bring about change and we should expect initiatives from a remote and unfamiliar Directorate General to have a limited impact, as compared with more immediate and powerful masters such as national education ministries. Yet if it is important not to exaggerate the Union's influence, it is no longer impossible to ignore it completely.


## Learning in a wider world

No education system has ever been completely shut off from outside influences, of course. Indeed, the association of education with a particular nation state is itself a comparatively recent development, dating back, essentially, to the period of the Englightenment, the French Revolution and the Industrial Revolution. Even then, during the late nineteenth century, often seen as the high point of nation-state creation in the western societies and their colonies, people interested in building a national education system took a very active interest in what was going on elsewhere. Geography matured as a central element in the school curriculum. Colonial administrators, whether in Sierra Leone, Silesia or Ireland, invariably looked to the mother country for inspiration (Adick 1992). British government reports gave space to descriptions of education and craft training in Germany, France or America. African, Czech and Irish nationalists looked abroad for inspiring examples of how the schooling and training of young people might help strengthen national culture and foster economic independence.

In education and training the most important modernising tendencies have always been international in nature. The best example of this trend is, perhaps, the creation of the modern education and training system itself: despite very significant variations, the institutions and content of education and training are remarkably similar across a range of countries that are otherwise notable mainly for their diversity. But why, particularly, should we spend time and effort considering the education and training policies of the European Union? Is there anything new and noteworthy in what often seem to be a scatter of seemingly unrelated initiatives, often known by half-comprehensible acronyms, invented and supported by a remote body that has very little presence in today's busy, crowded, noisy classroom? Surely we have heard all this before? And aren't there more pressing things to worry about?

National governments, in Europe at least, continue to play a considerably more important role in education and training policy than any inter-governmental body. What is more, for every inter-governmental body that is growing in power and influence, like the EU, others – UNESCO is an obvious example – are becoming increasingly marginal and irrelevant. Teachers and trainers are also constantly brought up against local realities; families, local youth cultures, churches, local political structures, neighbourhood influences and the job market all have to be taken into account. Yet it is precisely where these local cultures and structures come into play with globalisation that we can see important changes. These changes will continue to reshape the way in which we identify our learning challenges and try to meet them for some time to come. The European Union is one of the most powerful of these arenas; its trials and troubles and achievements all represent a concerted attempt to mobilise and co-ordinate a balance of local, national and transnational resources in the face of increasing globalisation.

We live in a world where globalising tendencies are increasingly visible and influential. For western Europeans, and, to an extent, for central and eastern Europeans as well, the process of European integration is one of the most decisive symptoms of globalisation. It is a powerful force in the reworking of the nation state, at least among its own members, and a growing influence on nations to its eastern and southern borders. The EU often presents itself, and with some justification, as a brake on the globalisation process: only by banding together, the argument runs, can we Europeans remain key players in the next century. These processes are complex and their outcomes remain uncertain. Yet the implications are already so far-reaching that it would be astounding if education were not to be affected by them.

Education and training, far from being a safe haven protected by the classroom walls, occupy an exposed position on the front line. Education and training are, after all, strongly bound up with our sense of who we are: we want young people to learn, not solely how to read, write and labour, but also to be good neighbours and loyal workers. Our definitions of education and training – and of schools above all – are largely framed in the context of the nation state. Sometimes these connections are explicit, as in France where the creation of French citizens is not just widely regarded as a sensible thing for schools to do but is also a statutory constitutional requirement. In some countries teachers are treated as civil servants, engaged on the nation's behalf to do the nation's bidding. In virtually all nations where the curriculum is centrally regulated, and in most where it is not, the content in several subjects – particularly languages, history and literature – is designed to provide a formation in the national identity. Public spending on education and training is usually justified by their contribution to the national good: it helps maintain our culture and boost our productivity. This is commonplace. Why question it?

Globalisation matters because it poses an explosive challenge to these widely-held beliefs about why our education and training systems exist. After all, education and training arose as part of the nation state and are largely regulated, planned and financed by the nation state. Yet many now believe that 'the international economy has outgrown the political, economic and intellectual resources of the nation state' (Avis *et al.* 1996, p.2). That is to say, international economic forces cannot be controlled any longer by a single nation; the vulnerability of sterling in the early 1990s is often cited as an example of the way in which international financial exchanges are now beyond the control of single nations. Similarly, multi-national corporations are often regarded as being beyond the reach of the nation state since, if conditions become intolerable in one jurisdiction, they are able to pull up their roots and go elsewhere. Within the European Union this explosive challenge to the nation state's capacities has become increasingly explicit as education and training have come towards the forefront of the integrationist agenda.

This has been a rather uneven process. Vocational training was the first to be considered a legitimate matter of European concern; it featured in the original Treaty of Rome in 1957, where it was closely tied to the basic aims of creating a common market for goods, services, capital and labour. Education, by contrast, did not feature in the Treaty of Rome at all and was, therefore, strictly none of the EU's business until 1992 when the Treaty on European Union (more widely known as the Maastricht Treaty) devoted an article to educational issues. This did not stop either the Commission or the Council of Ministers from becoming involved in educational issues; well before 1992 the EU had both a policy on education and a wide range of action programmes. The Union is continuing to seek further competences in both education and vocational training and all the evidence of past experience suggests that it will probably be successful.

Much of this has limited relevance in most classrooms, lecture theatres and workshops. It still sounds like high policy settled in smart restaurants and sealed in flag-decked chambers and celebrated in conference halls. Certainly that dichotomy between policy and practice is real, if hardly unique – it doesn't stop us from paying attention to the policies of our own government, for a start. Nevertheless, we can still speak of a remarkable process of Europeanisation in education and training. After all, the EU directly influences the shape and coverage of much vocational training: since the European Structural Funds are used to subsidise training for the unemployed in every member state, as well as for some categories of employee, it is European regulations – and not British, Danish or Greek decisions – which determine the structure and principles of eligibility of most national or regional training programmes. In education, and in vocational training, the Union has provided incentive measures to promote transnational partnerships: European student and teacher exchange programmes are now a normal feature of university life and are increasingly common in vocational training institutes and thousands of Europe's firms have joined transnational training partnerships sponsored by the EU. The European dimension is being built into the national curriculum in several countries and is an influence on teaching content in others. Museums, voluntary bodies, broadcasters and educational researchers are all to be found in European networks, pursuing activities that reflect current EU policies. Increasingly, then, our education and training systems are being asked to function in a wider, more European world.

## Where is Europe?

But where did Europe come from? How did the continent become transformed into a geo-political entity? And how do our ideas of Europe relate to the formal institutions of education? This apparently elderly continent is, in fact, younger than it appears: the idea of Europe as a clearly-defined entity derives, effectively, from the nineteenth century, while the language of a European domain only came to be widely used in the fifteenth century – usually in contradistinction to the domain of the Osman Turks (Boer 1993). The phrase 'European civilisation' was, reportedly, first aired in 1766 in a work on the North American colonies, as part of an argument in favour of turning the natives into good Frenchmen and women (Boer 1993). The idea of Europe thus arose from an earlier geo-political conception, that of Christendom, and was articulated in opposition to a non-Christian – and, increasingly, 'non-civilised' – external world.

Does all this matter? I think it does. First, European politicians are themselves fond of appealing to the positive values of European civilisation (Brine 1995; Wilterdink 1993). They do so, as one might expect, in a somewhat selective manner, but that is not the point I wish to emphasise now. At this stage it is important to note that the ideas which led to the Treaty of Rome were born during the Second World War and in the immediate post-war years, a period in which politicians from the victorious European powers were canvassing the possibilities of a 'third way', independent of a necessary but somewhat unreliable and, for some, unappealing ally in the USA and also in opposition to an increasingly menacing Soviet Union (Urwin 1995). One attraction of positively emphasising European civilisation as a unifying force for the 'third way' was that it offered the prospect of integrating post-war Germany into a wider negotiated coalition of western European nations. If the idea of a European civilisation was a magnet, though, it also represented a polar opposite to the twin barbarisms of Nazism and the USSR, as well as drawing attention to Europe's cultural distinctiveness from its American ally. Education and training have played a central part in this discursive construction of the European Union.

The second reason why the idea of a European civilisation matters is that its history is bound up so closely with the emergence of what is recognisably the modern European education system. More than that, educational institutions played an active and formative role in shaping the idea of a Christian, civilised and learned community. Universities in medieval Europe were themselves the offspring of the Christian church, its authority centering on Rome but with important theological and scholarly outposts throughout Christendom. As universities were few and scattered, it was normal for their students (and teachers) to travel in pursuit of their studies and to move from one set of teachers to another –

a pattern of purposeful wandering that became institutionalised
in the medieval *peregrinatio academica*, which, in turn, helped to
spread and develop the scientific and humanistic ideas of the
fifteenth and sixteenth centuries (Corradi 1988). By the seven-
teenth century, following the Reformation, the university system
split on a confessional basis: some universities were associated
with counter-Reformation Catholicism and some with Protestantism, while some tolerated a number of different perspectives.
Leiden, the largest international centre of Protestantism, counted
itself a tolerant institution; foreign students rose, at times, to 50 per
cent of the total (Corradi 1988). Humanism had a similarly powerful influence on European education, helping to establish a
classical education which covered and was, at least partly, taught
in the classical languages and which helped embed a particular
definition of European civilisation as tracing its lineage back to
the cradle of Greek antiquity (Wilterdink 1993). A desire to lay
claim to this inheritance is evident in the EU's choice of titles for
its educational action programmes – in adopting the names of
SOCRATES, ARION, ERASMUS, COMENIUS and LEONARDO
DA VINCI, the Union was consciously emphasising the continuity
of the European cultural inheritance. Similarly, when the member
states selected Florence as the home of the European University
Institute, the choice of site was itself an appeal to the humanistic
tradition (Kreher 1996). Of course, this is largely a symbolic ges-
ture: it represents an attempt to devise emblems of a common
European citizenship, sometimes without looking too closely into
their provenance. Some may find it rather ironical that the EU is
commemorating the philosophical greats in a period when
educational philosophy has largely been expelled from the
curriculum for apprentice teachers. As we shall see, the EU's
action programmes are relentlessly vocational, utilitarian and
instrumental in their emphasis, sharing the tendency towards the
'technological option' which characterises so many other EU policies and activities (Szerszynski, Lash and Wynne 1996). Yet the
Union has pursued the 'technological option' while emphasising,
through its symbolism, its attachment to the humanistic tradition
of education. This tension between instrumentalism and humanism has dogged the EU's human resources policies since their
genesis, just as it has characterised a wider and continuing conflict
within European educational thinking.

The third reason why this inheritance matters is that Europe's colonial expansion ensured that its institutions and values were superimposed on non-European societies. The idea and institution of the school, though it had its origins in the Middle East, spread across the globe in the last two centuries as an element of a modern world system which was dominated by European conceptions of teaching and learning. In planter societies, such as Australia and America, the language of educational institutions harked back to a classical Europe of the distant past: a Lyceum or an Athenaeum could be found across the new world. In the colonised regions of the world, the European model had to adapt to and co-exist with established institutionalised forms for socialising the young (Adick 1992).

Europe's sense of itself is grounded in its nations' histories. In reality, those national histories sit uneasily with one another; it does not require a leap of the imagination to see that the citizens of Denmark, Germany, Austria, Italy, Greece, Finland, Sweden, Britain, Ireland, Belgium, France, Portugal, Spain and the Netherlands must interpret the history of the twentieth century in very different ways. In one way we could view the Union as an heroic attempt to break with Europe's quarrelsome past and create something new. It is true that, as Nico Wilterdink (1993) has pointed out, 'The concept of European unity did not become politically important until Europe's position in the world was no longer one of dominance' (p.125). And yet, in important ways, the EU's leaders see themselves as helping to build a new civic identity in the old continent. If Europe's sense of itself has always been constructed in relation to other non-European cultures, then the Union, as an attempt to construct a new order with its own sense of itself, is designed to protect its citizens from more successful, more innovative competitors in the shape of Japan, the USA and the nations of the Pacific Rim.

## Globalisation and the Europeans

Globalisation has deeply affected all industrial societies since the 1970s. An explosive combination of rapidly developing communications with dramatic expansion in international competition in the world's markets had clearly led to a relocation of economic decision making. But globalisation has also affected our culture. It isn't just that, as many people will tell you, the world today is becoming a smaller place, though, like all clichés, this does point to an important aspect of daily reality. My own daily life, to take an example close to home, is a tapestry of international influences: I live in Ireland, drive a Malaysian car, have a Dutch sound system, watch American movies and enjoy Indian – or, more accurately, Pakistani – food and my younger son follows the fortunes of Manchester United – a club with barely one English player. Like most people, I could go on to offer plenty of other examples. Some of the more popular signifiers are drawn from the new information technologies, particularly as they affect our leisure and business behaviour: the Internet has become a symbol of high modernity itself. Other signifiers come from our new awareness of environmental interconnections: the image of a blue and green planet moving through space is matched by new fashions in tourism and trading which bring diverse ethnic cultures into every shopping centre. Globalising tendencies have offered us a new iconography, broadcast through the media and occupying a central place in the discourse of hypermodernity.

Hype to one side, globalisation encompasses two broad tendencies that are central to the argument of this book. First, conventionally, it is widely used to describe the way in which the world's trading and manufacturing activities are woven increasingly closer together. Vincent Cable (1995), for example, defines globalisation as the tendency towards 'economic integration' across national borders, a process he ascribes to greatly reduced transport costs and improved international information flows. It follows that just being physically close to other economic resources – raw materials, innovative scientists, imaginative investors or a range of skilled labour – no longer conveys a significant competitive advantage over other nations. Lester Thurow (1994), previously Dean of Business at the Massachusetts Institute of Technology, addressed this topic in a lecture in London:

> The unskilled living in the first world are going to have to compete with the unskilled living in the third world, head to head... In the economy ahead, there is only one source of sustainable competitive advantage – skills. Everything else is available to everyone on a more or less equal access basis. (pp.51–2)

This diagnosis is widely held by policy makers, including many who are influential within the European Union. A recent joint report from Europe's university rectors and its major business forum argued that:

> Globalisation means that many jobs that do not add much value are exported to poorer and cheaper countries... The only way for rich countries to stay rich in the long term is to have people who are more productive – which often means that they are better educated. (Cochinaux and de Woot 1995, p.22)

Here, then, is the first consequence of globalisation for western Europe: in a ferociously competitive world market, high-cost labour inputs must rest upon high quality generating high levels of added value. The difficulty with this, of course, is that it assumes that nations elsewhere do not opt for a similar strategy. Yet the available evidence is that, particularly among the nations of the Pacific Rim, education and training are regarded as vital aspects of competitiveness (Reynolds 1995). Nothing stands still; on the contrary, globalisation means permanent insecurity.

It follows from this that governments world-wide face very similar challenges. Among these challenges there is substantial agreement among governments and inter-governmental agencies such as the World Bank or UNESCO that the raised economic significance of high quality human resources is probably the most important (Watson 1996). Yet, according to several leading globalisation theorists, the same economic processes that have created these challenges have also tended to reduce governments' abilities to find effective solutions (Avis *et al.* 1996; Cable 1995; McGrew 1992).

Mostly, governments themselves are understandably reluctant to confess to their voters that they are powerless in the face of globalising tendencies. One way out for national leaders, it seems, is to create transnational coalitions that will counterbalance the uncertainties arising from globalisation. Thus the German federal minister for education and science, Dr Jürgen Rüttgers, told a Dutch academic audience in 1996 that:

> From the viewpoint of a national government, it is striking to witness how wide a gulf is opening between globalisation and the capacity for political management. As the world is networked, so the capability of solving the world's problems

is reduced... With a united Europe, we are able to create a counter-balance.

Germany, it should be noted, is particularly vulnerable to global competition, thanks to its relatively high labour costs. One study of labour costs in 1992, undertaken by the Federal Institute of Economics, reported that the hourly labour costs for workers in South Korea were 22.6 per cent of the German levels and in Hong Kong were 16 per cent of those in Germany. Most alarming of all, those in the neighbouring Czech Republic and Poland were around 5 per cent of the German levels (*Die Zeit*, 10 September 1993). Elsewhere in Europe the debate has been more muted; the same pressures are there, different only in their degree. According to McGrew (1992), the nation state is undergoing a complex and uneven process of dissolution in at least four respects:

- it is losing competence with the erosion of traditional boundaries between 'internal' and 'external' policy areas, though this is partly counterbalanced by a wider influence outside the nation's traditional borders

- there is a growing number of international regimes and inter-governmental organisations, leading to the creation of 'transgovernmental coalitions of bureaucrats' who face similar problems and propose similar solutions

- as state autonomy is reduced, the strength of global markets grows

- citizens can see the global context of domestic problems, and it becomes more difficult to maintain the authority and legitimacy of the national government. (pp.87–91)

While it remains true that most firms remain stubbornly national in their ownership and control, and even to some extent in their markets (Ford and Coca-Cola still earn more in the USA than in the rest of the world put together), even relatively cautious observers confirm that the globalisation of economic activity is a measurable reality (Grant 1993). For smaller nations in particular, but also for those who are accustomed to behave as regional powers, regional inter-governmental groupings are, therefore, an attractive and apparently feasible vehicle for retaining some global status. Certainly this argument is widely used to justify the growing influence of the EU, which remains by far the largest and most comprehensive of the world's regionally-based economic inter-governmental organisations. It plans, moreover, to become larger still.

The economic challenges of globalisation influence much of the Commission's thinking. Indeed, so great is the concern, and so complex the challenges, that the Commission has seemingly lost interest in some of the more political and cultural aspects of European integration. Ideas of a 'people's Europe' or a 'Europe of the citizens' have given way to an emphasis on enhanced competitivity and growth in response to the fierce pressures of a new world economy. Others have pointed to the cultural aspects of globalisation: the English sociologist Anthony Giddens, for example, who defines globalisation as 'action at distance' which tends to transform space and time, emphasises that it embraces environmental risks and life-style decisions as well as the emergence of large-scale economic systems (1994, pp.4–5). Predictably, given the importance of economic policy in the EU's creation, this aspect of globalisation plays a relatively minor role within the EU's thinking. It can be discerned in aspects of broadcasting policy where the EU aims to promote European film and televisual industries for reasons of cultural autonomy rather than economic gain. It can also be seen in the attempts to develop the European educational multimedia software industry and thereby avoid the risk of further increasing American influence over the young (CEC 1996k; Riché-Magnier and Metthey 1995). Generally, though, globalisation has acted to reinforce the EU's tendency to focus on the potential economic contribution of its policies for education and training, and to regard other aspects as secondary.

## The learning challenges

How does globalisation affect education and training? Alternatively, is it simply a remote process going on somewhere 'out there' beyond the classroom? At one level, it is relatively easy to sketch out some of the educational consequences of globalisation. As one Canadian university president puts it, 'nations around the globe confront a similar educational options map' whose binding process is the growing 'social imperative of lifelong learning' (Morrison 1995, p.193). In societies that are heavily committed to economic growth and a stable or preferably rising standard of living – and that certainly encompasses every member state in the EU –

the impact was visible in the public debates over education and economic performance that followed the sudden recession of the early 1970s. British commentators usually start their account of this period with a speech by Prime Minister James Callaghan at Ruskin College in 1976, launching what became known as 'The Great Debate' about the role of schools in fostering positive attitudes towards industry among their pupils (Avis *et al.* 1996). Similar linkages between education and economic performance were being made by policy makers in a number of Western nations, as well as within the EU itself – which commissioned a report on education and training issues in 1972 (this episode is dealt with in more detail in Chapter Two).

Since the 1970s a number of national education and training systems have been more or less comprehensively restructured. In general terms, earlier liberal and humanistic conceptions of education have come under enormous pressure from those who prefer a more instrumental and vocational orientation, while a variety of organisational reforms have been undertaken in an attempt to bring the system more closely into connection with the world of employment. These broad trends are also visible within the EU itself as its development of policies for education and training has paralleled – and been conceived, in part, as a response to – the growing difficulties facing the European economies in an ever more competitive global market place.

One immediate challenge, therefore, concerns competitiveness. As new players enter the global market place for goods, services and finance, so the EU is required to identify ways of maintaining a competitive edge. If that edge can be found in Europe's 'abundant non-physical capital (education, skills, capacity for innovation, traditions)', as Jacques Delors put it in his preamble to a 1994 white paper on competitiveness, then one of the central learning challenges is that of continuously developing its stock of human capital (CEC 1994c). In the early stages of the EU's entry into this policy domain its role was a relatively limited one of helping fund measures to train the unemployed and, particularly, unemployed young people. It was also limited in the sense that the European level of intervention was confined to redistributing resources among the member states, who then managed the training programmes at local, regional or national level. In more recent years this set of learning challenges has acquired a higher profile as the competitive pressures of globalisation have intensified.

The rapid evolution of the new information and communications technologies also creates pervasive learning challenges. By now most European governments believe that everyone – or all young people, at least – should have at least a minimal grasp of the new information technologies. Increasingly, they also believe that the new technologies potentially offer a powerful and cost-effective means of delivering education and training to learners. Governments (and the EU) are rather inclined to blame teachers and trainers for being somewhat conservative in their approach to the new technologies. Education and training professionals, for the most part, appear to be perfectly happy to use certain technologies, provided that the equipment is accessible and reasonably user-friendly; broadcasting, video and now CD-ROM have all been taken up with some enthusiasm. Generally, the new technologies are welcomed by policy makers and professionals alike because of their direct relevance to the learners' employability and the competitiveness of Europe's economy. Although most policy makers and educationists still have a quite narrow perception of the new technologies, regarding them as a second-best option (if still an acceptable one for many purposes), increasingly technology-mediated teaching and learning is being taken ahead in ways which break out of conventional educational boundaries. More ambitiously still, some Union institutions have argued that technology-mediated learning and teaching have an important part to play in turning Europe into a central player in the global information society.

A rather more shadowy set of challenges arises from the uncertainty which is characteristic of globalisation. The German author Ulrich Beck (1992) has written compellingly of the ways that as knowledge creation accelerates, so our applications of knowledge – whether scientific, technological or social-scientific – tend to create unintended risks. Globalisation merely institutionalises and accelerates this trend towards risk and uncertainty, a tendency which is as evident in the money markets as in humans' influence on their natural environment. With the EU as anxiously commited as its member states to a drive for renewed growth and competitiveness, the risks of environmental depletion and degradation are particularly intense (as Delors himself acknowledged on a number of occasions, if not entirely convincingly). For many people the most obvious and distressing consequence is that their employment is insecure. If we can watch newsreels of angry strikes against redundancies not only in Sheffield and Dortmund but also in Japan and Korea, where the larger corporations felt able to guarantee workers a lifetime's employment, then our awareness of uncertainty is reinforced. If the only certainty is uncertainty and change, then education and training face demanding challenges. According to a number of influential figures, we now require a new balance between the acquisition of knowledge and skills on the one hand and the development of those capacities which enable us to replace outmoded knowledge and skills on the other (Cochinaux and de Woot 1995). Yet defining this appropriate balance is itself a risky business, beset by uncertainty, and our judgements are of course influenced by our new global awareness. Should we focus on social competence and personal adaptability? What happens to the basics – the three Rs? What about our national culture – its history, music, literature, our collective sense of place in time and space? And how about moral standards and religion, if flexibility and adaptability are the core capacities of the future?

Closely related to risk and uncertainty is the question of the welfare state. According to Delors, the 'soundness of its social model' was a significant factor in Europe's past economic success (CEC 1994c). In the same year, an EU White Paper on social policy argued that Europe's prosperity and its capacity to support social cohesion are mutually interdependent: each makes the other possible (CEC 1994a). More recent policy documents have been more pessimistic; the Comité des Sages, a group convened by the European Commission Directorate responsible for employment and social policy and consisting of established figures such as the veteran British politician Shirley Williams, noted that the welfare state was 'under threat' and accepted that 'A reformed social protection system must be more flexible, reflecting a more fragmented industrial economy subject to rapid change' (CEC 1996l, p.31). The Comité des Sages agreed with other critics that a globalised universe poses a direct challenge to the virtuous circle of Europe's social model, placing welfare systems under financial constraints and bringing to an end the long period of full employment that made Western welfare systems briefly sustainable. Several of the EU's leaders have argued that education and training can make a helpful contribution towards the maintenance of the European social model since they represent active rather than passive welfare measures: that is, instead of financing welfare dependency, it is preferable to support measures which build the capacity of the excluded individual or community.

In its White Paper on competitiveness, in an analysis accepted by the Council in its Essen meeting, the Commission placed human resources at the centre of its objective of job-creating growth (CEC 1994c). Indirectly, though, welfare systems are also undermined by the way in which individual lifestyles and life cycles become more fluid and reflexive in a globalised order of things (Giddens 1994). This would seem to pose rather sharper challenges to the European social model, which rests on an earlier notion of universal citizenship, than those identified so far by the EU institutions (see Chapter Six). This brings us to the next area of challenge, that of citizenship.

Citizenship, or membership of the wider national society, has been seen as a focus of education since the nineteenth century. This linkage is increasingly strained by globalisation. The origins of many modern education systems lie in the eighteenth- and nineteenth-century struggles over democratic participation, whose success brought about a concern to build a body of educated citizens who could share in the government of the nation. This helps explain the important relationship which persists between the nation state and its system for educating and training the young. How should we educate citizens in a globalising society, where national frontiers become ever more irrelevant to many important decisions and a specific linkage between citizenship and a single national state appears to be anachronistic and ineffective (Turner 1990)? Conceptions of a wider European citizenship that embraces Scottishness or Irishness or Danishness and a more continental identity are expressed, albeit rather limited and perhaps superficial, in the way that some individuals now describe themselves and their identities (Wilterdink 1993). More formally, the Union has enshrined the concept of citizenship into the Treaty on European Union, building on earlier discussions of the idea in the 1980s (Closa 1992). Unsurprisingly in view of the history of national education and training systems, the discussion in the Union has been closely linked with its development of policies in these areas.

Finally, globalisation poses cultural challenges. In many ways these are, perhaps, the most profound consequences of globalisation. Giddens (1994) has described the way in which 'Globalising influences have been directly bound up with far-reaching changes happening in the tissue of social life' (p.42), affecting the way that we understand our own individual identity and our most intimate relationships with others. Some of these changes seem more fundamental than others but even such relatively superficial issues as the quality of children's television have become the subject of controversy. David Reynolds (1995), a director of the international schools' effectiveness research project, has identified the anti-educational influence of American cartoons such as *The Simpsons* or *Beavis and Butthead* as helping bring down the standard of schooling in Britain. Cultural policy generally is rather weakly developed within the EU; in so far as it does exist, it is largely focused on the deregulation of broadcasting and telecommunications services with a small number of cultural heritage action programmes on the margins (Venturelli 1993). Nevertheless, the EU has adopted some of the trappings of a nation state (a flag and anthem and so on), its political leaders have advocated the virtues of 'a Citizen's Europe' and some of its leading education and training policy makers have commented on what they see as the threat of American cultural influence over such areas as broadcasting and educational software design (Riché-Magnier and Metthey 1995; Schuringa 1988).

If globalisation helps us place the EU in a wider context, its consequences are nevertheless very uneven. In sectoral terms we could expect that the impact will be different for universities than for primary schools, different for training in large multi-national companies than for people in small firms or on schemes for the unemployed and different for open and distance learning and the classroom-based variety. All of this mirrors the broader unevenness of globalisation and its impact upon our lives. However, just as none of us are untouched by globalisation in our daily lives, though the impact may differ, so no form of education and training is unaffected by the challenges of globalisation. In many fields tendencies towards an international role for education and training are already quite advanced; in others, globalisation has prompted a return to older values and behaviour, as in the calls for greater attention to the high points of national history in the schools' curricula. If the challenges of globalisation are uneven, and often unexpected, they have nonetheless proven surprisingly pervasive.

## Decision making in the EU

Globalisating tendencies have, in turn, disrupted existing inter-governmental institutions and helped create new ones. Because they are relatively new and reflect compromises arising from a series of sometimes conflicting pressures, those institutions do not have the legitimacy that is usually available to the institutions of the nation state. In particular, they must depend upon their nation-state members to provide what the nineteenth century English constitutional expert Walter Bagehot called the 'dignified' part of government: the European Commission is rather short on bear-skins, coaches and palaces but long on committees and procedures. As a relatively new supra-national organisation, yet one which has acquired real power, the EU has had to evolve a set of institutions which allow for extensive consultation and compromise before any decision can be taken and which may then implement those decisions across all the member states – each of which has its own national arrangements for any particular field of policy. Hussein Kassim has described the Union's decision making system as:

> ...characterised by a high degree of flexibility, fluidity and improvisation. Decisions are taken in a range of different and constantly changing institutional settings and at different levels, their locus itself often being the subject of negotiation and compromise. Coalitions between institutions and inter-est groups tend to be short-lived and shifting. (1996, p.20)

In reality, then, even in a field where the decision-making proce-dures are clearly outlined in an agreed Treaty (education and vocational training are such an area), policy making follows a complicated pathway.

At any rate, it is probably helpful at this stage to provide a brief description of the decision making institutions in the EU. Four organisations have particular importance: the European Commis-sion, the Council of Ministers, the European Parliament and the European Court of Justice. In addition, the Union has created a number of ancillary and advisory bodies, as well as a wide range of external organisations that are independent of the EU but which try to influence its decisions. Each will be briefly described in turn.

The Council consists of representatives of the governments of the member states. At its highest level (the European Council), it consists of the heads of state or government who meet at least twice yearly to formulate overall policy guidelines and to reach the more significant decisions on the Union's future. In addition, a number of specialist councils have evolved, dealing with particular policy areas and attended by the relevant government ministers (agriculture, social affairs, finance and so on). Most education and training decisions are taken either by the Education Council (before the Treaty on European Union was ratified, its sessions were formally described as 'the Council of Ministers of Education meeting within the Council') or, in respect of European Social Funds (ESF), the Social Affairs Council. The presidency of the Council circulates among the member states on a six-monthly basis.

The Council serves as the final decision making body. Since the Single European Act, many of its decisions have been taken by what is known as a 'qualified majority' – that is, it must command at least 70 per cent support. However, the Treaty on European Union allowed the Council to reach a number of its decisions on the basis of a simple majority. Even this is not entirely clear-cut, though, as all voting is on a weighted basis; the larger states (Germany, France, Italy and the UK) are counted as ten votes apiece, Spain has eight votes, and so on, with the smallest member state (Luxembourg) having two votes. In practice, ministers often delegate their powers on a week-to-week basis to civil servants, whose role in the Council of Permanent Representatives (COREPER) is particularly influential. COREPER consists of national officials of ambassadorial rank; essentially, it acts as a filter between the Council and the other institutions. In turn, it functions through specialist committees such as the Education Committee, which meets monthly and consists of national civil servants from the member states.

The Commission is the Union's executive institution. Its members are political appointees nominated by member states for five years at a time; larger member states appoint two Commissioners while smaller states name one. In 1995, then, it was agreed that there would be 20 Commissioners for 15 member states. Although the Commissioners depend on the member states for their position, in theory the Commission functions on a collegiate basis independently of the member states. It is supported by a civil service divided into 23 departments or Directorates General. DGXXII is charged specifically with implementing Union policies for education, training, human resources and youth; the Commissioner responsible for DGXXII (Antonio Ruberti in the last Commission under Delors and Edith Cresson under Santer) is also responsible for science, research and development policy. DGXXII, in turn, comprises three sections or Directorates: one for education policy, one for training policy and the third for other matters (including relations with third countries – that is, nations that do not belong to the EU). In addition, some aspects of training and education also fall into the responsibilities of several other departments. The most important of these is DGV, which handles employment, industrial relations and social affairs policies; DGV's Directorate C is responsible for the implementation of the European Social Fund and a number of related programmes within the member states.

Under the Treaties, the Commission has three main functions. First, it initiates all proposals for legislation, which it usually prepares after wide-ranging consultation with experts, specialist associations and the member states. Second, it is the 'guardian of the Treaties' and must ensure that all Union legislation is implemented by the member states. Finally, as the Union's executive body, it is required to deliver its policies. In practice, the member states administer most of the larger programmes – such as the Structural Funds. However, a growing number of activities are administered directly by the Commission or its agencies.

The Parliament has 626 members who are directly elected for a five-year term. It sits in broad party-based groupings, of which the largest are the Party of European Socialists (which includes most of the social democratic parties as well as the Labour Parties of Britain and Ireland) and the European People's Party (made up largely of Christian Democrats). It has a right to be consulted and deliver opinions on legislative proposals; in some areas it may introduce amendments (the so-called 'co-operation procedure'), while in others its agreement must be given before any legislation is approved by the Council (known as the 'co-decision procedure'). In particular, the Parliament must agree to the annual budget before it can be adopted by the Union.

Much of the Parliament's work is carried on by its standing committees. By 1996 it had 20 permanent committees, including a committee on Culture, Youth, Education and the Media; in addition, its Committee on Social Affairs and Employment had oversight of the ESF among other issues. So far, the Parliament has proven more important for its symbolism than its power. However, it has shown a willingness to engage with the Commission and Council, if need be by disrupting the Union's budgetary process, and some of its members believe that, as the only directly elected institution of the EU, the Parliament should have a greater say over policy. Certainly some lobbyists have started paying greater attention to influencing the Parliament, but whether it actually will be able to carve out an increased role for itself remains to be seen.

The European Court of Justice (ECJ) is responsible for interpreting the legal side of the Union's activities. Its 15 judges are required to give judgements on the interpretation of the treaties and other Union legislation, and on their application by member states, by the Union institutions or by other parties. As Chapter Two shows, ECJ decisions have been particularly important in the field of education and training. It should not be confused with the European Court of Human Rights, which has no formal connection with the EU. The ECJ has, since 1989, been supplemented by a preliminary chamber, the Court of First Instance.

Finally, the Union has created two consultative committees that sit alongside its own institutions, but whose members are nominated through the member states. The Economic and Social Committee (ECOSOC) is the oldest, having been established alongside the other Union institutions. It consists of representatives of employers' associations, trade unions and consumers. The Committee of the Regions (CoR) was created under the Treaty on European Union and consists of representatives of local and regional government in the member states. Under the treaties, the opinion of each committee must be considered on a number of policy issues. Thus Article 198a of the Treaty on European Union specifies that CoR must be consulted on all proposals for education, but not training, which, in some member states, is not a regional but a central responsibility. CoR has, nevertheless, created a working group on both education and training (known, confusingly, as 'Commission 6'), later requesting that it should have the same formal consultative status in respect of vocational training.

ECOSOC and CoR may also decide to give an 'own-initiative' opinion on any topic, regardless of whether or not the Commission and Council have decided to consult them. There is some rivalry between the two committees, who share premises and a common secretariat, and between the committees and the Parliament, which sees itself as the representative of Europe's citizens.

As in all major policy areas, there is also a range of lobbying groups in and around the Union. Some of these were created specifically to influence the EU's policies. Others were created to serve other purposes but undertake lobbying alongside other functions. Particularly important groups in the education and training fields include the European Round Table, an association of employers that has established close relations with a number of leading officials in the Commission, and the Conseil des Recteurs d'Europe (the committee of European university rectors), whose membership includes all the national rectors' associations as well as a high proportion of third level institutions in all of Europe, as well as some from outside. CRE increased its lobbying role significantly in the 1990s and is now consulted on all major proposals affecting the sector. Similar specialist groupings exist on the European level for a number of other professional associations, teachers' unions or other interest groups (notably the European Network of Women, which has lobbied successfully on training and education issues). In addition, many professional associations now appoint an officer or sub-committee who is responsible for European policy matters and some have permanent offices in Brussels. On the other hand, education and training is a relatively large area, and one which is diffused across several Directorates, and most of the professional bodies and other interest groups have yet to make much of an impact.

## Policy making in a global context

At first sight, the decision making structures of the EU seem complicated and cumbersome. These are certainly reasonable ways of describing the formal system but, in practice, the process is slightly more open and indeterminate than first appears. As a transnational civil service, the Commission is remarkably open to direct approaches from professional bodies and speciali‹ : associations of various kinds – partly, no doubt, because these groups can provide a much-welcomed counter-weight to the influence of the member states. More important, perhaps, is the fact that the EU is doing something new. It represents the first time that any group of states has come together freely and peaceably to adopt what is effectively a federal structure that combines elements of inter-governmentalism (co-operation between states) and transgovernmentalism (shared sovereignty over specified areas).

This process of institution building and policy forming has taken place largely in response to the challenges of globalisation. At the same time, it also represents a globalising influence in its own right. Seen in this wider context, it is possible to view the EU neither as a sinister plot to undermine national sovereignty nor as the bright star of innovative modernity but as the response of an aging continent that feels itself under threat. In many ways, globalisation continues to flow round and through the EU. Compared with the growing global influence of the USA, or the sudden springing up of the 'little dragons' of the Asian-Pacific region, the EU can sometimes seem rather puny and ineffectual.

Despite the general caution of this analysis, it is significant that at a time when more established inter-governmental agencies are declining in influence – the Council of Europe and UNESCO are good examples – the EU continues to consolidate its position at the same time as slowly expanding its membership. No other regional trading coalition (the North American Free Trade Association, the Asian Pacific Economic Conference) has devolved key legislative and judicial functions to new, shared institutions; none has evolved towards political union; none has created significant policies for areas such as education and training. For all its weaknesses and shortcomings, then, the EU has embarked upon a course that remains unique.

# Chapter Two

# Developing Policies for Education and Training 1957–1992

The history of EU policy on education and training is one of a changing balance of power between the Union and the member states. Although the EU had considerably increased its stake in, and powers over, education and training by the time that the Treaty on European Union was ratified in 1993, the outcome of this contest nevertheless remained undecided. At most of the decisive moments the member states have managed to assert their sovereignty over these fields, most notably in recent years in the context of the Maastricht Treaty itself, which appeared to be quite specific and unambiguous in identifying education and training systems as lying within the responsibilities of member states rather than the Union. In so far as the founding Treaty had referred to the area in 1957, it had been to charge the Union with some competences in the field of training while leaving education entirely in the hands of the member states. Between 1957 and 1992 every Commission proposal was faced with assertions of sovereignty by the member states, usually acting through the Council but sometimes resorting individually to legal challenges to the Union's proposals. Yet the Union's stake in this area, and the scope of its decision making, have, nevertheless, grown steadily.

The growth of the Union's interest in education and training has passed through four distinctive stages. In the period between 1957 and 1973 education and training were relatively minor interests. From 1974 to 1985 the Union showed some interest in education, but its major concern was with vocational training. From 1986 to 1992 education and training became significant areas of policy, with a stream of action programmes contributing to the steady achievement of the single market. From the ratification of the

Treaty on European Union, the EU has adopted a more radical approach seeking to promote the concept and practice of the learning society. As in a number of other areas, this process has often been incremental and uneven but the result has been a transfer of competences to the European level (Pollack 1994). This chapter traces the creeping extension of European competence in the field of education and vocational training between 1975, when the Union was created, and the debate over the Treaty on European Union in 1992.

## Education, training and the creation of the Common Market

The Treaty of Rome made virtually no reference to education and very little to vocational training. Essentially, it provided for three broad types of intervention: closer co-operation between member states, a common European policy and financial subventions to member states. Article 41, for example, allowed for co-ordination of vocational training activities within the Common Agricultural Policy, while Article 57 referred to the 'mutual recognition of diplomas, certificates and other evidence of formal qualifications' between the member states. Article 118 required the Commission to promote 'close co-operation between the member states in the social field, particularly in matters relating to...basic and advanced vocational training'. Article 123 of the Treaty required the Commission to create a European Social Fund, which was to 'have the task of rendering the employment of workers easier and of increasing their geographical and occupational mobility within the Community' (Lenaerts 1994, p.18). Finally, the most explicit statement of European competence came in Article 128, which stated that:

> The Council shall, acting on a proposal from the Commission and after consulting the Economic and Social Committee, lay down general principles for implementing a common vocational training policy capable of contributing to the harmonious development both of the national economies and of the common market.

In the field of vocational training, which was treated as an adjunct of the common economic market, the EU had quite extensive powers; in the field of education, it appeared to have none at all.

It was one thing, though, for the Treaty to give the EU powers, or competences, in respect of education and training. As might be expected, the central issue was how these powers were used. Articles 118 and 128 were very important in the long term, as we shall see, as was the new European Social Fund (ESF). Article 57 subsequently provided the basis for a number of Directives on the mutual recognition of qualifications and the Commission also decided to fund a number of studies of comparability. From the mid-1960s, aggrieved workers started to use the Article in court cases against authorities or employers who they claimed had refused to accept their qualifications. In the short term, though, the priorities of creating a common market did not include education and training.

In general, the member states remained reluctant to allow a common policy to encroach upon what they regarded as discrete and autonomous fields of national policy. National resistance was evident even in the field of vocational training, where the existence of European-level competences was indisputable though their exact scope remained ambiguous. In an effort to clear up the uncertainties over Article 128, the Council of Ministers reached a Resolution in 1963 which identified the responsibilities of member states under the Treaty of Rome as being to ensure:

- access to adequate training for all workers
- access to continued training and retraining as necessary throughout the working life
- a balanced training which combines personal development with economic and technical requirements
- a smooth transition between initial general education and vocational training
- information and guidance services for workers and young people
- suitable training for teachers and trainers, especially in the least favoured regions of the common market
- the provision of data to the Commission on the future need for workers in certain sectors of the economy.

As well as collecting these data, the Resolution identified the Commission's responsibilities as being to propose measures for implementing a common policy and to encourage exchanges between vocational training specialists (*Official Journal of the European Communities*, 2 April 1963).

Very little came of these proposals. As a newly-created institution, whose future remained uncertain, the Europe of the Six concentrated largely on economic matters: its achievements in this early period were in such areas as reducing trade tariffs, creating the European Investment bank and establishing the basis of a common agricultural policy. The one major area where nothing was done, despite the powers granted by the Treaty and the important precedent of retraining within the European Coal and Steel Community before 1957, was in setting up the Social Fund.


## The 1970s: early steps

If the Common Market's first fifteen years were spent on other matters, the early 1970s witnessed a sudden upturn of interest in education and training. A number of factors led to this development. First, a number of Europe's politicians saw education as a means of creating the new European citizens of the future. This view was particularly widespread among the generation who were directly, personally influenced by the experience of crisis and war in Europe. The idea of a European university, as a means of building a common citizenship among young people, was mooted in the mid-1950s, but little came of the idea until the early 1970s. In 1972 nine states agreed to create the European University Institute (EUI), which opened in Florence four years later as a centre for postgraduate teaching and research concentrated exclusively in the social sciences and humanities. In fact, the Institute is not an EU institution; partly because of the legal position of education in the Treaty and partly to secure the Institute's independence, it was created outside the Union's framework by agreement among the member states (Kreher 1996). As a way of creating even the élite minority of a future generation of European citizens, the EUI was too small to make a great difference; as a symbolic declaration of intent, it anticipated the stream of education programmes which flowed from the mid-1980s onwards.

If the idea of nurturing young European citizens was somewhat nebulous, growing economic uncertainty among Europe's politicians – precipitated initially by the 1973 oil crisis – proved a rather more influential factor. Most EU members depended heavily upon imported fuels and the oil shock profoundly affected their sense of economic security. Like many Western nations, the member states started to question the extent to which education and vocational training were achieving their full potential in helping sustain the levels of growth that had helped fuel the prosperity of the post-war years. Perhaps more subtle in its consequences for policy thinking, the early 1970s also witnessed a turning point in public awareness of environmental constraints upon growth. The publication in 1974 of the Club of Rome report, *Limits to Growth*, had a greater impact upon policy élites and academics than on the public more generally, but it raised for the first time in many people's minds the possibility that environmental constraints could limit economic growth in the prosperous Western nations. Policy makers' minds turned increasingly towards the role of (renewable) human resources and knowledge-based innovation and growth, rather than focusing primarily upon the manipulation of (depletable) natural resources.

Stimulated largely by these economic disturbances, the 1970s witnessed a lively international debate over the contribution of education and training towards social and economic development. This discussion was prompted by growing evidence that the massive post-war investment in primary and secondary education had done little to reduce social inequality and had made less of a contribution towards productivity and economic growth than expected. Unusually, though, the key agencies in stimulating controversy over the future of education and training were specialists working for international governmental bodies. Most notable was the group of educationists working for the Organisation for Economic Co-operation and Development (OECD), whose Centre for Educational Research and Innovation favoured a radical switch of investment away from what it described as the 'front-loading' of education into the early years towards a 'recurrent alternation' for individuals between education, work and leisure throughout their lifespan (OECD 1973). Specialists within the United Nations Educational, Social and Cultural Organisation (UNESCO) were more ambitious still, promoting a design for lifelong learning that had even more radical implications than the OECD's recurrent education. The Council of Europe, meanwhile, evolved the concept of 'education permanente' – that is, planned learning from cradle to grave. In this heated international atmosphere the Commission

asked Professor Henri Janne, a former Belgian minister of education, to formulate the first principles of a Community education
policy. Janne invited a number of educational experts to join him;
the subsequent report identified the possible scope of a policy at
European level.

At the time, the Janne report attracted relatively little attention.
It acknowledged the limited competences allowed by the Treaty,
which it saw as permitting only a piecemeal approach. Given the
economic, scientific and social policies already arising from the
Treaty, it argued, the need was now to develop a coherent strategy
with the ultimate goal of gradual harmonisation of the educational
policies of the member states. As well as the establishment of an
Educational and Cultural Council, the Community's specific responsibilities within this strategy should include promotion of
foreign languages, staff and student exchanges between schools
and universities and a pattern of lifelong learning (referred to as
'education permanente' but actually rather closer to the OECD's
recurrent education strategy) through each individual's working
life. However, the Janne report coincided with the expansion of the
Union to a membership of nine as the Republic of Ireland and the
United Kingdom were followed by Denmark into membership in
these years. Enlargement, in turn, brought new difficulties in
achieving agreement on the major issues facing the Union; the
prospects of agreeing a common education policy among the nine
member states seemed remote. Vocational training was, however,
another matter. In preparing for the entry of the three new members, the Council had agreed in 1972 that the Union should take
steps to improve the quality of life of its citizens. The chief result
was the creation of the ESF, launched in 1974 and primarily concerned with employment and retraining – especially in so far as
these were needed to redress the impact of other EU policies.

In responding to the Janne report, the Commission proposed a
Resolution to the Council on co-operation in education. In a 1974
communication on education in the European Community, the
Commission proposed a series of pilot projects to develop staff and
student exchanges at primary, secondary and third levels, special
measures to support the integration into schools of the children of
migrant workers and the encouragement of a European dimension
in education through studies of foreign language learning, provision of information and materials to support the study of Europe,

higher education co-operation and the establishment of European schools. The Commission also proposed the creation of a European Committee for Educational Co-operation. Such thinking was hardly likely to commend itself to the member states, who adopted the view that harmonisation was not an option. In rejecting the Commission proposals as the basis for a European education policy, the member states intended to act decisively to maintain education as a field where competence lay fairly and squarely at national level. This pattern was to be repeated on a number of occasions over the following decades.

The member states' response was drafted by their Ministers of Education, meeting *not* as the Education Council but as the 'Ministers of Education meeting within the Council of Ministers'. This convoluted verbal formula was designed to emphasise the EU's lack of competence in the field of education and was used to describe the formal sessions of the Education Ministers until the Treaty on European Union was finally ratified. In their lengthy Resolution of June 1974, the Ministers of Education robustly reminded the Commission that education was about far more than the economic domain and that each member state had its own policies and systems which must be respected. They therefore proposed first that any measures should take place on the legal basis of co-operation between the member states in a field where they held unquestioned authority, rather than as a formal EU measure under the terms of the Treaty of Rome. The Ministers approved the establishment of an Education Committee, comprising representatives of each member state and the Commission, to foster co-operation in seven specified areas:

- improved training and education for nationals of other member states and their children
- promotion of closer relations between the member states' education systems
- compilation of educational documentation and statistics
- increased co-operation in higher education
- improved recognition of academic diplomas
- encouragement of freedom of movement and mobility of teachers, students and research workers
- equal opportunity for free access to all levels of education. (*Official Journal of the European Communities*, C38/1, 1976).

Given the limited competences available to the EU, much of this was little more than exhortation. The 1976 Action Programme was marked by its modesty. In it the Council agreed that the Commission would organise exchanges of views and experiences between the member states, conduct pilot projects of activities which would smooth the transition from school to work for young people, provide vocational training to young workers and young unemployed persons and establish an Education Committee to bring forward future proposals.

Despite its modesty, the 1976 Action Programme was nevertheless significant. For the first time, it marked an acceptance of education as a legitimate area of policy interest for the EU; previously this was limited effectively to the establishment of 'European schools', which were to provide for the children of EU staff in Luxembourg, Brussels and Strasbourg. Organisationally, it resulted in the decision in 1981 to shift responsibility for education policy from DGXII (Research, Science and Education) to DGV (Employment and Social Affairs), which already covered vocational training; as a result, Ministers for Education joined the relevant meetings of the Council alongside their colleagues from Employment and Social Affairs ministries (Brine 1995). Moreover, the Council approved a second action programme (1982–1987) concerning the transition of young people from education to adult and working life, which, in turn, fed into the developing range of education and training action programmes in the later 1980s (OJ, 6 July 1988). Alongside this specific policy development in respect of education, the Commission also conducted a reform of its structural policies, leading to a proposal to create a European Regional Development Fund (ERDF), with the aim of tackling spatial inequalities arising from variations in the regional economies of member states (Preston 1994).

Such developments came, though, in the 1980s. Other than the creation of the ESF, little happened directly at the time in respect of training policy. Perhaps this was as much as could have been achieved at a time when the EU was coming to terms with three new members – Ireland, Denmark and the UK – where substantial numbers of the public hotly opposed the very idea of Community membership; in the case of the UK, a minority Labour government had come to power pledged to renegotiate the terms of membership. As the Janne report itself noted, it was important to allow the new members to 'assimilate the consequences of the Treaty without any interpretation which would increase intervention measures by the Community' (Janne 1973, p.18). In these circumstances, it was, perhaps, inevitable that the Commission had little desire to pursue the Janne recommendations to the full.

## 1976–1986: turning the tide

Within a decade of Janne, the Commission had lost its reticence. Swept up in the debate over the single market, education and training were carried along by the integrationist tide. By the mid-1980s the Janne agenda was superseded by a wide range of measures in education and training, complemented by increasingly ambitious policy discussions within the Commission itself. Clearly, the experience of the 1976 Action Programme was itself important. As in so many other policy areas, having established the legitimacy of its policy interest through an agreed programme of co-operative measures, the Commission then moved on to develop more ambitious ideas and proposals. We cannot help wondering about the pattern of cause and effect in this process. Did the Action Programme express a deliberate attempt to push a wedge into the crack of Article 128 or was it only after witnessing the potential of a policy at European level that the Commission developed ambitions of its own? At this date, when memories are already fading and archives are closed, we can only guess at the answer – which may well be that a mixture of both intention and reaction was at work.

Certainly, the context favoured a more active approach to policy. The oil shock of 1973 was rapidly followed by dramatic rises in unemployment levels across European society, particularly among young people. After three decades of full employment, the collapse of youth labour markets came as a surprise for which no one had planned (other than the dwindling band of Western Marxists, whose oft-repeated predictions of capitalist crisis at last found a target). Perhaps understandably, most European policy makers initially regarded youth unemployment as a short-term consequence of the oil shock and their responses were largely geared towards short-term and localised measures. Eric Hobsbawm has remarked that 'until the 1980s it was not clear how irretrievably the foundations of the Golden Age had crumbled' (1994, p.404).

Yet as the severe rise in unemployment persisted across Europe through the 1970s, so the member states – followed soon by the European institutions – began to formulate a more strategic response. For member states, this response invariably formed part of a wider package of measures designed to tackle their growing domestic economic problems. The downturn was also important at European level, for if the EU failed to assist member states survive economic crises of this kind then its entire foundations would be open to question. In 1983 the Council decided that the ESF should have two major goals: reducing youth unemployment (at least three-quarters of the Fund was to be spent on the training and employment of the under-25s) and job creation in the most disadvantaged regions, such as Ireland, southern Italy, Greece, Portugal and parts of Spain.

In most member states ESF grants were largely allocated to training programmes run by the government – such as the Youth Opportunities Programme (YOP) in England. As high unemployment levels persisted into the mid-1980s, and were accompanied by a steady growth in adult unemployment and steep declines in manufacturing employment in the industrial heartlands of France, Germany, Italy and the UK, so the role of the ESF expanded to cover adult training. This experience, in turn, fed into the reform of the Structural Funds more generally, as is described in the following section.

In the field of education policy the fruits of the 1976 Action Programme came under the scrutiny of the Education Ministers at their June 1980 meeting. As might be expected given the economic situation, the Ministers did not address merely the report on the Programme's results but also discussed the wider context of unemployment among young people, proposing further research studies and exchanges of experience at European level in response. From the early 1980s, though, the debate suddenly broadened out from the immediate question of providing training or guidance to the unemployed. As unemployment itself became part of a wider agenda that was to result in the 1986 Single European Act, so the Union started exploring its powers in respect of vocational training – powers that it had previously ignored. In 1983, for example, the Council passed a Resolution on vocational training measures which emphasised the role of the new technologies in increasing the employability of unemployed people (*OJ*, 20 July 1983). Later in the same year the Council urged that all young people should become familiar with the new technologies at school (*OJ*, 24 September 1983). This process widened still further as the Commission's proposals matured for an inter-governmental conference that would revise the Treaty of Rome and set out a clear timetable for achieving the single market.

In moving towards the single market, the Commission identified education and training policy largely as a complementary area. That is, it was not in itself central to the process of achieving the single market but the Commission identified several ways in which it might underpin that process. Most directly, mutual recognition of qualifications would facilitate the mobility of labour. So far, the Commission had pursued this goal mainly through a series of legally-binding Directives covering specific occupations. By 1985 this had covered a number of professions such as nursing, midwifery, dentistry, veterinary medicine, pharmacy and architecture. Each Directive was accompanied by the creation of an advisory committee which monitored its operation and suggested updating measures to the Commission. Aggrieved individuals, professional institutes and national authorities all invoked the Directives in appeals to the courts, a number of which ended up for a ruling in the European Court of Justice. This was, in other words, an increasingly cumbersome process and, in 1985, the Council agreed that the European Centre for the Development of Vocational Training (CEDEFOP) should undertake a transnational study to establish the comparability of the member states' different vocational qualifications systems (see Chapter Four).

Labour mobility was also the subject of a number of highly-publicised court cases. In each case the European Court of Justice (ECJ) interpreted the law in such a way as to extend the EU's competences (McMahon 1995). In a 1974 case involving the son of Italian immigrants in Munich, the Court ruled that the Free State of Bavaria had no right to restrict educational bursaries to German nationals, stateless aliens or political refugees. In this case the principle involved was non-discrimination and the Court treated the case as one concerned with the rights of migrant workers and their children; the fact that it was at variance with a member state's education policies was neither here nor there. Subsequently, the Court started to treat parts of the education system as though they fell under Article 128 of the Treaty of Rome, which defined the EU's competences as including vocational training.

Crucial here was the case of Gravier, a French national who enrolled on a four-year course at the Academie Royale des Beaux Arts in Liège which then charged her the foreign student's enrolment fee. Jacqueline Shaw (1991) has even suggested that the Gravier judgement directly triggered the ERASMUS programme, as worried member states sought to control what might otherwise have been an uncoordinated flood of student transfers. While this is surely to overstate the impact of the Gravier decision, it was nonetheless an important instance of judge-made law. In its judgement the Court ruled that:

> any form of education which prepares for a qualification for a particular profession, trade or employment or which provides the necessary training and skills for such a profession, trade or employment is vocational training, whatever the age and the level of training of the pupils or students, and even if the training programme includes an element of general training. (293/83 [1985] ECR 593, p.614)

As Gravier's course was a form of vocational training (she hoped, apparently, to work as a strip cartoonist), it followed that it was contrary to the provisions of the Treaty to charge a fee which was not payable by Belgian nationals. Following the Gravier decision, a number of foreign nationals studying in Belgian higher education institutes initiated legal proceedings against the practice of levying a foreign students' fee on the citizens of other member states. In ordering repayment of the fees, the ECJ further broadened its definition of vocational training to the point where it was virtually impossible to identify any higher education course which would not fall within this rather elastic category.

In turn, this judgement became the basis for an appeal by the Commission itself over the legal basis on which the Council had approved the ERASMUS programme. ERASMUS, or the European Action Scheme for the Mobility of University Students, appeared to have nothing whatever to do with vocational training; its purpose was to encourage university students to study, and lecturers to teach, for short periods in another member state. In its original proposal the Commission had identified Article 128 of the Treaty as the basis for the new programme. Article 128 allowed the Council to act by a simple majority vote after consulting the

Economic and Social Committee (ECOSOC), which represented the interests of the social partners; it did not require any consultation with the Parliament. In approving ERASMUS in 1987, the Council therefore added Article 235 to Article 128 in providing a legal basis for its decision. As Article 235 required unanimity in the Council, as well as consultation with the Parliament, the Commission asked the ECJ to annul the Council's decision, claiming that as the ERASMUS programme targeted vocational training, Article 128 provided a sufficient legal basis. This was a battle over turf, and the Commission won. In its judgement the Court pointed out that it had consistently held that any form of education which prepares for a qualification enabling the holder to enter a particular profession was vocational training, even if it includes an element of general education. As university studies mainly met this criterion, the Court ruled that the ERASMUS programme was, therefore, an attempt to meet the Union's objectives as laid out in Article 128 (Lenaerts 1994).

At this stage, then, the Union was only able to develop policies for those parts of the education system which the Court might regard as a form of vocational training. While it could include much higher education (and the Court made it clear that it would generally treat higher education as a form of preparation for professional life), it clearly did not include compulsory schooling or general adult education and pre-school education. Even after its amendment by the 1986 Single European Act, the EEC Treaty granted no competence to the Union to develop a policy in the field of education. Given that the Union was required to act within the powers laid down for it, this should have meant that the Union did not touch upon education policy – other than by agreeing specific acts of co-operation between the sovereign member states (Lenaerts 1994). The cumulative impact of the ECJ's decisions on the development of a broad and coherent education policy in the EU, therefore, should not be underestimated.

As well as directly supporting the single market by enabling greater mobility, education and training also came to play a part in the wider strategic thinking of the Commission. As the process of European integration took on speed, so there were growing public expressions of anxiety over the implications. In 1984 the Council created an *ad hoc* committee on a People's Europe (the so-called Adonnino Committee, after its chairman), charged with

identifying ways of improving the EU's image – above all, by
suggesting measures which would make the single market both
more real and more attractive to individual citizens. In its first
report the Adonnino Committee suggested that the most attractive
aspect of the single market for individuals was the first to enjoy
freedom of movement, emphasising the importance of mutual
recognition of qualifications and strengthening the general right
of residence. In its second report, which was endorsed by the
Council in Milan in June 1985, the Committee called for measures
to 'involve and interest young people in the further development
of Europe' (CEC 1985a, p.23). In the same year, a Commission
White Paper in preparation for the Single European Act noted
(almost as an aside) that as part of the process of economic
integration, the Commission intended to develop an education
programme with a view to 'helping young people, in whose hands
the future of the Community's economy lies, to think in European
terms' (CEC 1985b, p.26).

Initially, little came of these ideas. However, in May 1988 the
Education Ministers agreed on a path-breaking resolution on the
European dimension in education, which called for action both at
the level of member states and on a European basis. In addressing
the European dimension in education, the Ministers made it clear
that they had schools rather than universities or vocational training in mind. In a paragraph which shows the influence of the
Adonnino proposals, the Ministers stated that a major purpose of
the European dimension was to:

> strengthen in young people a sense of European identity and
> make clear to them the value of European civilization and of
> the foundations on which the European peoples intend to
> base their development today, that is in particular the safe-
> guarding of the principles of democracy, social justice and
> respect for human rights. (*OJ*, 6 July 1988, p.5)

Most of the practical recommendations were addressed to member
states, who undertook to publish a document setting out their
policies for integrating the European dimension into the curriculum, ensure that teaching materials promote the European
dimension and place a greater emphasis upon the European
dimension in teacher training. To support these activities, the
Commission proposed to sponsor information exchanges on experience across the member states, encourage the production of

teaching materials and introduce the European dimension into teacher training by making greater use of the ARION study visit programme and the ERASMUS exchange scheme. It also undertook to convene a working party, representing the member states, to co-ordinate these activities (*OJ*, 6 July 1988). In practice, the results of this Resolution were often rather limited: the idea of involving trainee teachers in ERASMUS, for instance, often ran foul of national requirements for teacher training, which effectively meant that study abroad could not be recognised in the member state concerned. Nevertheless, the Resolution marked an important transition. The EU still lacked any legal competence in the field of education; indeed, the Resolution itself was passed not by a Council of Education Ministers but by something officially called 'the Council and the Ministers of Education meeting within the Council', in acknowledgement of its ambiguous legal status. Nevertheless, the Resolution represented an acceptance that the Union could, by consensual agreement, act on a collective basis to influence the schools system. If it did not represent, as yet, a clear statement of Union policy on education, it was a clear step towards the development of such a policy.

By the mid-1980s, then, the EU was devoting a much higher level of energy to education and training policy than might have been anticipated a decade earlier. To a large extent, this higher profile for education simply reflected the drive towards the single market – a drive which was, generally speaking, supported vigorously by all twelve member states. In completing the single market, education and training came to acquire a prominent supporting role as mechanisms for facilitating greater mobility and helping develop a generation of European citizens who would see in the single market a positive development. At the same time, a series of legal judgements meant that the Commission had acquired competences in the field of education, whether it wanted them or not. Nevertheless, its largest instrument in the field of human resources remained the European Social Fund; even by 1992, the ESF was allocated sixteen times the yearly budget available to the Commission's education and training action programmes and occupied considerably more attention within member states. It is, then, not surprising that the ESF was subjected to the same broad pressures which stimulated the growing interest in human resources issues more widely.

## Human resources and the Structural Funds

In the run-up to the 1992 Treaty there were four elements in the Structural Funds: the European Social Fund (ESF), the European Regional Development Fund (ERDF), the Agricultural Guidance and Guarantee Fund and the Community Initiatives. A fifth – the Cohesion Fund – came into effect in 1993. The first three (ESF, ERDF and the Agricultural Fund) are managed by the member states but are organised around a set of common objectives that have been proposed by the Commission and approved by the Council (those approved in 1988 are shown in Figure 2.1, p.43). The Community Initiatives are a loose grouping of programmes established to meet specific priorities and are managed by the Commission. Together, the Structural Funds comprise almost one-third of the Union's total spending. As they account for a considerable share of the Union's budget, they tend to attract relatively high levels of attention.

Both the Social Fund and the Agricultural Fund were established through the Treaty of Rome. As the Agricultural Fund's role is primarily concerned with the improvement of agricultural productivity, through modernised structures and procedures rather than through investment in human resources, it need not concern us too greatly. The ESF, on the other hand, was created in order to improve employment opportunities for workers by supporting vocational training and to help increase their mobility within the EU. The ERDF was established in 1975 and included within the Treaty by means of the Single European Act; it provides for infrastructural investment in lagging and disadvantaged regions. For the main part, responsibility for administering the Structural Funds has lain with DGV (the Directorate General responsible for Employment, Social Affairs and Industrial Relations). However, DGXVI (Regional Affairs) also customarily plays an important role and this was strengthened when the goal of reducing regional 'disparities' was included in the Single European Act.

Young people were the main victims of the slump of 1974–75; in particular, unemployment levels were highest among school-leavers trying to find their first job. Preoccupied as they were with unemployment among the young, European leaders focused primarily upon the transition between school and work. Underlying this approach was the assumption that unemployment was persisting – against expectation – because there were frictions within the labour market. These might be related to the growth of new occupations for which there were too few qualified applicants (or 'skills shortages') or, more generally, to the failure of schooling to prepare young people for the world of work. European policy and programmes, therefore, focused on improving the transition to employment for young people by increasing investment levels in training and guidance.

European policy was mainly implemented through the European Structural Funds, whose redistributive nature meant that the EU's role was perceived externally as being secondary to that of the member states. Nonetheless, the Commission's powers to establish the regulatory framework under which the Funds operated meant that it – above all DGV – acquired a growing body of knowledge and experience in administering vocational training policy. Institutionally, this experience was acknowledged during a 1981 restructuring within the Commission, as a result of which DGV – the Directorate for Social Affairs – acquired responsibility for the EU's education and vocational training policies. In the recession of 1982–84, which particularly affected heavy industries such as coal, iron, steel and shipbuilding, adult workers were affected as much as young job-seekers; governments also became increasingly aware of the problem of long-term unemployment, particularly among young men. Once more, training and guidance programmes expanded on the basis of ESF support. Although the ESF was largely seen as a form of support for member states' internal policies, then, its significance during the period of recession had helped widen the EU's interest in education and training.

Inevitably, given their raised importance, the Structural Funds were caught up within the move towards the single market. Indeed, the Single European Act specifically required the Commission to review the operations of the Structural Funds and to develop proposals for their reform. In 1987 the Commission responded with a set of proposed framework regulations for the Funds, laying a quite new basis for their future operation. First, in what was probably, in part, a trade-off to build support for the single market among the poorer member states, the Commission proposed that the Structural Funds should double in size by 1992 (a proposal known as the 'Delors One' package). Second, in calling for stronger social and economic cohesion, the Single European Act singled out greater effectiveness of the Structural Funds as central in reducing the gaps between the various regions and the Delors proposals were intended to ensure that their contribution was clear, visible and strategic. Essentially, there were five dimensions to the 1988 reforms:

- assistance was concentrated on specific policy objectives
- integrated programmes at regional level
- partnership between Commission, member state and other 'competent authorities' at national, regional and local level
- congruence with member states' regional economic policies
- improved administration and evaluation of the Funds.

Since the Funds were devoted largely to supporting measures taken at national level, and were channelled through the respective national government departments, there were direct and immediate practical consequences for the vocational training programmes of the member states (Preston 1994).

In establishing five objectives for the Funds, the Commission created a framework that would remain largely intact until the late 1990s. Indeed, the only significant innovation in 1994 was the integration of the previous third and fourth objectives (concerning training and guidance for the unemployed) into a single Objective Three and the creation of a new Objective Four (see Figure 2.1). This framework ensured that the Union's structural investment would be concentrated in the poorest regions. Objective One was designed to focus effort on those regions whose development was lagging behind that of the rest of the EU (including Greece, Portugal, parts of Spain and Italy and the whole of Ireland). Some 63 per cent of the total allocation for the Structural Funds was devoted to this first objective (Matthews 1994). Objective Two was intended to assist restructuring in frontier regions or urban industrial regions (which included a number of regions that were likely to be disproportionately affected by the single internal market). The other objectives might support activities across all member states. The 1988 reforms also provided for member states to bring forward multi-annual development plans, which, if supported from the Funds, might then operate over a longer timespan than the year-by-year allocations that had operated hitherto. This was intended to ensure greater continuity in the programmes supported from

**Objective One:** in the 'lagging' regions of the Union, to support employment growth through training and guidance, especially for unemployed people and to help strengthen training systems, promote technology transfer and help training for small- and medium-sized enterprises.

**Objective Two:** in border regions and regions of 'industrial decline', to support employment growth through training and guidance, especially for unemployed people, and to promote technology transfer.

**Objective Three:** in all regions, training of the long-term unemployed (out of work for 12 months or more) aged 25 and over.

**Objective Four:** in all regions, training for unemployed young people under the age of 25.

**Objective Five (a):** adaptation of agricultural structures (not usually interpreted as encompassing education or training measures).

**Objective Five (b):** in rural regions, to support employment growth through training and guidance, especially for unemployed people, and to promote technology transfer.

*Figure 2.1: The European Structural Funds: the objectives after the 1988 reform*
*Source:* Preston (1994, p.34)

the Funds, though many member states continued to complain of delays in the annual approvals that were still required.

Although human resource investments were only one among a number of areas supported by the Structural Funds, they have always constituted a very considerable share of the total. In the case of the Community Support Framework agreed with the Republic of Ireland between 1989 and 1993, it is estimated that of the £3191 millions in Union assistance, at least £1220 millions were directly spent on human resources – roughly 40 per cent (Matthews 1994). Indirect spending on human resources within other operational programmes, such as the STAR programme for increasing access to telematics in rural areas, probably brings the overall share to roughly one-half of all expenditure. In member states such as France, whose allocation came mainly under Objectives Three and Four, of course, the vast majority of the Structural Funds allocation was for human resource programmes. The importance of the Structural Funds for the Union's stake in vocational training, then, should not be underestimated.

As part of the 1988 reforms, the Commission also confirmed the status of a small number of highly-focused programmes to support specific priorities. The first five of these Community Initiatives provided support for retraining programmes for coalmining areas (RECHAR), cross-border collaboration (INTERREG), technology transfer and research development (STRIDE), environmental protection in Objective One regions (ENVIREG) and a programme for the Union's territories overseas (REGIS). A further series was launched in 1990, including training for women (NOW), rural development programmes (LEADER), the development of cross-national qualifications (EUROFORM), the use of telecommunications in Objective One regions (TELEMATIQUE) and training for people with disabilities (HORIZON). A number of existing specific measures were also grouped together with the Initiatives, including retraining in declining textiles regions (RETEX) and in declining iron and steel regions (RESIDER). Taken together, the Initiatives accounted for a total of almost 10 per cent of the Structural Funds in the period between 1989 and 1993.

Economically, the Community Initiatives were designed to alleviate negative consequences of the single market process and tackle the specific difficulties faced by problem regions. They also helped the Commission politically, in two ways. Internally, as Pollack (1994) has pointed out, the Initiatives gave the Commission the capacity to redistribute resources without having to strike side-bargains with individual member states. This was a useful addition to the Commission's toolkit, though it also opened up the possibility of criticism from MEPs and the Council over the way that the Community Initiatives were managed. Externally, they contributed to the wider process of building up a constituency of popular support for European integration. The Commission claimed that the Initiatives helped it to 'make a specific and focused response to problems which threaten the livelihood of its citizens, or frustrate their ability to break into the virtuous circle of rising prosperity offered by the internal market...' and thus 'bring the Community closer to its citizens' (CEC 1993a, p.3). Behind this lay a fear that ordinary citizens had no idea that the Union was supporting practical measures such as the Youth Opportunities Programme. One local government official in an English Objective Two region subsequently said that:

Every time someone visited one of our projects, like when we opened the training centre for Asian women, they'd complain that we didn't have a sign up saying that this had been supported by such-and-such a fund, or our sign was too small, or something. Then we heard that they had decided what size signs had to be, they'd even decided on the colours you'd to have. It drove us mad, but we didn't mind as long as we got the money. (Interview, February 1995)

Certainly the Delors period was marked by a concern not only to bring 'the Community closer to its citizens' in its activities but also for it to be *seen* to be delivering practical support at the local level.

## Supporting mobility: education and training up to Maastricht

Between 1986 and 1991 the European Commission launched nine new education and training action programmes with a combined budget of well over a billion ECUs (see Table 2.1, p.48). In addition, at least eight of the new Community Initiatives developed within the Structural Funds from 1988 until 1992 had a substantial education and training dimension. In the two years before the 1992 conference at Maastricht the Commission prepared separate policy memoranda on open learning, vocational training and higher education; it also produced discussion papers on the future of the Community Initiatives and the European dimension in education. The period between the ratification of the Single European Act and the presentation of the Treaty on European Union saw education and training continue their rise up the policy agenda, concluding with their formal inclusion into the Treaty itself. With hindsight, much of this activity achieved little of lasting value other than awareness-raising, and that was often patchy. However, its value was certainly demonstrated after 1992 when the process of European integration started to permeate the farthest reaches of the education and training system.

The 1980s generation of action programmes started rather hesitantly. In 1983 the Council and the Education Ministers issued a joint declaration on higher education. Anticipating discussions within the Commission, the Stuttgart declaration called for greater mobility in European higher education and urged member states to assume the responsibility of funding student exchanges when the present Commission programme expired. Two years later the Ministers and Council were faced with the Commission's White Paper proposals, as well as the Adonnino recommendations on student mobility. Yet the first two programmes approved, EURO-TECNET in 1983 and COMETT in 1986, were primarily related to the new technologies rather than student mobility. EUROTECNET, which can stand as the EU's earliest attempt to develop a training programme that was clearly its own, was concerned to bring new technologies into training; since it was clearly based on Article 128, the programme simply marked an extension of the EU's activities rather than its powers. COMETT (European Community Programme in Education and Training for Technology), the EU's first programme in education, was established to promote university-enterprise partnerships to promote transnational training and work placements linked to the new technologies. Despite the fact that it involved universities rather than vocational training, the Commission managed to avoid legal challenges by basing its proposals not only on Article 128 of the Treaty but also Article 235 (which is concerned with research and technology development). COMETT was followed rapidly by ERASMUS. This decision was to mark a new stage in the development of programmes and policies for education, representing the first major programme following the European Social Fund that had a significant impact upon educational institutions and individual teachers and students in the member states.

ERASMUS aimed specifically to promote greater mobility among staff and students, support inter-university curriculum projects and encourage wider mutual recognition of academic qualifications. Its practical consequences are discussed in greater depth in Chapter Four. Like many other EU initiatives, ERASMUS got off to a shaky start. In a particularly public bout of in-fighting, two months after the Council approved the new programme, the Commission challenged its decision in the Court of Justice. With the ECJ deciding in favour of the Commission, there was then an acrimonious fight over the level of budget that ERASMUS required. Nevertheless, the ERASMUS programme had enormous symbolic importance. As with COMETT, individual institutions could send proposals under ERASMUS without any reference to the national ministry or to regional authorities. It had high visibility at institutional level, not least because of the practical difficulties involved in integrating foreign students into the university system on an unprecedented scale. Financially, it was by far the largest of the EU's action programmes, with a budget between 1987 and 1992 of 307.5 million ECUs; COMETT, the second largest in financial terms, enjoyed a budget of 206.6 millions. It therefore marked a significant milestone in the gradual development of the EU's competence in the field of education and training.

ERASMUS also acted as a path-breaker, enabling the Commission to pursue new initiatives, claiming that these were needed if ERASMUS were to succeed. One early example was the European Credit Transfer Scheme (ECTS), established with ERASMUS funding to enable students not only to study in another member state but also to be certain that their achievements would be recognised when they returned to their home university. A pilot scheme was established in 1988/89 to identify the kinds of mechanisms that might be helpful when considering a credit system across Europe, limited, for practical reasons, to five disciplines: Engineering, Chemistry, Medicine, Business Administration and History. An 'inner circle' was established, comprising two representative Universities, within each of the five disciplines, from each of the member states, with a remit to exchange students within the ERASMUS scheme. The credit terms were based on one academic year of study and dual qualification was seen as permissible.

As ECTS was developed within ERASMUS, the number of entirely new action programmes expanded rapidly from 1988 onwards. Table 2.1 gives an overview. As can be seen, ERASMUS remained the flagship – both in terms of its budget and in terms of the attention it attracted. It also provided something of a model for other programmes; all involved the creation of collaborative arrangements: FORCE, LINGUA, PETRA, TEMPUS and YES all devoted the bulk of their resources to subsidising exchange programmes. COMETT and FORCE differed from the other programmes in that they were expected to be led by employers rather than educationists, so that the EU's investment was closely geared to the needs of business. That was the theory, at any rate. The reality – discussed further in Chapter Five – was that projects were often fronted by employers but developed and driven by educationists. In other respects there were important differences. ERASMUS and TEMPUS primarily involved higher education institutions;

PETRA, LINGUA, IRIS and COMETT involved vocational training providers (which could certainly include universities and, in
fact, predominantly did so in the case of COMETT); LINGUA
could include schools as well as other providers of education and
training; IRIS, PETRA and YES addressed very specific target
groups defined in terms of gender or of age. Thus while the process
generally followed a familiar pattern – incentive funding, voluntary participation, direct relations between institutions and
Commission, transnational partnerships and exchanges – the different action programmes tried to pursue distinctive objectives
and audiences.

### Table 2.1: Main EC Education and Training Action Programmes, 1986–1992

| Programme | Period of approval(s) | Total budget | Purpose |
|---|---|---|---|
| COMETT | 1986–1995 | Ecu 206.6m | University-enterprise co-operation in the field of technology training |
| ERASMUS | 1987–1994 | Ecu 307.5m | Mobility of university students and staff and joint curriculum projects |
| EUROTEC NET | 1983–1994 | Ecu 7.0m | Promote innovation in training in respect of the new technologies |
| FORCE | 1991–1994 | Ecu 31.3m | Promote continuing vocational training |
| LINGUA | 1990–1994 | Ecu 68.6m | Promote foreign language competence within teacher education, secondary and higher education and vocational training |
| PETRA | 1988–1994 | Ecu 79.7m | Promote vocational training of young people and preparation for adult life |
| TEMPUS | 1990–1994 | Ecu 194m | Mobility scheme for university studies between EU and central/eastern Europe |
| YES | 1988–1994 | Ecu 32.2m | 'Youth for Europe' – exchanges of young people and centres |
| IRIS | 1988–1995 | Ecu 0.75m | Networking between vocational training projects for women |

*Source*: Various EU documents (particularly CEC 1993c, passim).

## 1990–1992: policy proposals

By 1990 it was possible to argue that the Union had achieved a critical mass. It had a large stake in member states' vocational training programmes, had created a number of Community Initiatives which were implemented in the member states – several of which were centrally concerned with human resources – and it had overcome apparent legal difficulties to establish a number of action programmes supporting staff and student exchanges and curriculum development projects in higher education and vocational training. It appeared high time that these disparate developments were reviewed and that the Union's competences were clarified. By coincidence, a number of decisions were to be taken in 1992: a number of the action programmes (including ERASMUS) expired in 1992 and the Commission was required to bring forward new proposals before any successor could be approved, 1992 marked the completion of the single market programme and there were plans for an inter-governmental conference (IGC) to approve a reform of the founding treaties. The two years before 1992, therefore, witnessed a flurry of activity in DGV and the Task Force on Human Resources in an attempt to ensure that new policies were in place, or at least before the member states, by the time that this series of decisions had to be taken.

In the period 1990–1992 the Task Force published five key documents on its education and training policies. They included three Commission memoranda – on higher education (CEC 1991a), open and distance learning (CEC 1991b) and vocational training (CEC 1992b) – as well as a widely-debated report on skills shortages in the European labour market and a series of proposals on university-industry co-operation entitled *Advanced Training for Competitive Advantage* (CEC 1992c). Taken together with the 1993 report on the results of the EU's training and education programmes between 1986 and 1993 (CEC 1993c) and the Green Paper on the European dimension in education (CEC 1993b), these amount to a substantial attempt to generate debate around, and support for, the Union's role in education and training.

In the end the debate tended to consolidate rather than innovate. This was not because the debate itself was unimportant but rather because the Commission's proposals did not greatly stray beyond the existing borders of its stake in education and training. Superficially, the published proposals were far-reaching and challenging. However, this was more because rather modest proposals were set against an iconoclastic analytical backdrop in which the Commission freely passed judgement upon matters that belonged without question to the sovereignty of member states. Essentially, the Commission's approach was to create a discourse of crisis, which then made its own proposals sound eminently reasonable under the circumstances. In this case the perceived crisis was Europe's shortage of skilled labour, arising from the development of new economic forces which required higher levels of skill and knowledge from the workforce. In particular, the Commission appears to have been greatly influenced by its Industrial Research and Development Advisory Committee (IRDAC), a body dominated by senior industrialists and created to advise the Commission on strategic issues related to its policies for research and development. Completed in November 1990, its report on skills shortages was published in time to influence the Commission's three education and training memoranda.

IRDAC's decision to prepare the report was apparently stimulated by:

> *evidence* now *that higher investment in technological R&D* – a crucial area in which Europe must keep and improve its competitive position – *might not produce the expected economic benefits due to lack of qualified people* both to develop and exploit advanced and innovative products and processes. (IRDAC 1991, p.1; emphasis in original)

IRDAC concluded that the output of training and education systems – higher education especially – were the prime determinant of competitiveness and that the threat posed by skills shortages was so serious that 'immediate action is required from all parties concerned' (IRDAC 1991, p.2).

This line of reasoning was followed closely in all three Commission memoranda. The *Memorandum on Higher Education* provided a sketch of the demographic, scientific, technological and policy changes, concluding that these showed the need for wider participation in higher education, a strong partnership between higher education and industry, upgrading of the existing workforce through continuing education, greater use of distance and open learning and renewed attention to the EU dimension, which should, above all, comprise improved student mobility, curriculum development and language teaching (CEC 1991a). Similarly, the Task Force argued in its *Memorandum on open Distance Learning* that Europe was entering a critical period of global competition, in which 'the Community's major trading competitors in the developed world are concentrating very heavily, and to a greater extent than in Europe, on improving the skills and knowledge of their existing and potential labour force' (CEC 1991b, p.3).

Like the *Memorandum on Vocational Training* (CEC 1992b), it made relatively few specific proposals; those it did make – such as the creation of a trans European network on open distance learning, or greater promotion of distance open learning across other EU action programmes – were considerably less radical than many open learning professionals had anticipated. Much the same might be said of the Communication which the Task Force prepared for the Commission on higher education–industry co-operation, which again provided a wide-ranging analysis of the status quo combined with a recommendation that the EU in future should emphasise its contribution to 'the Europeanisation of existing and future higher education–industry networks' through student and management exchanges and placements (CEC 1992c).

The discussion documents and reports of the early 1990s helped provide a general legitimation of the Union's policy interest in the area. All five documents were widely discussed and the Commission duly received responses from a broad range of interested parties, which it subsequently summarised for circulation to member states and others. Few of these responses, except, perhaps, those of some member states, denied the Union's right to be discussing these matters and formulating its own policies for the future; quite the reverse, a number criticised the timidity of the Union's proposals. More than this, they also alerted administrators and professionals to the Union's potential role in determining education and training policies in the future. Those who responded to the memoranda included not simply national education ministries but most of the major educational trade unions, the national associations of university rectors and vice chancellors and a number of professional institutions as well as other established interest groups. Thus these groups at member state level – and, where these existed, their European umbrella organisations – started to include the EU within their own policy discussions and lobbying activities. This was probably the major achievement of the discussions that the Commission launched in the period between 1990 and 1992.

In generating debate the Union followed a pattern which can also be seen in later policy-oriented publications. The number of specific proposals for future action were few – sometimes bafflingly so. They were preceded by a discourse of crisis; in this case the sense that things had come to a turning point was provided by the IRDAC report with its alarming talk of skills shortages that were now so serious as to inhibit Europe's competitiveness. They were accompanied by a magisterial diagnosis of the challenges consequently facing the entire system – and, despite its lack of specific competences, the Union certainly did not shrink from specifying what it believed to be the appropriate responses for universities, member states and other relevant parties. Yet any recommendations for its own future action were few and couched in rather general terms. This may have been an unusual way of consulting over policy but it allowed the Union both to seem remarkably sensible, indeed restrained, and to test the water – to see what responses it got from the member states and also the other parties affected before then drafting its own plans.

## Overview

By 1992, then, the EU's interest in education and training had come a long way. If the European Social Fund was largely devoted to funding training schemes for the unemployed, the principle had been accepted that the Commission could devote around one-tenth of its Structural Funds' budget to other priorities through the Community Initiatives, most of them concerned with human resource programmes. In addition, the Union had developed a range of action programmes in the fields of vocational training and education, winning in the process a series of legal battles which legitimated its policy interest in this area. The action programmes were wide-ranging and reasonably well-embedded. In a review of the earlier programmes undertaken in preparation for the development of new proposals, the Commission's Task Force on Education, Training and Human Resources concluded that 'The combined achievements of the programmes put in place since 1986 can clearly be seen to have been considerable, in terms of the numbers of people who have participated; the trans-national activities generated; and their impact on policy thinking in the different member states' (CEC 1993c, p.29). Allowing for some pardonable exaggeration, this achievement is all the more remarkable given the fate of other transnational education policy bodies. Following the publication of a series of reports on recurrent education in the early 1970s, the OECD's Centre for Educational Research and Innovation made little, if any further, impact.

Even more striking was the virtual eclipse by 1992 of the United Nations Educational, Scientific and Cultural Organisation (UNESCO), which had been created a year after the end of the Second World War with the hope of harnessing international co-operation in education, science and culture on behalf of peace, security and human rights. Throughout the 1950s and 1960s, UNESCO continued unchallenged as the central place for international debate, information exchange, research, co-operation and aid in respect of education policy and practice. By the end of the 1970s, however, UNESCO had been replaced as the key agency of multilateral educational aid by the World Bank (or International Bank for Reconstruction and Development), which was clearly dominated by the Western powers and, specifically, by the USA. The withdrawal of the United States and the United Kingdom from its membership ensured that by the time of Communism's collapse in the late 1980s, UNESCO was already marginal to the extent where its future role was seriously in doubt (Baumert *et al.* 1994). The contrast with the EU's role in promoting multilateral policies and programmes for education and training could hardly be greater.

Yet the EU's achievements, though considerable, remained limited. Financially, as Table 2.2 confirms, the EU's commitment to its human resources policies was still relatively small. Ignoring the subventions to member states through the Structural Funds, the total budget for the EU's own education and training policies and programmes was barely over a half of one per cent by 1992. Agricultural policy was still the big item on the EU's shopping list and it would remain so through the 1990s. The Commission itself recognised that the co-ordination of its education and training programmes had rarely been systematic. Indeed, the Commission's own attempt to provide a coherent policy framework for its action programmes – *Education and Training in the European Community: guidelines for the medium term* – appeared in 1989, somewhat late in the day. Externally, a growing lobby of employers, trade unions and education professionals was arguing that the Union should place a higher priority upon education and training than it had done hitherto. Internally, such criticisms were frequently articulated within ECOSOC as well as within the Parliament. IRDAC, in its report on quality in education, urged the Union to do more to promote lifelong learning (IRDAC 1994). Externally, the increasingly influential employers' lobbying body, the European Round Table of Industrialists, argued in a joint paper with the European Council of Rectors that the EU's activities lacked coherence and were focused narrowly upon young people: 'there is no Europe-wide programme of Lifelong Learning... This will endanger Europe's competence position' (Otala 1992, pp.83–5). Moreover, despite the sympathetic rulings of the Court of Justice, the Union's competences were constrained by the lack of references to education in either the Treaty of Rome or the Single European Act. It had no real role in respect of pre-school education or primary education, its role in secondary education was limited to the LINGUA programme (though LINGUA was confined in the UK to post-compulsory education) and it had no role in general adult education.

**Table 2.2: EU Spending on Social Fund, Education and Training Programmes as a Percentage of Total Yearly Expenditure, 1987 and 1992**

| Activity | 1987 | 1992 |
|---|---|---|
| Education, training, youth | 0.20% | 0.57% |
| European Social Fund | 7.30% | 8.10% |

*Source:* General Reports (for 1987 and 1992) of the Activities of the European Community

Resolving these difficulties was, in turn, likely to create new problems. While the member states were willing to cede some sovereignty over vocational training matters, they regarded education and, above all, their schools systems as quintessentially national in character. Yet the Commission's president throughout the move towards the single market, Jacques Delors, was keenly aware of the parallels between European integration in the late twentieth century and the building of nations that had taken place in the century after 1789. Under his ambitious and visionary presidency it was most unlikely that the Commission would turn away an opportunity to expand its remit into an area which had such a close association with the shaping of national identities. With the Treaty on European Union, that opportunity appeared to have arrived.

Chapter Three

# Educating a Europe of the People
## The 1990s

Until 1992, European policies in education and training developed rather haphazardly. Member states continued to regard education and, to a lesser extent, training as a matter of national sovereignty; yet throughout the 1980s in particular, the Commission increasingly believed that education and training were vital instruments of EU policy. Member states, independently and through the Council, constantly set out to protect their sovereignty; and where they agreed to an extension, either of the EU's competences or the use that could be made of them, they restated their belief that the Commission's powers in this area were strictly limited. It was a one-sided struggle. Despite the fact that the member states appeared to have right – or at least law – on their side, to use Pollack's term, this was a perfect example of 'creeping competence' at work (Pollack 1994). The Treaty on European Union appeared to offer an opportunity to clarify definitively where competence lay, not only in respect of education and training but in other disputed policy areas as well.

This chapter traces the development of the EU's policies towards education and training in the period following the completion of the single market. If the starting point must be the treatment of education and training in the Treaty on European Union, the central questions which follow might be expected to concern the nature of the large framework programmes for education and training which followed: the SOCRATES action programme for education and the LEONARDO DA VINCI programme for vocational training. Certainly these programmes occupy a central place, but within months of their launch the EU was reviewing its policy towards the area – first through the publication of an innovative but widely-criticised White Paper (*Towards the Learning*

*Society*) and subsequently through the highly-provocative work of the Study Group on Education and Training, a team of specialists appointed directly by, and responsible to, the Commissioner. In terms of policy development, then, the Treaty seems to be less of a turning point than one more milestone on a rather lengthy pathway.

In the event, the 1992 Treaty failed even to end the struggles over definitions and competences. Admittedly, the Articles which covered education, training and culture were designed to ensure that each party's domain was clearly identified; more generally, the Treaty's provisions on subsidiarity and on the role of other European institutions (notably the Parliament and the newly-created Committee of the Regions) were intended to build in safeguards against trespassing. Yet shortly after the member states agreed to ratify the Treaty there were complaints that, once more, the Commission's proposals for education and training had crossed the boundaries of its agreed competence. As for the supposed safeguards, the creation of the new Committee of the Regions (CoR) and the extension of the Parliament's powers had created a dense fog where all should have been light. Instead, the CoR immediately became embroiled in an intense rivalry with both the Parliament (who saw the CoR as attempting to usurp the Parliament's representative functions) and the Economic and Social Committee (ECOSOC), which was asked to share its premises with the new upstart. For its part, the Parliament was not only fighting off the CoR's pretensions but was also engaged in constant disputes with the Council and the Commission, both of which were reluctant to cede any of their decision making powers to the Parliament. On several occasions the Parliament showed that it was willing to use education and training policies as a bargaining chip. At the same time, growing enthusiasm and interest among educational institutions and the employers' lobby further raised the visibility of education and training as a policy issue. For its part, the Commission showed growing ingenuity in identifying those problems of education and training which it could present as amenable to solution only at the transnational level. By the late 1990s education and training remained an area of conflict and controversy. It was also marked by a strong contrast between the depth and scale of the challenges as identified by the Commission and the modesty of its concrete proposals for action.

## The treaty on European union

With the 1992 Treaty in force, the Union acquired clearly specified responsibilities for education and training policy. Article 126 set out the EU's role in respect of education. Article 127 deals more specifically than its predecessor (Article 128 of the Treaty of Rome) with vocational training. The new Article 128 sets out the position with respect to culture. Though they were covered in the 1979 Social Charter, education and training do not feature in the Protocol on Social Policy (originally written as a chapter in the draft Treaty but subsequently treated as an addendum signed by eleven member states only following vigorous objections from the UK). The main consequences of the Treaty, therefore, were to provide separate and different legal bases for education and training so that the Commission felt obliged to organise distinct programmes for the two areas, to broaden the EU's competences in respect of the development and implementation of a common vocational training policy while respecting member states' sovereignty over its content and organisation and to identify education as lying within the Union's competence while respecting the member states' sovereignty over its content, organisation and linguistic and cultural diversity and explicitly ruling out the possibility of harmonisation. These provisions were specifically limited by requirements that the Commission should follow specified procedures in each case, including prior consultation (CEC 1992a).

The Treaty provisions are sufficiently important to warrant closer discussion. The most innovative is Article 126, which requires the Union 'to contribute to the development of quality education by encouraging co-operation between member states and, if necessary, by supporting and supplementing their action while fully respecting the responsibility of the member states for the content of teaching and the organisation of education systems and their cultural and linguistic diversity.' (CEC 1992a, p.47). It also allows the Union and member states to promote co-operation with third countries, such as Japan or the USA, as well as with other inter-governmental organisations like the Council of Europe or UNESCO. It explicitly excludes harmonisation of national education systems, including curricula.

In developing its activities in education the Union was to aim at the types of activity that were pursued previously through such programmes as ERASMUS. Essentially, the Union's competence extends to providing incentives to member states to co-operate with one another by:

- developing the European dimension, particularly through language teaching
- encouraging student and staff mobility, including measures to encourage academic recognition of diplomas and periods of study
- promoting co-operation between educational establishments
- developing exchanges of information and experience on issues common to the education systems of the member states
- encouraging exchanges among young people and among 'socio-educational instructors' (a phrase designed to encompass a rather diverse group of occupations, including, for instance, community youth workers in Britain, 'animateurs socio-culturels' in France and health information providers in the Netherlands and Germany)
- encouraging the development of distance education.

Interestingly, the Parliament took the view that this list was indicative rather than exhaustive and that other areas might be developed as required (Lenaerts 1994). There was no evidence in the SOCRATES programme that either the Commission or Council shared this interpretation.

Finally, the Treaty specifies the procedure by which the Union exercises its powers: namely, by 'co-decision'. Any proposals must be initiated by the Commission and agreed by the Council by qualified majority voting, following consultation with ECOSOC and CoR, and with the formal involvement and support of the Parliament.

In the field of vocational training the Treaty provided a more detailed and specific restatement of the existing Treaty provisions. Article 127, while explicitly ruling out harmonisation of the member states' 'laws and regulations', required the EU to 'implement a vocational training policy which shall support and supplement the action of the member states while fully respecting the responsibility of the member states for the content and organisation of vocational training.' (CEC 1992a, p.48). Where Article 126 referred to 'incentive measures', Article 127 specified that the Union may take 'measures' to implement its policy. As in education, the Union and member states were to co-operate with what the EU calls 'third countries' (that is, non-members) and international agencies.

More explicitly, the Union's aims in developing a vocational training policy were to:

- facilitate adaptation to industrial change, in particular through vocational training and retraining
- improve initial and continuing vocational training in order to facilitate vocational integration and reintegration into the labour market
- facilitate access to vocational training and encourage mobility of instructors and trainees and, particularly, young people
- stimulate co-operation on training between educational or training establishments and firms
- develop exchanges of information and experience on issues common to the training system of the member states.

Again, the Treaty specifies the process of decision making but, in the case of vocational training, the process is 'co-operation'. That is, not only must the Parliament and ECOSOC be consulted but the Parliament may also introduce amendments. Although CoR may produce 'own-initiative opinions' on policy proposals affecting vocational training, there is no statutory requirement that it be consulted. This reflects the situation in a number of member states where vocational training is a national responsibility while education policy often involves local government.

As previously, the Treaty acknowledged a greater role for the EU than in respect of education. While it excluded harmonisation of laws and regulations, it did not state, as such, that other areas could not be harmonised; it also required the Union to develop a policy of its own in respect of vocational training, rather than limiting it to supporting developments in the member states as Article 126 did in respect of education. In principle, then, the vocational training provisions offer the Union a somewhat wider field of action than is open in the case of education. Yet both are based on the complementarity of Union action with the ultimate responsibility of the member states. Formally, the Union's role is limited to supplementing national policies and providing incentives to co-operation among the member states.

Far from expanding the Union's competences, then, has Maastricht actually done the reverse? By ruling out harmonisation, restating the competences of member states and allocating a major role to the Parliament and consultative bodies, the Treaty initially seemed to have placed clear limits to the future development of the EU's education and training policies. Catherine Bernard (1992) states simply enough that the educational provisions of the Treaty were not radical: Article 127 closely mirrors Article 128 of the Treaty of Rome while Article 126 simply extends to schools education the provision made for higher education under judge-made law. Yet the Treaty did slightly more than tidy up a minor muddle.

As one expert has argued, while legally this appears to mark a return to the 1974 position in respect of the division of competence between the Union and member states, the major difference is 'that since 1974 an acceptable role had been carved out for the Community in education' (McMahon 1995, p.117). One judge in the Court of First Instance has, moreover, pointed out that the Treaty on European Union allows for a measure of co-ordination of vocational training where it is deemed necessary for their mutual recognition. In view of the ECJ's past treatment of vocational training, this could afford 'a sufficient legal basis for...a measure of harmonization' (Lenaerts 1994, p.35). The longer term consequences, therefore, remain to be seen. In theory, subsidiarity should place strict limits upon the Union's freedom of manouevre. However, the exact meaning of subsidiarity – including its legal definition – remains unclear and, in the past, the Court of Justice has consistently extended the Union's powers (Hrbek 1994; Lenaerts 1994; McMahon 1995; Meehan 1993). The general overriding principle of subsidiarity is written into Article 3b of the Treaty. This states that:

> In areas which do not fall within its exclusive competence, the Community shall take action...only if and in so far as the objectives of the proposed action cannot be sufficiently achieved by the member states and can therefore, by reason of the scale or effects of the proposed action, be better achieved by the Community.

In the field of education the Treaty both clarified the existing position and gave the Union new and explicit powers. The Union's field of operation was enlarged to include sectors of education that were in no sense forms of vocational training, such as pre-school, primary and liberal adult education. All of these were previously affected by Union policy, but only through non-binding resolutions or conclusions of the Council and the Education Ministers or, indirectly, in that they were sometimes able to participate in action programmes in other policy areas. This means, first, that there is no need to dissemble: the Union no longer needs to base its education policy on its powers in relation to vocational training. Action programmes such as ERASMUS may continue as before (indeed, part of Article 126 seems to be worded in such a way as to ensure that ERASMUS will not be constricted in any way) but on a firmer and clearer legal footing. Second, the introduction of education into the Treaty had enormous symbolic significance, at least among specialists. Two university European officers described Article 126 during interviews as a 'milestone' which made them feel that their work had taken a new direction, while the Director of a national professional association claimed that when a colleague pointed out the implications of Article 126, 'it made me take the Community seriously, I suppose for the first time really' (Interview April 1995).

Third, the new Article reinforced the boundaries between education and vocational training. This was manifested shortly afterwards when the Commission proposed two separate integrated action programmes: the SOCRATES action programme in education and the LEONARDO DA VINCI action programme in vocational training. An early example of the difficulties to come appeared when the existing COMETT programme on university–enterprise co-operation had to be divided into two, one falling into the definition of vocational training found in Article 127 and one falling into the new definition of education in Article 126. Later measures, including the European Year of Lifelong Learning, sought to span the boundaries between vocational and general learning, but the fact that two different decision–making procedures were required for the two areas made it unlikely that the Union would develop larger-scale proposals based on both Articles (Lenaerts 1994). Fourth, it removed the need for the Union's education policies to focus exclusively on the economic implications – though, in practice, as the ERASMUS programme demonstrated, the linkage was already somewhat vague.

On balance, it seems that the Treaty essentially confirmed the status quo. This was the view of one senior legal official who wrote, shortly after ratification in 1993, that so far as education and training policy were concerned, 'To date, priority has been given to applying a light touch and the Union Treaty has enshrined this approach in the constitution' (Lenaerts 1994, p.38). While consolidating the *acquis communautaure* – that is, the existing body of competences and policy interests – the Treaty also confirmed the primacy of the member states' sovereignty in both areas.

## Restructuring after 1992

Far from clarifying the process of policy formulation, in the short term the Treaty muddied the waters yet further. However, the climate of change which surrounded the Treaty did allow the Commission to reorganise its administrative responsibilities as well as restructure the action programmes, in ways which were very much to its advantage. The first fruit of this period was the designation of a new department within the Commission, with specific responsibilities for education and training. DGXXII had previously been rather bizarrely known as an 'empty Directorate', having lost its original functions some years previously. Thomas Ó Dwyer, head of the Task Force on Education, Training, Human Resources and Youth, now became Director General; his staff were transferred with him from DGV to DGXXII. With the creation of two large framework programmes for training and education, the Commission was able to shift staffing resources away from the separate technical assistance units which had previously helped administer the disparate action programmes and increase the internal staff of DGXXII.

The new arrangement also changed the Commissioner's role. Instead of having to disentangle education and training from the wider, and often more pressing, concerns of DGV, the Commissioner responsible for DGXXII now had greater room for manouevre. For the Commissioner and her Directorate-General, the new role of the Committee of the Regions and Parliament helped create a new set of uncertainties – though if the Commissioner happened to be good at political in-fighting then the pressures from these two representative institutions could prove extremely helpful in extracting concessions from other

Commissioners and even the Council. Edith Cresson, whose career as Socialist prime minister of France may have been brief and inglorious, was very different in both her politics and her approach from Padraig Flynn, Commissioner responsible for most of DGV's activities, who sometimes gave the impression of hankering after a return to domestic politics rather than taking Europe to the leading edge. Cresson brought to the position of Commissioner a modernising instinct and a degree of energy and vision that made her a natural ally of the European integrationists in the Commission. An innovator rather than an incrementalist, she had little patience with the idea that the sovereignty of member states should invariably be allowed to hinder Europe's collective development as a global power – a development in which education and training had a vital role to play.

By the time that Cresson assumed her position, the EU's post-1992 action programmes had already taken shape. By and large, the new Directorate-General succeeded in grouping its education and training programmes into two broad frameworks corresponding to the competences granted in Articles 126 and 127 of the Treaty. The Commission set out its response to Article 126 in a 1993 Green Paper on the European dimension in education, arguing that its interpretation should take place in a 'wider context featuring the completion of the Single Market and its impact in the area of education and training, as well as changes in the need for human resources in the light of social and technological changes' (CEC 1993b, p.2). Accepting that responsibility for most of the consequent decisions lay with the member states, the Green Paper argued that Union attention should focus on three main areas: (a) educating young people for citizenship through experience of the European dimension (through language learning or transnational projects), socialisation in a European context (through exchanges) and helping improve their understanding of Europe and its development, (b) 'offering opportunities for improving the quality of education' by sharing information and experience, arranging for transnational co-operation and supporting collaboration on the development of teaching materials and (c) preparing young people for the transition to adulthood and working life by helping build transnational partnerships of schools, businesses, local authorities and other bodies, and fostering transnational networks between general educational institutions and those providing initial vocational training (CEC 1993b, pp.5–7).

As its authors frankly acknowledged, the Green Paper lacked detail and offered no specific proposal. This did not prevent an irritated UK minister from rejecting the idea of a new 'statutory curriculum, modules or themes which would be commonly used throughout Europe' and calling for 'common-sense not common education' in the new Europe (*Department for Education News*, 2 November 1993). In fact, the Commission had made no such proposal. Rather than innovating in terms of content, the new SOCRATES action programme was, effectively, a collection of the existing programmes (ERASMUS, LINGUA, ARION and YOUTH FOR EUROPE in particular) with a new but small-scale programme for schools partnerships (COMENIUS). Its focus on higher education was confirmed by its budget: 55 per cent was allocated to Chapter One actions (higher education) and 10 per cent to Chapter Two (schools education); 25 per cent was allocated to 'horizontal activities' (LINGUA, exchanges of senior managers and specialists under ARION, open and distance learning). SOCRATES made no reference to early-years education and a line respecting adult education was added at a later stage, following concerted lobbying by the Deutscher Volkshochschul-verband and the Danish government. If the Commission's proposed budget was modest, it was, nevertheless, reduced further in the process of negotiation between Commission, Parliament and Council.

In short, the proposed scope of SOCRATES, and the means by which it was to be furthered, were conservative in the extreme. By June 1996 the Commission had approved some 109 co-operation projects under SOCRATES, involving around 700 partners from 18 nations (the details given here are as reported in a Commission press release of 27 June 1996). The only new areas in SOCRATES concerned the schools partnerships under COMENIUS and co-operation in adult education; 37 of the first 109 co-operation projects were in adult education, accounting for a budget of nearly 3 million ECUs. In addition, 41 of the approved projects concerned the introduction of the European dimension into open and distance learning, including, for instance, the use of multimedia materials in teacher training. As foreshadowed in the 1991 *Memorandum* (CEC 1991a), the emphasis here was upon the use of new technologies in conventional educational settings. Under

COMENIUS,the Commission worked quickly to support, in 1995, some 500 school partnerships, 800 teacher exchange schemes and 500 study visits for head teachers (CEC 1996e). Otherwise, most of the activities supported by SOCRATES bore a strong similarity to those that had existed under the previous action programmes.

LEONARDO DA VINCI was even less innovative. This was not surprising as it was little more than a collection of existing pro- grammes (essentially FORCE, PETRA and elements of LINGUA and COMETT) with a clearer emphasis upon transnationality and what the Union called 'transversal partnerships' (that is, consortia which brought together the different types and levels of training organisation). Nevertheless, its cumulative scale was substantial. Following what was, by now, the customary wrangling between Commission, Parliament and Council, the total budget allocation for the period 1995–1999 was 620 million ECUs. From 4542 re- sponses to the first call for proposals, issued in May 1995, the Commission decided to support 749, with a combined grant of 89,656,442 ECUs (details taken from the Commission press release of 14 December 1995). By and large, the pattern followed that of the previous action programmes, though with some significant, if limited, new trends. As before, training establishments (including universities and vocational colleges as well as private bodies) formed the largest single group of initiators, constituting 32 per cent of the principal promoters. Also as before, almost all the approved projects were pilot projects (555 in total), with the inten- tion that the 'lessons' should be absorbed by the partners once LEONARDO funding came to an end (though one of the main lessons from the earlier generation of projects was that the most successful partnerships would usually submit an application for further funding from the EU). An important new development was the increased role of small- and medium-sized firms (SMEs), who now constituted some 21 per cent of all partners in approved projects; though this was still a considerable under-representation, it was rather better than in the earlier action programmes where the absence of SMEs had caused some policy makers and experts considerable concern. Other significant features, all of them pre- sent in the earlier programmes but accentuated further in LEONARDO, included a strong emphasis on the new technolo- gies, a focus on social disadvantage and the extension of social- partner networks (see Chapter Four for a further discussion of social partnership) and sectoral networks such as those in agri-food and automobiles.

Rather surprisingly, the changes in status did not greatly alter the EU's financial support for education and training. As Table 3.1 shows, the proportion of total EU spending which was allocated to DGXXII (and before it, the Task Force) and its programmes actually *fell* after 1992. Even in 1992, which witnessed both the Maastricht conference and the completion of the single market, the share devoted to education and training represented considerably less than half of one per cent of the EU's total annual spending. To put this in perspective, the Common Agricultural Policy in 1994 consumed just over 49 per cent of the Union's annual spending while the ESF took just over 8 per cent and the Community Initiatives something under 3 per cent (CEC 1995d). Although the Union had certainly increased the visibility of its education and training policies, and persistently claimed that it had enhanced both their status and priority, it had done absolutely nothing to shift its pattern of spending in their favour. This might imply that the Union was simply speaking with a forked tongue, and, to some extent, no doubt it was. To leave it at that would, for all its appealing simplicity, be inadequate. Alternative or – more accurately – complementary explanations need to be considered. One of these is the pressure on some of the smaller, discretionary areas in the Union's budget arising out of the Council's insistence on financial prudence after Maastricht; particularly after Delors had been replaced by the more pragmatic Santer, colourful flagships

**Table 3.1: Proportion of the total EU budget allocated to Education, Training, Youth 1990–1995 (based on the annual General Reports of the EU)**

| Year | Percentage of total budget |
|------|---------------------------|
| 1990 | 0.32% |
| 1991 | 0.39% |
| 1992 | 0.46% |
| 1993 | 0.42% |
| 1994 | 0.43% |
| 1995 | 0.40% |

*Source:* General Reports of the Activities of the European Community/European Union

tended to take second place to a search for ways of identifiably adding value at a European level. Another was the growing recognition that it was easier and often more effective for the Union to pursue its policy goals in education and training by reshaping other human resources measures, such as ESF, so that they were consistent with those policy goals.

The changes brought about by the Treaty thus affected the EU's policies in related fields, with inevitable consequences for its overall spending on training and education. The Structural Funds were not much affected directly by the Treaty; indirectly, the Union's revised powers over training and education were bound to affect the Funds indirectly since it was through the ESF and the Community Initiatives that much of its total spending on the area was channelled. Spending on the ESF and Community Initiatives dwarfed the sums allocated to education and training programmes, as has already been noted. Moreover, even though they too were affected by the more constrained financial regime that followed 1992 – particularly visible in the changing balance of spending between the ESF and the Initiatives – as a share of total spending, they continued together to account for well above 10 per cent of the Union's total budget (Table 3.2). If the Union's emerging human resources policy goals were to have any serious influence within the member states, the ESF and Initiatives were the most logical places for this impact to take effect and become visible to

**Table 3.2: Proportion of the total EU budget allocated to the European Social Fund and Community Initiatives, 1991 and 1995**

| Year | ESF | Community Initiatives |
|------|-----|----------------------|
| 1991 | 8.99% | 2.38% |
| 1995 | 7.11% | 3.33% |

*Source*: General Reports (for 1991 and 1995) of the Activities of the European Community

actors outside the charmed circle of the Union's own institutions. In the mid-1990s the Union started to revise its larger human resources programmes. Between 1994 and 1996, for example, the Union brought together several existing Community Initiatives into a common framework (EMPLOYMENT) which was specifically aimed at promoting employment growth through the development of human resources. EMPLOYMENT comprised four distinct but interrelated strands:

- promoting equal employment for women, particularly in respect of training, access to growing occupations and to management ('Employment – NOW')
- improving the employment of the disabled ('Employment – HORIZON')
- integrating young people into the labour market, especially those with no basic qualifications ('Employment – YOUTHSTART')
- enhancing the employability of vulnerable groups such as migrants, refugees and people living in disadvantaged urban areas ('Employment – INTEGRA').

As well as placing a stronger strategic emphasis on human resource development in its policies for employment creation, by bringing the four measures into one framework initiative the Union hoped to increase the effectiveness and visibility of its intervention, not least because EMPLOYMENT placed a much heavier stress upon transnational activities than had the earlier programmes (*OJ*, 10 July 1996).

Similar hopes informed the development of another, parallel Initiative in 1994, aimed at helping European companies to adjust to industrial change. The ADAPT Initiative was targeted at four specific goals:

- helping companies improve their training strategy and content
- gearing training and guidance to support competitiveness
- helping safeguard existing jobs by improving general skills levels
- developing training and guidance which anticipate future industrial changes.

Like EMPLOYMENT, ADAPT is chiefly concerned with funding projects in the member states; those projects must involve links between partners in at least two member states and they must fit national priorities. Thus the UK priorities focus particularly on promoting the growth of jobs in small firms and in high-growth sectors such as services, tourism, and arts and culture.

In addition, in 1993 the Union revised the ESF Regulations to strengthen and widen the Fund's activities. Administratively, the new Regulations were designed to ensure a more strategic relationship between allocations under the Fund and the policies of the member states. Member states were required to draw up a plan for the programming period (1994–1999 in this case) which outlined their own policies and spending plans and indicated where the additional allocations fitted into the national picture. The Commission and each member state were then to draw up an agreed Community Support Framework (CSF) detailing the operational programmes for which funding was requested. One national civil servant involved in this delicate negotiation said, after drafting a Single Programming Document (combining both the plan, the CSF and the operational programmes), that 'the trick is in the wording – you've got to bring down the money and, at the same time, give your departments as much discretion as possible' (Interview, February 1995). The same interviewee's experience was also that the negotiations were real, with constant redrafting after meetings with the Commission.

Most importantly, the Union merged two existing objectives concerned with training the unemployed and secured additional resources for a new Objective Four with the aim of 'facilitating adaptation of the workforce to industrial change and changes in production systems'. This was the first time that the ESF had a substantial and general commitment to training for those who were already in a job. Essentially, the Union's aim in introducing this measure was to direct attention and resources towards *preventing* unemployment by targeting employees in sectors and organisations where there were risks of redundancy or closure, rather than simply trying to rescue the unemployed. It provoked opposition from the UK, whose government argued that it amounted to subsidising lame duck companies and that any company which was involved would effectively be publicised as a failing concern. The Union therefore agreed that the UK could spend its Structural Funds' allocation on other Objectives, though monitoring this was as ever to prove difficult (Barnett and Borooah 1995). A new sixth Objective was introduced covering support to regions with an extremely low population density; the only areas meeting the criteria for Objective Six support were in the north of Finland and Sweden, both new entrants to the Union. The new

Objective Six was small-scale, accounting for less than half a per cent of all Structural Funds' spending. More substantially, the Union sought to ensure that the new Objective Four complemented the transnational measures supported under ADAPT. Because of the size of these two innovative programmes, and because of their direct impact within the member states, it could reasonably be concluded that they were at least as important in terms of their overall influence as the SOCRATES and LEONARDO action programmes.

**Table 3.3: Breakdown of the European Social Fund,**
**1994–1999 (percentages)**

| Objective 1 | 47.6 |
|---|---|
| Objective 2 | 7.8 |
| Objective 3 | 27.4 |
| Objective 4 | 4.9 |
| Objective 5 | 2.0 |
| Objective 6 | 0.4 |
| Community Initiatives | 9.0 |

*Source:* General Reports of the Activities of the European Community for 1994

## The 1995 White Paper

Completion of the post-Treaty reforms did not exhaust the Union's interest in human resources issues. If anything, the Commission, frustrated by the limited nature of the changes which it had been able to make, started to place education and training more firmly towards the centre of its strategy for continued integration. As ever, a range of different reasons can be discerned for this process: some of these had to do with the internal political process within the Union as different actors repositioned themselves in respect of further European integration and others were more directly concerned with the potential role of education and training as a means of solving other, often pressing, problems which faced the Union (the chief of which was, for most of the leading politicians, its contribution towards European competitiveness). Given the Union's limited competences in this area, perhaps it was inevitable that the contrast between the discourse of crisis which permeated its analysis and the limited nature of its proposals should become ever sharper. The publication, in late 1995, of the Commission's

White Paper, *Teaching and Learning: towards the learning society*, did little to resolve the resulting tensions.

Organisationally, the White Paper arrived by a rather unusual route. As two of the Commission's officers mentioned during interviews (November 1996), the White Paper was not preceded as is usual by consultation over a Green Paper. Rather, it was drafted by the Study Group on Education and Training, a gathering of specialists appointed personally by Mrs Cresson in the autumn of 1995 and responsible directly to her. The final report – influenced heavily, so it is said, by its French chair – was wideranging in the extreme. The title, with its reference to the 'learning society' (*société cognitive* in French, *der kognitiven Gesellschaft* in German), signals both the direction and the scope of its ambition.

In a number of ways, *Teaching and Learning: towards the learning society* was a new departure for the European Union. For a start, the White Paper represents the Commission's first policy statement based on the responsibilities it was given for education and training under the Maastricht Treaty. Perhaps its most significant aspect was its focus on lifelong learning. As is so often the case, this emphasis was justified by the discourse of crisis, but alongside the rather familiar language of crisis the White Paper also employed a discourse of social transformation: we read that we are in a 'period of transition and profound change', a time of 'historical opportunity for Europe', a period 'in which one society gives birth to the next', even the dawning of a 'new age'. This discourse was also pursued by the President of the Commission; in a speech to the employers' federation, UNICE, in the week following the Commission's adoption of the White Paper, Santer described 'our epoch as a phase of transition towards a new society' (Santer 1995b). Yet while recognising the importance of lifelong learning, the Commission largely defined its significance in terms of employment and the economy.

In the opening sections of the White Paper the Commission noted the wide range of challenges facing the European economy. In particular, it identified three 'factors of upheaval':

- the impact of the information society upon employment and learning
- the internationalisation of the economy
- the development and dissemination of scientific and technological knowledge (CEC 1995e, pp.21–6).

As a result, no one individual or organisation could expect to remain untouched. Instead of a job for life, individuals had to be as adaptable and flexible as their employers had to be innovative. In response to the uncertainty and risk introduced by these upheavals, the White Paper proclaimed that 'The society of the future will therefore be a learning society' (CEC 1995e, p.16). In defining this objective, the White Paper painted a rather general and imprecise picture of the learning society: 'Tomorrow's society will be a society which invests in knowledge, a society of teaching and learning, in which each individual will build up his or her own qualifications' (CEC 1995e, p.5). In places it used the term 'knowledge-based society' as though the two were interchangeable (see, for example, CEC 1995e, p.9).

While its primary focus was upon employment and competitiveness, the Commission also argued that education and training were vital 'to the preservation of (Europe's) social model' (CEC 1995e, p.49). Arising from the three 'factors of upheaval', there was an 'urgent need to avert a rift in society' (emphasis in original – CEC 1995e, p.48). European society had to avoid a division 'between those that can interpret; those who can only use; and those who are pushed out' (CEC 1995e, p.26). A new principle of post-industrial social organisation was emerging: 'the 'learning relationship' will become an increasingly dominant feature in the structure of our societies' (CEC 1995e, p.17). Consequently, for reasons of both competitiveness and social solidarity, all must be able to seize opportunities for improvement and fulfilment 'throughout their working lives' (CEC 1995e, p.17). The White Paper contrasted this lifelong learning approach with the traditional emphasis upon once-and-for-all qualifications gained at school or in initial training and lasting, with minor adaptation, for a lifetime.

Second, the Commission expressed a robust view of the need for action across the entire Union. As well as the prospective impact of labour mobility throughout Europe, the nature of the three 'factors of upheaval' justified action at the European level. Indeed, globalisation and the spread of new technologies, according to the White Paper, create 'the risk of cultural uniformity' (CEC 1995e, p.18). Cultural uniformity was defined as the risk that new communications technologies in education will lead to a 'lowest common denominator', so that people 'lose a common heritage of

bearings and reference points' (CEC 1995e, p.30). European civilisation is, according to the White Paper, particularly under threat
at present from American domination of multi-media products
and, above all, of the educational software market. Thus 'to a
greater extent than before, promoting the European dimension in
education and training has become a necessity for efficiency in the
face of internationalisation and to avoid the risk of a watered-
down European society' (CEC 1995e, p.51).

Third, the White Paper attempted to sketch a human resources
strategy across the Union. Much of this analysis is now well-established in the Western nations, encompassing such issues as the
changing age-structure of European society, the rise in the number
of working women, technical innovation in all areas and awareness of the environmental constraints on growth. In response,
Europe's success was said to depend on the need to instil a *broad
knowledge base* and building up *abilities for employment and economic
life*. In essence, this involved a call for measures such as greater
flexibility of delivery, wider access to continuing training, closer
school–business partnerships and the recognition of prior learning. It is notable that this agenda was evidently designed to match
the Commission's proposals in other policy areas. These include
its policies for the information society, for research and technology
development, for social solidarity and regional regeneration and,
above all, for employment and growth.

Following the sustained analysis of human resource issues
across the Union, the White Paper then turned towards specifics.
As well as calling for a debate throughout the European Year of
Lifelong Learning on the issues connected with the creation of a
learning society, it urged the pursuit of five 'general objectives'
across the Union:

- promoting the acquisition of new knowledge – with an
  emphasis on breadth rather than narrowness – along with
  improved recognition of skills and knowledge (e.g.
  through a new European accreditation system), greater
  ease of student mobility and support for software
  development

- building closer relations between schools and business,
  including a new European apprenticeship scheme with
  trainee mobility along the lines of ERASMUS

- combating social exclusion, through the creation of 'second chance schools' in deprived inner city areas and the creation of a European voluntary service

- demanding proficiency for every citizen in three Union languages, with a new 'European quality label' for schools which meet agreed criteria for language development, and continued support for teacher mobility

- treating capital investment and training investment on an equal basis, with the EU measuring performance in member states and publishing the results, and sponsoring an investigation of the legal and administrative changes needed if companies are to treat training expenditure as an investment.

The White Paper noted that the Commission can only fund new initiatives by reallocating existing funds for education and training. Anyway, under the principle of subsidiarity, in many cases action would have to be taken by member states, local government or trade unions and employers.

Compared with the ambition of the White Paper's title, these measures seemed humble and conservative. The White Paper itself contended that the creation of the learning society 'entails radical change' (CEC 1995e, p.74). Yet the White Paper's proposals failed to live up to this challenge, a failure which was apparent on a number of levels. First, although the White Paper referred throughout to the need for learning to occur throughout one's working life, its primary focus remained the initial education system. Of course, schools and entry-level training can hardly remain unaffected by the requirements of a learning society (for example, through far greater attention to the ability to learn independently and critically from a wide range of information sources, including the mass media), but what was proposed failed to address these issues. Further, although the White Paper paid due lip-service to the need for personal development and social learning, and even active citizenship, as well as training, there was no sign that the Commission had any concrete proposals in these areas. In fact, the White Paper simply replicated the established boundary between vocational training and general education (at a time when firms like Ford, Michelin and Lucas were reporting the commercial benefits from blurring the boundaries between training and more general learning). Third, as Coffield (1996) has noted, the White Paper gave the pivotal role in constructing the learning society to the individual, downplaying the role of more collective arrangements in promoting or hindering lifelong learning (as examples, he cites CEC 1995a, p.48 and p.51). Finally, the fear of cultural uniformity was less than helpful, representing the implicit xenophobia that appears to continue to drive much of the EU's fear of Japan and the USA.

Within the Union, the White Paper's reception was lukewarm. The Education Council gave it very short shrift indeed. Formally debating the White Paper at its May 1996 session, the Education Ministers expressed their views in the form of some carefully-worded, but sharply critical, 'Council Conclusions'. In their opening remarks, rather than offering the conventional words of welcome for the White Paper, the Education Ministers chose 'to thank the Commission for this further contribution to the analysis of the major issues facing the development of the Member States' education and training systems' (*OJ*, 6 July 1996, p.1). Having politely, but firmly, reminded the Commission that this ground belonged to the member states, the Ministers then proceeded to attack the White Paper for its vocational emphasis and instrumental approach, indicating that the Commission had fallen victim to 'an Enlightenment view of social change, in which excessive hopes are placed in knowledge as an end in itself' (*OJ*, 6 July 1996).

In the Ministers' opinion, the Commission's linear view of the relationship between learning and economic growth had led it to focus overmuch on globalisation and the new technologies, thus ignoring 'significant demographic changes, the confrontation of cultures, environmental issues, threats to the ways we live together in democracy, and the serious problem of social marginalization, which is largely the result of the divide in terms of knowledge and the use of capacities to master it' (*OJ*, 6 July 1996, p.2). Again in measured terms, the Ministers noted that it was apparently necessary to restate the Treaty's clear declarations on national sovereignty in this area, as well as on the principle of subsidiarity. They then reminded the Commission that the same problems were being debated, from perspectives which embraced cultural and 'purely educational' as well as economic issues, in the Council of Europe, UNESCO and the OECD (the Ministers did not see fit to labour the point that these transnational bodies, unlike the EU, may not make decisions that bind their members). Essentially, the Council had given as clear an indication as it could that it did not intend to take the White Paper further.

The Committee of the Regions was not quite so negative. Its opening comment likewise broke with convention: rather than a welcome, the Committee decided to say that it 'notes that the White Paper provides food for thought' (*OJ*, 24 June 1996, p.16). Representing regional and local levels of government, CoR expressed similar views to those of the Council on what it saw as the Commission's disregard for the principle of subsidiarity, adding that 'the objective of the EU is not to set up a European Planning Authority for training and education '(*OJ*, 24 June 1996, p16). It also took issue with the Commission's narrow conception of education and training. Unlike the Council, which had found little to welcome in the five objectives listed in the White Paper, CoR expressed guarded interest in all five. Thus it believed that the idea of the 'second chance school' for young people was inadequate in the context of a 'continuous lifelong learning approach'. It reminded the Commission of the importance of lesser-used minority and regional languages and pointed out that encouraging enterprises to invest more in training was a matter for member states (*OJ*, 24 June 1996, pp.19–20). It concluded with a call for education and training to promote mutual understanding and tolerance and foster 'participation in the democratic decision-making process' – issues which the White Paper had not addressed (*OJ*, 24 June 1996, p.21).

Was this lukewarm reception justified? Certainly, the White Paper was a rather uneven document. On the down side, it was dominated by old agendas for action. It aimed at old targets, trying to encourage a sharp growth in Union-wide labour markets. It used old weapons such as student mobility. Yet, as we have seen, labour market researchers have repeatedly shown that transnational labour migration is a phenomenon of the relatively unskilled or takes place within international firms; in either case, student mobility schemes are largely irrelevant. Moreover, student mobility systematically excludes a range of groups, including most adult students and virtually all those that suffer from social exclusion (like the unemployed and single parents). The most innovative proposal – that of treating spending on training as a form of capital investment for fiscal purposes – also caused greatest annoyance in the member states, partly because it was plainly a case of Commission encroachment onto an area of national sovereignty and partly because previous attempts by some nations to do this had foundered on the genuine practical difficulties. This was, according to the President of the European Parliament, a 'hot issue' which involved 'an area where the EU has no influence' (Kops and Hänsch 1996, p.3). Temporarily backing down on this contentious proposal, the Commission tried to avoid further controversy by asking its vocational training development agency, CEDEFOP (described in more detail in Chapter Five), to carry out a series of case studies of vocational training funding systems. Finally, the White Paper was widely criticised during the consultation process for its lack of vision, its focus on the schooling process and, above all, its emphasis upon continuing training as the major form of lifelong learning. Such criticisms were particularly common not only among the professional adult education community (e.g. Deutscher Volkshochschul-verband 1996), but as we have already seen the Council and CoR had expressed similar misgivings.

Nevertheless, the White Paper did restate the far-reaching diagnosis of Europe's human resources challenge. It also took it for granted that the idea of a learning society now commands widespread support. Overall, though, like the discussion documents which had preceded the 1992 Treaty and the Green Paper on the European dimension in education which followed it, the 1995 White Paper was essentially a conservative document. In this it stood in contrast to the European Year of Lifelong Learning, in which the Commission showed a willingness to take risks and support demonstration projects that raised important questions about the nature and direction of the Learning Society. In using the White Paper to float ideas which plainly encroached upon national sovereignty, moreover, the Commission may unintentionally have done its cause more harm than good.

## Policy development in the mid-1990s: expanding the agenda

The decision to organise a European Year of Lifelong Learning was first flagged in Delors' White Paper on competitiveness. In the White Paper the Commission had signalled a strong interest in lifelong learning as the indispensable condition for a competitive economy:

Preparation for life in tomorrow's world cannot be satisfied by a once-and-for-all acquisition of knowledge and know-how... All measures must therefore necessarily be based on the concept of developing, generalising and systematising lifelong learning and continuing training. (CEC 1994c, pp.16, 136)

In its earlier forms, the Commission's proposal for a year of activities to celebrate and promote lifelong learning continued to pursue the emphasis upon competitiveness and its focus was initially upon continuing vocational training. However, in agreeing to support the proposal, both the Council and the Parliament emphasised the need to go beyond this immediate concern to embrace lifelong learning as a means of achieving personal fulfillment and promoting multicultural tolerance and active citizenship.

One Commission official's judgement was that the Year was a success in other ways as well. Although some of the more than 5000 projects had been extremely unusual (pub-based learning in West Yorkshire, to take one example), this was inherent in the intention of the way the Year was organised. The whole purpose of funding demonstration projects was that they should catch people's attention. In the event, the demonstration projects appear to have had some effectiveness not only in the member states but also within the Commission itself. According to an official in DGXXII:

They are reaching a level of policy profile and visibility inside the Commission and to some extent in the member states which they have not had before, and this is bound to have an influence on the way my colleagues view lifelong learning. (Interview, November 1996)

If this was the case, however, the idea of lifelong learning was also increasingly part of a wider raft of education policy goals being promoted within the Union as the whole area started to come once more under review.

Following the ratification of the 1992 Treaty, it became apparent that the Article on education posed constraints to further developments in Union policy. Initially, few of the Union's institutions proposed anything but relatively minor adjustments. In a 1994 interview, for example, the chair of the Committee of the Region's commission on education and training suggested that the exclusion of training from the areas where CoR was formally consulted had created 'rather an anomalous situation and one which may need to be redressed in future' (Farrington 1994, p.5), a perspective subsequently incorporated into CoR's proposals for the next Treaty revision (*OJ*, 2 April 1995). Otherwise, generally speaking, the Union's political leaders tended to work around the constraints – a tactic that ranged from an emphasis upon cross-national factors such as multimedia technologies through to the restructuring of other measures such as the Structural Funds – rather than propose further constitutional changes. A more radical approach was left to the Study Group on Education and Training, in its 1997 report, *Accomplishing Europe through Education and Training* (CEC 1997a).

Originally convened in June 1995 to help complete the drafting of the education and training White Paper, the Study Group's members were appointed by Edith Cresson and reported to her. Chaired by a senior French academic, Prof. Jean-Louis Reiffers of the Université de la Méditerrané, most of its twenty-two members were highly-regarded and experienced academics specialising in human resources issues: David Marsden, for instance, a Reader at the London School of Economics, has written widely on aspects of the labour market and John Coolahan, Professor of Education at St Patrick's College, regularly acted as a senior policy adviser to the Irish government. The fact that the Group's membership was not appointed by member states ensured that they had a degree of independence from national governments, who sometimes regard service on Union committees as carrying an obligation to express views in line with national policies. Yet the fact that the Group owed its continuing existence to Mme. Cresson, and was serviced by a secretariat that was appointed by DGXXII, meant that it had to work within constraints and boundaries that were at best ambiguous and unclear. At the same time, the Commission could always emphasise the unofficial nature of the Study Group, and the breadth of its remit, if its ideas caused offence elsewhere. In short, the Commissioner had created an ideal vehicle for developing potentially controversial ideas and proposals while minimising the risks of being seen to overstep the limits imposed by the Treaty.

In its report, which appeared in early 1997, the Study Group called for a fundamental overhaul of the education and training system (CEC 1997a, p.50). Four broad aims were identified for the education and training system as being central to this process of transformation:

- constructing European citizenship, by such means as promoting active pedagogies, encouraging mutual understanding, countering discrimination, extending foreign language teaching and removing the focus upon 'nationally-based views' in history and geography

- reinforcing Europe's competitiveness and preserving employment, by adopting pedagogies which develop 'the collective can-do', focusing on behaviour as well as knowledge, strengthening business–education partnerships, defining new occupational profiles and encouraging continuing lifelong training

- maintaining social cohesion, by guaranteeing a strong base of knowledge and skills to all young Europeans and strengthening pre-school and adult education

- taking full advantage of the information society, whose influence (the Study Group believed) will develop more slowly than elsewhere (CEC 1997a, p.50).

Bridging these four broad goals was a strong emphasis upon 'added value' and quality.

In particular, the Study Group called for a guarantee that all young Europeans will leave school with a clearly specified foundation of 'recognised basic knowledge and skills'. According to the Study Group, education and training were now out of step with the wider process of integration:

> The past twenty years have seen a notable convergence of production costs, relative product prices, currencies and incomes. Yet age-specific educational targets, the teaching and learning methods, curricula and assessment methods have hardly converged at all. This makes no sense... It is particularly important that at the critical ages (end of compulsory schooling/upper secondary/each university cycle) Europe specifies its aims unambiguously and informs all young Europeans where they stand personally, as well as how their school or college is performing with respect to those aims. (CEC 1997a, p.29)

Very clearly, then, the Study Group report went substantially beyond the concern with competitiveness which had predominated in previous discussions of Union policy.

The Study Group's report also deliberately breached the boundaries laid down in Articles 126 and 127 of the 1992 Treaty. The report explicitly addressed this problem:

> Article 126 of the Treaty limits the European Union's avenues of action as regards the organisation and operation of education and training systems, which clearly fall within national competence. The Study Group takes the view that this is an advantage, given the desirability of having a number of pathways to achieving similar ends. On the other hand, no interpretation of the concept of subsidiarity should be so restrictive that it prevents Europe...from declaring what the main common aims of our education and training systems are to be. Europe must also contribute, through initiatives and projects, to the wide dissemination of best practice and must encourage progress towards those aims. The Study Group takes the view that these efforts require more close collaboration with the member states than has been the case to date (CEC 1997a, pp.137–8).

It therefore proposed that a common aim for education and training across the Union should be rooted 'either in the Treaty or in another legal foundation' (CEC 1997a, p.138).

Because of its ambiguous status, the Study Group was able to explore ideas without too much homage to the Treaty restrictions. Yet it would be ingenuous to treat the Study Group's report as mere academic kite-flying. By dealing with citizenship as well as social cohesion, competitiveness and the information society (and indeed by expressing reservations over the significance of the latter), the report took a somewhat different approach from that of the Delors White Paper on growth, competitiveness and employment, and even from that of the Cresson/Flynn White Paper on education and training. Of course, there were also many continuities: in particular, in defining the objectives of the Union's interest in this area, the report took competitiveness as given which requires little further elaboration. Similarly, although it paid the obligatory lip-service to the learning society, its sole concrete reference to lifelong learning concerned the desirability of general adult education in redressing social exclusion; as an example, it cited the historically significant French extra-mural movement, the *universités populaires* – rather than the vibrant and more contemporary Spanish *universidades populares* – which suggested a somewhat conservative vision of lifelong learning. This impression was reinforced by the extent to which the report focused on the initial education system.

Nevertheless, in calling specifically for a revision of the Treaty in order to expand the Union's competences, the report set down a marker for the future. Moreover, the creation of study groups of this type is characteristically one of the routes taken by the Union in seeking to create a coalition of support for an expansion of its competences (this is considered further in Chapter Four). Typically, it adopted some of the discourse of crisis that has been so widely used by the Union's politicians to justify their involvement in education and training. And in great contrast with the White Paper on education and training, the Study Group's chief proposals were for action at Union level in order to 'lend concrete expression to the European vision that we offer to our young people and to develop lifelong learning' (CEC 1997a).

## Discussion

Between 1992 and 1997 the policy debate over education and training acquired a new momentum within the Union. In part, it benefited from the impetus that it had acquired during the move towards the single market when the Delors Commission had started to press for education and training to occupy a more central place in the Union's preoccupations. By continuing to couple its far-reaching analysis of the present education and training system with the discourse of a crisis of competitiveness, the Union's institutions gave their relatively modest proposals an air of obviousness, even of historic inevitability. Where more fundamental change was desired, the Union preferred quietly to redirect resources within its own programmes than to risk the chance of reversal in any public debate over the limits to its competences. By 1997, though, the tensions within this position were increasingly apparent.

Yet much remained unchanged, and frequently unchallenged. Above all, the Union's *modus operandi* had changed little since the mid-1980s. Although the range of eligible institutions had been widened substantially, the action programmes were essentially

incentive schemes which rested on voluntary participation in
transnational partnerships of organisations. This *modus operandi*
had a number of virtues from the Union's perspective. One was
that it allowed the Union's institutions to build up relationships
directly with actors on the ground, rather than filtering decisions
through the screening mechanisms of the member states. Another
was that any such partnership had the active assent of all the
partners; in theory at any rate, there were no conscripts, only
willing volunteers. Frequently the Commission gave the impression that the activities themselves were sufficient justification for
their existence; for all its insistence on evaluation by others, it has
rarely learned systematically from its own experiences. This impression was misleading, though. What the Commission had
learned was how to work with educational and training institutions and systems with a minimum of involvement by the member
states and how to push the boundaries of its competence forward
on an incremental, step-by-step basis.

Second, competitiveness remained the central concern
throughout. Speaking at the launch of the SOCRATES programme in November 1995, for example, Commissioner Edith
Cresson emphasised the contribution of education as a 'key
factor' in European competitiveness:

> Non-tangible investment, that is notably education invest-
> ment, is clearly felt to be a priority at Union level: it has
> become obvious that it is through the quality of its human
> resources that Europe can face up to global competition
> while maintaining its own distinctive social model. (Cresson
> 1995)

This view had plenty of detractors – though as many of the critics
also benefited from participation in the Union's programmes, their
comments were sometimes muted. This was not always the case.
Despite its active involvement in the SOCRATES programme, the
German Folk High School Association opened its response to the
White Paper with an attack on the fact that 'in the White Paper,
general continuing education is primarily justified on grounds of
its occupational benefits for individuals and its economic benefits
for society' (Deutscher Volkshochschul-Verband 1996, p.1). Yet the
focus on competitiveness is highly serviceable for the Union's
political leaders. Quite apart from any other consideration, economic growth is widely accepted by the member states as a

legitimate goal of Union activity and any policy proposal which complements this aim is likely to win a hearing. Hence the merit of introducing a wide-ranging, even visionary, analysis of the potential role of education and training in overcoming the present crisis of competitiveness.

For all the ambition of its analysis, the Union is still bound by the terms of the Treaty. Achieving the necessary compromises on any Treaty revision was difficult enough with 12 member states; in an enlarged Union it is difficult to see how there can be any coalition sufficiently strong to widen the Union's legal competences in respect of education and training. The suggestion in this chapter is that when the scope of the Union's policy thinking exceeds the limits of its Treaty competences, it often seeks to pursue the implications through its own more important areas of activity – the Structural Funds or the Research and Technology Development programmes – than to engage in open conflict with the Council and the member states. The following three chapters explore some of these issues in greater depth.

# Chapter Four

# Education, Training and European Integration

For over thirty years the EU has steadily developed its interest in human resources issues. From being a provider of indirect support for vocational training through subventions to the member states, its competences have steadily widened to embrace policies and programmes covering almost the entire field of education and training. Spending on the area, though still modest, has grown steadily in recent years and education and training are regularly taken into account when determining policy and spending on such areas as research and technology development, regional policy or equal opportunities. Leading European politicians, moreover, now routinely state that the quality of Europe's human resources will be a key factor – perhaps even the central factor – in determining the future of the Union. In consequence, they have come to propose a radical overhaul of the education and training system as a necessary step in the achievement of a learning society. In practice, though, what has the EU achieved?

If the analysis pursued so far is accurate, then answering this question will not be a simple matter. Although education and training have been given the status of a formal and discrete policy area within the EU, overseen by a separate Directorate-General, this has not brought about an end to the adoption of education and training measures as a complementary element within other policy areas – environmental protection, regional policy or promotion of the audiovisual industry, for instance. Social policy remains the largest single area for EU spending on education and training; EU policies for research and technology development have also had a considerable impact on education and training. To determine more fully the overall influence of the EU on the direction of education and training systems across Europe, then, we will need to look across different areas of activity, and the following three chapters in turn consider the Union's policies for labour mobility, its social policy and its policies for research, development and innovation – all of which have directly touched upon the fields of education and training. This chapter has a more narrow focus, providing an analysis of those policies and programmes which are primarily concerned with education and training in themselves. As the previous chapter has shown, the range of the Union's initiatives expanded dramatically between the mid-1980s and the mid-1990s, and the focus here, therefore, is on three areas of interest: the impact of the student mobility schemes, support for human resource development in central and eastern Europe and the relatively new and untried area of schools partnerships.

If their public pronouncements are anything to go by, the Union's own leaders believe firmly that their intervention has been both substantial and positive. As early as 1992 Commissioner Vasso Papandreou claimed that the Union's action programmes had created 'an exciting network of partnerships which has already changed the face of higher education by involving it directly in the construction of a Citizen's Europe' (Papandreou 1992, p.5). Yet, as usual, we should treat such claims with all the caution we would apply to comestic politicians. For instance, the evidence available to Papandreou in 1992 showed that the EU's action programmes were falling well short of its own targets. In launching the ERASMUS programme, the EU had stated that it aimed to see one student in ten spending some of their studies in another member state by 1992; the actual level achieved in that year was around 4 per cent – a figure that, according to the Commission, represented 'significant progress towards the 10 per cent mobility target' (CEC 1993c, p.10). While there can be little doubt that the EU's policies and programmes have had some impact upon individual institutions and national systems alike, that impact has been both limited and uneven. Moreover, what we are currently witnessing is both the product of specific policies and measures within the EU and also part of a wider internationalisation of the education systems of the advanced nations as they respond to and, in turn, help to create the globalising tendencies of modern societies. This pattern will be seen repeatedly as we examine the three different areas selected for closer analysis in this chapter.

## Student mobility

In encouraging student mobility through such programmes as ERAS-MUS, COMETT and LINGUA, the Union believes that it is making a long-term investment. Its ideal is the creation of ever more graduates:

> who have had *first-hand experience of studying, living and working in another Community country*, who are proficient in a number of Community languages, who have begun to understand and appreciate the culture and mentality of other Community countries and for whom the whole of Europe as opposed to the single nation state is a natural area of activity. (CEC 1991a, p.28; emphasis in original)

Particularly in the mid-1980s, the Union's focus was on supporting mobility in higher education. For the Commission, undergraduates represented the future in at least three senses: they were young and could expect a reasonable shelf-life, they had less of an investment than older Europeans in the nation state system which the Union sought to complement and partly replace and, perhaps above all, they would eventually become Europe's decision-taking class. Regardless of the legal difficulties described in Chapter Two, influencing this group became an important element in the Delors strategy for achieving the single market. Has it worked?

For the Union's political leaders there is no question but that the student mobility programmes have been stupendously successful. Papandreou's successor as Commissioner responsible for education and training policy, Edith Cresson, has claimed that:

> For the 500,000 young people who have already benefited from ERASMUS, the image of Europe is no longer that of a distant abstraction or a bureaucracy hung about with regulations. For them, Europe has become a concrete reality, a wellspring of learning and opening out. (Cresson 1995)

Such judgements appear remarkably confident, if somewhat premature. The ERASMUS programme came nowhere near meeting the target originally set for it of providing, by 1992, a period of study abroad for 10 per cent of Europe's students. In fact, by 1992, even taking the 4 per cent who moved within ERASMUS together with students moving independently of the EU schemes, the total number who studied for at least part of their course in another member state reached, at most, an estimated 6 per cent or 7 per cent (CEC 1993c). In Europe's most popular destination, the United

Kingdom, other EU nationals accounted for fewer than 4.2 per cent of all higher education students (HESA 1996). Moreover, many more students than those benefiting from EU programmes study at a higher education institution in another EU member state (Gordon and Jallade 1996). It appears, then, that in this respect the planned Europeanisation of higher education has achieved relatively little.

Given the Union's ambitions for its higher education programme, this conclusion at first seems surprising. A closer examination of the figures suggests that it is also only partly accurate: progress towards the Europeanisation of higher education was uneven with much faster progress in some countries and subjects than in others. Table 4.1 summarises the position in the various member states (excluding Luxembourg, which does not have its own university system) in the period between 1986 and 1993. This covers the first seven years of the ERASMUS programme, which should be enough to give us some idea of its overall impact. In one case – that of the UK – the number of other EU nationals quadrupled. In all other cases the increase was rather

**Table 4.1: EU nationals studying abroad by host country, 1986 and 1993 (thousands)**

| Country | 1986 | 1993 |
|---|---|---|
| Belgium | 11 | 13 |
| Denmark | 1 | 1 |
| France | 19 | 25 |
| Germany | 20 | 27 |
| Greece | 0 | 0 |
| Ireland | 1 | 2 |
| Italy | 13 | 8 |
| Netherlands | 3 | 3 |
| Portugal | 0 | 1 |
| Spain | 4 | 4 |
| United Kingdom | 8 | 33 |

*Source*: EUROSTAT 1995, p.98
*Note:* All figures are given to the nearest 1,000. For Spain, the earlier figures are in fact for 1989. For Belgium and Greece the later figures are for 1991. For Germany, Ireland, Portugal, Spain and the UK the later figures are for 1992.

more modest, while in the case of Italy the number of non-EU nationals actually fell. A quick glance at these overview figures, therefore, suggests that the EU programmes may have stimulated some mobility, if not at the levels expected and hoped for by the Union's politicians. However, a more detailed look at three of the member states –Germany, Italy and the UK – suggests a more complex landscape in which the EU's programmes may have been very minor players indeed.

In the case of the UK, what is striking in the overview data is the growth in the number of third-level students from other EU nations (see Table 4.2). UK universities remain enormously popular with young people from elsewhere in the EU and ERASMUS is a major contributor of overseas students. Thus although the UK, in 1993/94, *sent* out some 18 per cent of all ERASMUS fellowship holders, it *took* some 27 per cent (Teichler 1996b). Yet, as Table 4.2 shows, within UK higher education the EU students are clearly outnumbered by other international students, with Asia, in particular, being a considerable contributor of incoming students (HESA 1996). Particularly significant numbers came from Malaysia (14,627 in 1994/95), Hong Kong (10,683) and Singapore (6326). Also important was the USA (8064 in 1994/95). The largest single

**Table 4.2: All overseas students in UK higher education by domicile and level of course, 1994/1995 (given as a percentage of all overseas students)**

| Domicile | Post-graduate | First Degree | Other under-graduate | Total overseas |
|---|---|---|---|---|
| EU 12 | 29% | 45% | 59% | 40.1% |
| Other European | 8 | 7 | 9 | 8.0 |
| Africa | 9 | 6 | 4 | 6.7 |
| Asia | 33 | 33 | 9 | 29.5 |
| Australasia | 2 | 1 | 1 | 1.0 |
| Middle East | 6 | 4 | 1 | 4.3 |
| North America | 9 | 3 | 17 | 7.7 |
| South America | 3 | 1 | 0 | 1.4 |
| Total Overseas (Numbers) | 69,844 | 69,858 | 24,011 | 163,713 |

*Source*: HESA 1996, p.7.

number of incoming students from the EU nations in the same year came from the Republic of Ireland (12,858, of whom almost one-third were studying in Northern Ireland institutions). The second largest number came from Greece (12,247) – with which the UK has long-established relations in a number of specialist and postgraduate areas, such as medicine – followed by Germany (11,054) and France (9916). In other words, this more detailed statistical examination does little to revise our view of the EU action programmes.

A similar picture emerges from a more detailed study of the German higher education system (Table 4.3). The proportion of other EU nationals among all foreign students in West German institutions fell slightly between 1980 and 1990, while the proportion from other European nations rose (this included Austria, not yet an EU member but participating in ERASMUS, and Poland, a major participant in TEMPUS). The number of West German nationals who studied abroad rose even faster than the number of incoming students, doubling between 1980 and 1990 to reach some 34,000. By far the fastest-growing destination was the USA, whose share of the total rose from 18 per cent in 1980 to over 20 per cent. Other EU member states took 37 per cent in 1980 and 37 per cent again in 1990. Austria's share meanwhile fell from 17 per cent to 15 per cent, while that of Switzerland fell from 14 per cent to 12 per cent (Baumert et al. 1994). At least three different processes were at work in Germany's case. The first is, clearly enough, the influence of the EU action programmes. This must be disentangled, though, from the growing number of students who had been

**Table 4.3: Foreign students in higher education in the German Federal Republic by nationality, 1980 and 1990 (as a percentage of all foreign students)**

| Region | 1980 | 1990 |
|---|---|---|
| EU 12 | 25% | 23% |
| Other Europe | 26 | 30 |
| Africa | 7 | 6 |
| America | 12 | 8 |
| Asia | 30 | 30 |
| Total foreign (numbers) | 56,733 | 99,760 |

Source: Baumert et al. 1994, p.170.

born or brought up in Germany by immigrants or were themselves refugees who hoped to settle in Germany; one authoritative source notes that around 50 per cent of the students who were registered as foreign nationals actually had a German domicile (Baumert *et al.* 1994). Hence the apparent popularity of German universities with the citizens of Greece (over one-quarter of the other EU nationals in 1990) and Turkey (by far the largest single number of foreign students with 9874 in 1990). The third process concerns the globalisation of study patterns among young people generally, a process influenced as much by the cultural attractions of the USA as by any particular set of policies or support programmes. This helps explain not only the growing attraction of the United States as a destination for German students but also the attractiveness of Ireland and the UK, who share a language with the USA.

The Italian case appears to point in quite a different direction. Although the Italian influence over the development of the ERASMUS programme was strong, as Sofia Corradi (1988) has demonstrated, alone in Europe the Italian university system has notably failed to attract as many foreign students as it did when ERASMUS started (see Table 4.1, p.89). Most of the fall came between 1986 and 1989, precisely the years when ERASMUS should have started to encourage greater mobility. However, this alone should not lead us to make a negative judgement of ERASMUS. Leaving aside such extraneous factors as unfavourable currency movements, one reason for other Europeans' indifference towards the Italian university system, according to European officers in German and UK universities, is the poor quality of the student experience in the vastly overcrowded and impersonal Italian universities, which deters many who might otherwise find Italy an attractive destination for cultural and climatic reasons (Interviews, February 1994; September 1995; September 1996; November 1996). Those who did attend Italian institutions were more likely to report problems with accommodation, financial matters and administrative matters; their views of the academic standing of Italian higher education, on the other hand, were positive (Teichler 1996b). The Italian pattern seems to suggest that experience of mobility has tended to create a more discerning, better-informed market among young Europeans.

Overall, then, ERASMUS appears to have made a limited impact. Generally speaking, those who have travelled with an

ERASMUS bursary appear to have enjoyed their time at another European university. The one major external study of the programme concludes that the vast majority of former ERASMUS students are generally satisfied with their experience and report increased subsequent mobility as a result (Teichler and Maiworm 1994). However, McNay's study of successful European higher education networks concluded that they were kept afloat mainly by means of the EU's financial support and that: 'There was insufficient intrinsic commitment by the corporate institution to continue the activity from its own resources' (1995, p.37). Moreover, the proportion of the ERASMUS awards that does not find takers was still growing in the early 1990s, to something like 47 per cent of all awards by 1993/94. Despite these difficulties, the total number travelling to study under the programme rose steadily from 3244 in 1987/88 to some 56,000 in 1993/94 (Teichler 1996a). To this extent, the programme has helped foster, to some degree, a sense of a common European identity among the small minority who are directly affected; it has also provided them with a positive experience of movement between the Union's member states. It has, moreover, helped promote a steady growth in the number of students who study elsewhere in Europe, though not to the extent anticipated by the politicians when they established ERASMUS. Speaking positively, we can agree with Teichler (1996a) that ERASMUS has helped ensure that study abroad 'is no longer a marginal phenomenon' in the member states of the EU.

From the Commission's perspective, the level of student mobility is a great deal lower than anticipated. This, it believes, arises chiefly from artificial barriers within the member states. In a Green Paper on the mobility of students and researchers published in late 1996 the Commission identified variations in the student funding systems between member states as one of the major deterrents (CEC 1996d). Other barriers include the acceptability of entry qualifications, variations in quality between institutions and systems, difficulties in determining the award of credit gained abroad and different national regulatory systems for the professions. Reportedly, the Commission viewed with interest the 1994 Nordic Council treaty which created a completely open market for university applicants in the five member countries (Egede 1994). Early experience suggests that this more open approach is proving popular with students. Given the evidence that demand for higher education abroad is rising, quite independently of such 'push' factors as restrictions on access at home, such an approach might appear attractive more generally within the EU. However, it is likely that most member states will continue to prefer the balanced and managed mobility offered under the EU's exchange programmes to the potentially turbulent higher education market epitomised by the Nordic Council agreement.

What is more striking, though, is the evidence of a general growth in international study. Much of this takes place on a regional or a linguistic basis. Examples might include the Conference of Rectors in Ireland, which brings together university managers from North and South alike, or the Danube consortium of university rectors, created in 1983 with 47 institutions in membership from nine countries including Italy and Germany (Leitner 1993). This general growth has been most remarkable between Asia and the rest of the advanced world, as the newly affluent young of Malaysia, Singapore, and Hong Kong have travelled to study.

Some writers seem to suggest that education and training systems are simply the passive victims of globalisation. Such forces as the new communications technologies, the internationalisation of capital and employment and cross-border environmental problems may often appear to be external to the education and training system. Yet, as Peter Scott has emphasised, universities in particular have always been international in at least their self-image and their aspirations; in recent years, their international outlook has been accentuated by growing international flows of students (and, I would add, staff), by the growing economic significance of symbolic and knowledge-based goods and by the impact of communications systems upon the dissemination and spread of information (Scott 1995). More speculatively, the expansion of higher education may have helped weaken the attachment of young people, in particular, to the local relationships in which they find themselves – both as a place and, more importantly, as a site of unquestioned wisdom about the world (Giddens 1994). More broadly, consumerism and rapid communications (air travel, music, film, TV) have helped transform youth cultures.

Non-EU students have proven particularly attractive to Europe's universities because their tuition charges form a useful source of income. Thus, in part, the internationalisation of higher education is due to changes on the supply side. Member state governments sometimes also perceive political advantages, in the form of global influence, from encouraging non-EU citizens to study in their universities. Rather than sponsoring higher education places as a form of aid to poorer nations, the emphasis is increasingly on relationships with potential economic partners. The German government, which favours export-driven growth, is purposely encouraging universities to increase what it sees as a relatively small number of foreign students. Awarding a prize for international co-operation, the Federal Minister of Education and Science stressed that:

> A Germany with skills for the future requires an education and university system with skills for the future. In an economy that is increasingly globally oriented, that cannot be achieved without strong international cooperation by the universities in research and teaching (BMBF Aktuell, 30 November 1995).

Subsequently announcing his decision to invest 30 million DM in making German universities more attractive to foreign students, the Minister emphasised that the internationalisation of higher education was intended to serve national policy goals since 'in the epoch of globalisation Germany must not become a mere scientific province' (*Presse-Info*, 13 January 1997).

Far from helping construct a common European identity, then, the encouragement of international student mobility is entirely congruent with the interests of individual nation states. It is also, as a number of university managers have noted, entirely compatible with the aggressive promotion of individual institutional advantage (Gribbon 1994). Along with the other EU mobility programmes, ERASMUS may well have promoted the concept of the citizen's Europe. However, it is itself a part of a much wider internationalisation of the lives and aspirations of the young – particularly the more affluent and educated, who are the most likely to include a period abroad as part of their transition from school to employment.

## Human resources, aid, reconstruction and development

ERASMUS and the other action programmes were designed to promote exchanges of knowledge and understanding between what were, basically, equal partners. Even accepting differences of quality and resourcing between the higher education systems of member states, as well as in their economic structures and performance, the EU member states are recognisably Western and, by world standards, rich. The collapse of communism in 1989 created something of a dilemma for the Union. Coming as it did half-way through the single market process, the rapid democratisation and economic collapse of the nations of central and eastern Europe could hardly be ignored. The difficult circumstances of the newly democratic nations posed terrible risks to western Europe: in the short term there were the dangers of nuclear proliferation, ethnic conflicts, mass migration and international criminal trade and in the longer term there were anxieties over political instability, historically disputed borders, dependency on the USA and even a resurgence of militant Islam. With unaccustomed speed, the Union decided to enter on the stage as a collective supplier of aid – including educational aid – in support of social stability and economic reconstruction.

Since the 1960s there has been growing appreciation for the role of human resources in economic reconstruction and development. At the same time, the new importance of education and training has led to the marginalisation of bodies such as UNESCO, who tend to stress the general virtues of learning (for citizenship, social change or personal development), and their eclipse by bodies like the World Bank, who focus more on the 'bottom line' of economic growth (Watson 1996). The EU's role as aid donor has accordingly grown, though at a time of constrained public budgets generally this growth has been comparatively slow. Its role encompasses aid to the developing nations of the south (the so-called ACP states of Africa, the Caribbean and the Pacific) as well as to a number of peripheral nations that have been colonised by EU members (essentially, the French overseas Départements) through the Community Initiative REGIS. However, since the collapse of communism in 1989/90, this relatively modest contribution has been supplemented by a major role in channelling aid to the nations of central and eastern Europe. This section, therefore, focuses on this relatively recent function for the Union and, in particular, on the role of TEMPUS, which might be described as more or less equivalent to an ERASMUS programme for the nations of central and eastern Europe. Indeed, from the mid-1990s TEMPUS was increasingly regarded as a form of preparation for full entry into LEONARDO and SOCRATES.

With the collapse of communism the Union moved quickly to offer economic support to the former communist states. The Commission's starting point was the assumption here that the higher and continuing education and training systems of central and eastern Europe were both inferior to those of the EU and inadequate on their own to make an effective contribution to reconstruction and development. TEMPUS (Trans-European Mobility Scheme for University Studies) was created in May 1990 as an element within the wider PHARE programme of economic aid (PHARE standing for Pologne, Hongrie Aide à la Réconstruction Economique), with a view to helping transfer 'know-how' from Western universities and training bodies to their Eastern counterparts. It was extended in 1994 to the former Soviet states, within the framework of PHARE's sister programme TACIS (Technical Assistance to the Confederation of Independent States, being the Union's economic aid programme to the nations of the former Soviet Union). Together, PHARE and TACIS have been described by two French commentators as 'the instruments by which the European Union might exist politically, in competition with American hegemony and despite Germany's ambition to go it alone, within the reconstruction of these markets' (Lesniak and Le Billon 1996, p.122). The TEMPUS experience has strongly informed similar programmes such as MED-CAMPUS, the Union's inter-university co-operation programme between universities in the EU and twelve neighbouring nations in the Mediterranean (*OJ*, 27 June 1995).

It began with a budget allocation of 194 million ECUs for the period up to the end of 1992; a further 107 millions was allocated for the academic year 1993/94. Like ERASMUS, COMETT and LINGUA, the TEMPUS programme operated through voluntary participation in transnational partnerships; although the governments of recipient nations had to approve a shortlist of proposals, they could not direct particular individuals or institutions to participate. Unlike ERASMUS, networks between western and central or east European countries were not to be established on a reciprocal basis but for the purpose of transforming higher education in the newly democratic nations. The centrepiece of TEMPUS is its first Action: the creation of Joint European Projects (JEPs) involving universities from at least one eligible central or eastern European country in partnerships with universities from the Union member states. The JEPs promoted staff and student exchanges and joint curricula projects.

Unlike ERASMUS, COMETT and LINGUA, the Commission took it for granted that only minimal support would be available from the central and eastern European governments. Instead of an exchange of knowledge and know-how between partners, TEMPUS existed to promote a one-way transfer. Because it was developed within the framework of PHARE, the Task Force on Human Resources (then still within DGV) was required to co-operate with DGI (the Directorate-General for External Relations). Subsequently, with the extension of TEMPUS to seven of the newly independent states of the former Soviet Union in 1994, the Task Force was required to manage two parallel programmes, each financially distinct from the other but sharing the same broad educational objectives: TEMPUS PHARE and TEMPUS TACIS.

How effectively has this worked? On the positive side of the scales, the first systematic independent evaluation of the scheme between 1990/91 and 1995/96 concluded that TEMPUS had achieved considerable results in a comparatively brief time (Teichler 1996b). Among its successes, the programme had offered large enough grants – on average, over 400,000 ECU for each JEP – to make an immediate impact: eastern partners were enabled to modernise equipment, reform curricula and develop new skills among staff and students. Its impact was greatest in countries like Albania and Bulgaria, which had little access to the international community and were in desperate economic circumstances; in relatively prosperous Hungary, conversely, its impact was more marginal. Overall, the evaluators concluded that TEMPUS could continue to serve a valuable function and should not be replaced too hastily by full entry into ERASMUS and LEONARDO (Teichler 1996b).

However, TEMPUS has also attracted widespread criticism. First, most of the funding is made available not in the so-called beneficiary nations but to those who provide the 'know-how'. Within PHARE as a whole, the Commission claims that over 70 per cent of the programme budget returns to the member states of the EU (Lesniak and Le Billon 1996). One Polish official has emphasised that this inevitably means that the partners in the beneficiary nations are the junior members of the consortium, dependent upon the western partners for the continuation of the activity, and sometimes unable to influence such simple decisions as the choice of a consultant (Kozek 1994). Moreover, many academics and teachers in central and eastern Europe were unable to accept that they had a great deal to learn from their western colleagues; at least in terms of the basics, and often in terms of their specialist knowledge as well, as their young people tend to attain higher educational standards than in many Western nations. The behaviour of some western partners had made matters worse: as well as much evidence of dedication and commitment to east-west partnerships, the evaluation cited above also noted tensions arising from patronising attitudes, the use of second-rate staff and financial selfishness (Teichler 1996b). Unsurprisingly, there is strong resentment of the assumptions that underlie TEMPUS and often this is combined with a low opinion of the western partners in PHARE and TACIS projects (western consultants in Poland are known colloquially as the 'Marriott brigades', partly after the expensive Warsaw hotel where many of them stay and partly after the Communist habit of sending brigades of the young faithful to sort out agricultural or industrial problems). This widespread suspicion also helps ensure that projects remain *ad hoc* with little attempt to maintain contact once the immediate tasks are completed. The ephemerality of some projects can be guaged in the comment of a French trainer who left her post after two months of developing a management training project: 'I'd had about enough of backing programmes of the type, 'How to become a Supermanager in Two and a half Days', preferably in the countryside, in a sympathetic environment where you can eat well' (Lesniak and Le Billon 1996, p.124). Finally, the end of TEMPUS aid often meant that the spin-off from a JEP was less than it might have been: after the three years of support, new library purchases or subscriptions might be discontinued, for example, or software could not be updated (Teichler 1996b).

Second, TEMPUS has been widely criticised for its ham-fisted management. On the one hand, its administration is remarkably cumbersome, with detailed investigation of the smallest items of spending combined with lengthy delays in decision making and payments. Of course, this can be regarded as a minor problem; frustrating though it is for the partners concerned, it is a bureaucratic hindrance rather than a major defect. However, it is combined with much more serious management problems. There have been disturbing allegations of mismanagement. One example, cited in a recent report, was the approval of a proposal from an Anglo-Dutch consortium to retrain some 500,000 soldiers in the Ukraine. Although 2 million ECUs were paid over, it was reported that not one soldier was trained (Lesniak and Le Billon 1996). Critical audit reports have stimulated little comment, or apparent self-criticism, from the Commission.

More serious still is the failure to attend to the macro-economic impact of the programme. Judging by its published evaluations, the Commission is highly satisfied with TEMPUS. An interim evaluation in 1992 led to a number of changes in the programme's administration, including an attempt to ensure that it would operate within a 'strategic framework for higher education de-velopment within each country' identified in the context of the PHARE programme (Wilson 1993, pp.430–5). In June 1996, fol-lowing publication of an interim evaluation, the Commission developed proposals for an extension of TEMPUS until June 2000. According to the evaluators, the programme has made a signifi-cant impact on the reform and improvement of higher education, particularly in the associated states which have participated in TEMPUS since 1990. Its impact among the non-associate states and the newer independent states of the former USSR, who participated from 1993, was more limited (CEC 1996j). Yet these judgements rest on very little concrete evidence, other than the numbers of students and staff who participate, and whether spending claims are verified. It is left largely to the recipient states to consider whether project aims are achieved or not. Yet the Commission has persistently resisted attempts to decentralise the programme and involve the beneficiary states more actively in its management. On balance, it must be concluded that the conse-quences for development and regeneration in the nations of central and eastern Europe were not as substantial as might have been expected, given the level and range of investment.

However, economic regeneration was part only of the Union's objectives. According to Charles Wyplay, of the Institut des Hautes Études in Geneva, the Union's main achievement was symbolic, as much to do with visibility as substance: 'They (PHARE and TACIS) allowed the Union of the Fifteen a presence in Eastern Europe in competition with the Americans' (Lesniak and Le Billon 1996, p.124). The benefits were partly political, particularly after the December 1994 Council decision to gear PHARE spending partly to the eligible nations' planned entry to the Union, and they were also economic in that they provided member states and enterprises with a bridgehead in the newly marketised economies. Even then, the EU's assistance programmes were minimal compared with the role of the World Bank, and its influence was limited accordingly.

As the Union's largest programme of international educational aid, TEMPUS, for its first half-decade, performed patchily. In the difficult conditions which faced the PHARE and TACIS programmes, failures – sometimes dramatic failures – were to be expected. Moreover, some member states continued to pursue their national advantage through their own assistance programmes alongside those of the Union. Germany was the most flagrant example. Partly this was due to geography and, above all, the shared border with Poland and partly it arose from economic factors, with a sharp rise in German investments in its eastern neighbours. France and Britain also mounted sizeable international assistance programmes, often tied to trade missions, as did Denmark (for example, exporting the educational model of the folk high school as a foundation of democracy). In these circumstances, with massive political uncertainty and dramatic cuts in public finance (affecting individuals' salaries as much as institutional budgets) in all the recipient nations, what more could have been done? But the truth is that the difficulties arose partly from its clearly identified policy of transferring know-how and knowledge to university systems which did not always need western advice and expertise; many of the central and eastern European universities needed money to pay salaries, buy books, invest in technology and maintain buildings. The explanation appears to be that the Union's intention in PHARE and TACIS was, in large part, to establish a symbolic, visible presence in the new democracies and build a bridgehead for trade, and TEMPUS was, in the end, subordinated to those paramount goals.

## Schools and the European dimension

In contrast with higher education and vocational training, the EU's programmes for schools are of comparatively recent origin (Convery et al. 1997). For many years the Union had no competence in general education and until it was granted this competence under the Treaty on European Union it could only

develop limited initiatives in respect of either schools or general
adult education. Any activities which it did undertake either had
to have the full agreement of all member states, who were effectively choosing to co-operate multilaterally without the formal
constraints of the Treaties, or it had to take place within the
framework of another legal competence (most frequently, the
Union's competence in the field of vocational training). If the
Union opted for multilateral co-operation, any member state could
refuse to participate – as the UK did in respect of schools partnerships under the LINGUA programme. If it sought to include
general education under another legal competence, the Union
could expect to be challenged in the courts – possibly leading to a
defeat.

Notwithstanding the difficulties, by the mid-1980s the Union
was actively seeking to develop policies towards general education. A 1987 survey for the Commission of the European dimension
in schools level education showed that although governments in
the member states were generally satisfied with the existing
curriculum, specialist commentators took the opposite view
(Mulcahy 1992; Ryba 1992). In response, the Commission created
a small European Dimension in Education Unit within DGV, which
took on the organisation of a number of new, if small-scale, activities such as a yearly summer school, a teacher exchange scheme
and support for European teacher training networks (Ryba 1992).

In late 1991, when it had become clear that the Union's competences would be widened under the forthcoming Treaty, the Council
decided to fund a small programme of transnational schools partnerships. In a pilot programme that was designed to prepare the
ground for what later became the COMENIUS programme, the
Union supported some forty European partnerships over a period
of two school years. The partnerships were grouped under six
overall multi-disciplinary themes, the largest of which, in terms of
the number of activities supported, being 'Cultural Patrimony and
Shared Heritage', which covered projects such as Common Roots
(which focused on Greek and Latin as the sources of Europe's
patrimony). Other themes included 'Primary Education' (with projects on 'Our European heritage', 'European citizenship and the
child' and the production of a joint newspaper) and 'Environment
and Ecology' (which included a project on water supply problems
in Devon and the Maas-Rhein-Ruhr valleys).

In general, the school partnership pilot projects were primarily concerned with directly enhancing the curriculum. In themselves they were not mobility projects, although there were teacher visits for co-ordinating meetings and all the projects organised exchange visits for some pupils of between three days and two weeks. As the Commission noted in its report on the pilot phase, 'all partnerships played the mobility card (encounters, bilateral or multilateral exchanges), generally regarded as the only element able to consolidate the activities of the Multilateral School Partnership, by stimulating student motivation' (CEC 1996c, p.25). Rather than promoting mobility as a goal in its own right, the pilot school projects were concerned to build transnational partnerships around the development of activity-based learning in a number of specified, cross-disciplinary themes. Thus as well as fostering the European dimension within the curriculum, by emphasising active learning methods such as the production of portfolios, videos, games, exhibitions, newsletters or surveys, 'with the teacher acting as tutor and mediator...the pedagogy of the project forms part of the pedagogical philosophy of lifelong learning' (CEC 1996c, p.24). As in a number of other policy areas, the Commission was greatly concerned with the visibility of the programme, both within the participating schools and externally. Overall, the Commission expressed itself highly satisfied with the outcomes of the pilot projects, though accepting that their 'positive impact on the overall quality of education in Europe' would only come 'in time' (CEC 1996c, p.35).

As a pilot project, the European Schools Partnerships were relatively small-scale. With COMENIUS, the number of schools who were involved in transnational partnerships expanded considerably. Moreover, it was not as though the EU was starting from a blank sheet. Schools had also been involved in a small number of existing action programmes, particularly LINGUA (limited to the upper secondary ages). In a number of subjects – particularly languages and geography – there were a number of national, local and institutional initiatives in raising European awareness through the curriculum in the 1980s (Baumert *et al.* 1994; Hughes and Paterson 1994). Other transnational organisations had supported curriculum developments to promote the European dimension; the Council of Europe took a particularly active approach in such fields as history and human rights education

(Ryba 1995). Yet the immediate past also carried burdens. Many of these initiatives were developed in the late 1980s and early 1990s in a climate of European debate over the likely impact of the single market. As the UK inspectorate noted in 1991:

> The completion of the SEM by the end of 1992 is expected to bring major changes to patterns of trade and the movement of goods and people within the European Community, to technical standards and practices and to fiscal conventions and regulations. The European Commission has indicated that education and training will play a pivotal role in the successful implementation of the SEM. (HMI 1991, p.2)

Short-term enthusiasm, generated by the anticipated effects of the single market, was often followed by a loss of interest in the European dimension as the impact of the single market turned out to be less dramatic than anticipated.

Even by the time that COMENIUS was fully operational, in most schools the European dimension remained still more of an aspiration than a reality. Given the sheer number of schools in the EU, as well as the variety of curriculum structures, it would be surprising if the European dimension meant the same to all teachers and was implemented similarly across different institutions (Field 1997). In the final stages of the single market process, inspectors reported that in the UK further education sector, while many colleges aimed to promote awareness of other member states, 'SEM issues are not a high priority for the management of most colleges. Rarely do they appear in college strategic development plans, few targets and objectives are set, and there is little effective monitoring or evaluation of targeted curriculum development. Initiatives to respond to the SEM are largely ad hoc and uncoordinated' (HMI 1991, p.8). A similar picture prevailed in most schools, where the impact of the single market was even more remote than it was for further education institutions.

Nevertheless, despite the comparatively late entry of the EU into the schools arena, there were some striking new developments in the curriculum. In the UK these included a number of new qualifications: for example, the Southern Examining Group offered a GCSE in European Studies, often taken as an extra GCSE by sixth formers; the Southern Examining Group created a certificate in European Awareness; the Business and Technician Education Council's Level 3 GNVQ in Business included an optional unit on

'Business Within Europe'. However, these were isolated and somewhat marginal initiatives. For the most part, educational authorities and schools have preferred to treat the European dimension as a cross-curricular theme rather than as a separate subject (Buczynski 1993; Hughes and Paterson 1994). Even in such apparently unpromising subject areas as primary maths, teachers and publishers have identified topics which allow children to explore the European dimension. Arising from earlier experiences, a wide range of practical guidance has been published in Britain and elsewhere (e.g. NICC 1992). Overseas visits, schools exchanges and twinning arrangements have proliferated, though not solely within the EU. Often partnerships were most developed where a prior basis existed for a link – for example, as part of a wider town twinning initiative or because the institutions belonged to an international religious community such as those associated with the La Salle brethren or the Sisters of St Louis. In either case, the European dimension was often a secondary consideration; the La Salle schools are especially strong in the USA and Australia, for example. Nor are schools visits particularly concentrated within the EU; rather than political considerations, organisers are more likely to consider such factors as accessibility, language, cost and the availability of appropriate facilities (recreational as well as educational). But although such contacts have grown in the past two decades, the growth in international holiday travel has been considerably more striking. Compared with the impact of this fast-expanding market upon young people's experience and attitudes towards the wider world, the EU's influence was bound to be limited.

In most member states the development of a European dimension within the schools curriculum has been, at best, patchy. Among other unresolved difficulties, Raymond Ryba (1995) has noted that there is still no agreed definition of what the European dimension adds up to; there is no objective measurement of what has been achieved; nor is it clear that schooling can actually achieve the ambitious goals set out for it by the policy makers. While the EU's potential contribution in enriching the curriculum has convincingly been demonstrated, its emphasis upon the European cultural patrimony within the pilot projects (and later under COMENIUS) is at odds with the firmly national framework within which each member state determines the school curriculum. In trying to create the basis for a common European identity among young people, the Union's ability to influence the entire system across the member states is restricted. As member states seek to modernise the schools' curricula it becomes increasingly difficult to find space for the European dimension within an already-crowded curriculum. Furthermore, broader globalising tendencies have had at least as great an influence on schools and young people as the EU and its initiatives. For many teachers the relevance of the European dimension has still to be demonstrated; while this might be regrettable, it represents a rational response to the demands that they experience on a daily basis.

## The effects on education systems

In assessing the overall influence of the EU over education and training in the member states, we should recall both the recency and the fragility of the Union's stake in this sphere. Bearing this in mind, it is hardly surprising that Europeanisation seems to have made relatively little impact on the governance of education. Some member states separate responsibility for European policies, which is a matter for the relevant ministry, from the management and administration of European programmes, which they may choose to contract out to agencies. From the perspective of the EU, it does not particularly matter whether a member state chooses to manage the programmes through a ministry office or through a sub-contractor. What the Union requires is that a Technical Assistance Unit be appointed to manage the programme and advise potential applicants. In Germany, for example, many international programmes are managed on a contract basis by foundations such as the Karl-Duisberg Gesellschaft or the Deutscher Akademischer Austauschsdienst (DAAD). Similar arrangements are made by the UK government, acting through such quangos as the Central Bureau for Educational Visits and Exchanges and its host agency, the British Council. The French government is untypical in opting for central management of international programmes through the Ministry of Education; in 1994, the semi-independent Agence des Relations Internationales de l'Enseignement Supérieure had a staff of just five (*Times Higher Education Supplement*, 4 February 1994). One UK civil servant concluded that this type of organisation – highly desirable for the Commission in that it allows for direct contact with local and regional players – reduces the overall impact of the Union on education policy making:

> most of the money is allocated centrally from Brussels any-way, so there's very little opportunity for member state civil servants to get a purchase... There's an awareness in the member states that the way the university programmes are funded does leave the member state with very little voice, because of the way that Brussels funds that directly, but at the moment no one is very worried about it. (Interview, July 1996)

However, the same interviewee noted that there had been some signs of change after 1993. In particular, the Commission had taken the opportunity of launching SOCRATES and LEONARDO across the member states, thereby promoting the visibility of its pro-grammes. Furthermore, 'Now there's a separate DG, and those people have a policy agenda', which essentially involved 'trying to push the boundaries forward' (Interview, July 1996).

If European structures have relatively low visibility, Europe's policies rarely have a high standing among national civil servants. One civil servant who was seconded briefly to the Commission in order to help draft the regulations for a major new Community Initiative was quite blunt about the low status of the activity: 'I don't think there was a single person in the Department who thought the whole thing was worth a row of beans. They were totally cynical about them. I think Ministers were pretty cynical about it all as well' (Interview, November 1996). Perhaps one reason for the cynicism is the focus of civil servants upon 'the carve-up' of European resources. One UK civil servant said:

> You're talking about a member state that is basically Euro-sceptic. That's the starting point. The negotiating position was therefore to push the overall costs down while trying to get as much money as possible out of Europe for those activities which are in line with the policies of the member state. (Interview, July 1996)

In a number of the member states cynicism is combined with a perception that a 'European posting is...not a good career move' (Interview, July 1996). At national level we may safely conclude that in the larger member states at least, the impact of the EU has, to date, been peripheral.

Much recent policy discussion, though, has focused on Europe's influence not at national but at regional and local level (Paterson, L. 1994; Paterson, W. 1994). Since education policy often lies with regional or local government, as, in some cases, does training policy, this issue is potentially of considerable importance. How have the EU policies and programmes affected relations between different levels of government and the education system? So far as the higher education system is concerned, there has been a broad, if weak, tendency for the European programmes to foster a loosening of the relations between centre and individual institutions. A newly-appointed European Officer in one British university believed that the main reason for developing an institutional strategy for Europe was the availability of funding outside the direct control of the national Higher Education Funding Council (Interview, November 1996). In France, usually reckoned to be one of the more centralised of education and training systems, the necessity of allowing universities to formulate proposals to participate in the European programmes has helped create greater autonomy (Ministère des Affaires Étrangères 1995). The impact of this process has varied enormously. Within the larger member states its effects appear to have been limited and uneven, depending on such factors as the size of each individual institution and the weight of foreign students in its total population. Within the smaller member states the effect has probably been more significant. Thus one Dutch commentator suggests that in a non-residential university system which previously had few or no facilities for international students, ERASMUS had 'a great impact on the internationalisation of university education' with an increasing number of third and fourth year courses even being taught in English (Houwers 1994). As an example, she cites the University of Groningen which, in 1992/93, had 45 IUCPs under ERASMUS, two under LINGUA and 21 under TEMPUS; it also had 40 research projects funded by the EU with a total income of 1.8 million ECUs (Houwers 1994).

In the larger member states Europeanisation has usually been less dramatic. One German *Fachhochschulleiter* claimed that his *Land* ministry had blocked his efforts to obtain Structural Funds' support on the grounds that it would undermine the *Land*'s policy on student funding (Interview, September 1996). In an attempt to preserve central direction, the French Ministry of Education decided to concentrate international activities on a small number of what it optimistically called 'pôles européens' rather than allow all higher education institutions to apply on a free-for-all basis (Ministère des Affaires Étrangères 1995). In respect of higher education, then, there is a tendency for institutional leaders to perceive in the EU an opportunity to reduce their dependency upon the national ministry of education; their success in carrying this tactic to a conclusion is variable.

In contrast with its education and training measures, the EU's Structural policies have had a considerable influence over national systems. While this influence has been most visible in funding vocational training programmes for the unemployed, it has also affected the shape of higher education – particularly in the smaller and poorer nations which are eligible for Objective One support. Charles Adams (1993), drawing on interviews with senior government officials and university leaders across the Republic of Ireland, found that there was widespread knowledge in all universities of the Structural Funds and other EU training and education measures. He concluded that the considerable growth of student numbers in Ireland since the mid-1970s was largely attributable to the influence and financial support of the EU, which had also influenced the restructuring of the national higher education system. In the Irish case growth has been accompanied by a change in the higher education curriculum, with a marked expansion in applied and vocational areas, leading to fears among some academics that the system may lose its capacity for intellectual independence in the drive for utilitarian relevance (Dineen 1992). Broadly similar patterns can be seen in the growth since the mid-1970s of the numbers studying in the Regional Technology Colleges (RTCs). As one senior RTC teacher said, 'We wouldn't run a single new Diploma unless it was fully funded. I'd say more than nine times out of ten that money comes from the Social Fund' (Interview, December 1996). Ireland is a comparatively small country and its eligibility for support under Objective One means that it enjoys particularly high levels of support from the Structural Funds and the Union's influence is correspondingly greater than in larger states or states which receive relatively low levels of EU support (Matthews 1994).

Yet even in the larger and more affluent states the Structural Funds may exert an influence on the education and training system. The extent to which spending decisions are decentralised varies between and within member states, however. Thus in the UK the higher education institutions established a national ESF unit (managed jointly by the Committee of Vice-Chancellors and Principals and the other associations of institutional directors) to allocate and administer a sectoral allocation under Objective Three (and Objective Four before the 1994 reforms – see Chapter Two). At regional level the UK's further education system is eligible for funding under Objective Three, while some individual further and higher education institutions have secured capital grants as well as recurrent grants in regions eligible for support under Objective Two and Objective One. Although, compared with the smaller and poorer member states, these activities are relatively unimportant, there is no question but that they have influenced the system to some extent. To this extent, they have helped reduce dependency upon the national authorities and raised the visibility and importance of local and regional networks.

It is harder to discern any similar tendency in respect of schools' systems. Rather, member states remain generally reluctant to allow schools to develop greater autonomy than they have already. Nevertheless, there are signs that something of a struggle for power is taking place within member states as different levels of educational administration reposition themselves in response to the process of European integration. Because responsibility for education and training is usually shared between national and local or regional government, they tend to be affected by these internal struggles. Paterson (1996) has noted the way in which the German *Länder* used the Single European Act process to insert their regional powers – which include responsibility for education policy – into the Treaty and prevent any further erosion of their sovereignty; for its part, the federal Ministry of Education and Research has clearly used its position within the Union institutions to try to extend its role in respect of education and training over time. Within the UK a similar, albeit rather more muted, struggle has taken place over the position of Scotland: apparently, for some years during the 1980s an official from the Scottish Office Education Department was in the habit of attending Education Committee meetings uninvited and overtly distancing his department's policy from that being articulated at the Committee by the official UK representative. According to another member of the UK party, the

Scottish official usually occupied an empty seat belonging to Luxembourg (Interview, July 1996).

On balance, then, the development of the Union's education and training policies appears to have left the member states' powers largely unchanged. In a number of the Union's larger and important programmes local government has been entirely bypassed. It is, perhaps, predictable that local government has no particular role within the LEONARDO programme since vocational training policy in most member states (though by no means all of them) is the responsibility of central government. This is the rationale behind the Union's decision not to require the Commission to consult the Committee of the Regions in respect of vocational training, for example. While this has not prevented the Committee from offering its opinions under the 'own-initiative' procedure, it more or less guarantees that they will be received with courtesy and little else. Although local government is consulted on education policy proposals, through the Committee of the Regions, it otherwise has no particular function. Unlike central government, local authorities are not automatically involved in decisions on proposals under the COMENIUS programme – even though local government is, in most member states, responsible for schools. The role of local government is constrained even within those programmes which are concerned with promoting 'bottom-up' activities. Thus one sizeable early years programme in Belfast, funded by the Union's URBAN Initiative, was proposed and is managed by the Greater Shankill Partnership with minimal involvement with the City Council. In respect of education and training policy, at any rate, we see little evidence of an emerging Europe of the Regions; on the whole, the Europe des patries remains intact.

At a more practical level there is little doubt that the EU's policies and programmes have had an impact within the institutions at whom they are directed. Particularly within higher education, the late 1980s and early 1990s witnessed a marked institutionalisation of international relations. By 1989 the number of specialist managers dealing with international programmes in higher education was sufficient to generate a new professional body, the European Association for International Education; within four years it had gained over 800 members (Houwers 1994). Similar groupings have proliferated since the late 1980s, including the European Universities Continuing Education Network (founded 1989), the European Educational Research Association (1994) and the Academic Co-operation Association (1994). Most of these organisations have tried to influence EU policies: thus the European Association of Distance Teaching Universities gained impetus and membership in the face of a proposal from the Commission to establish a European distance university, against which EADTU successfully lobbied (Tait 1996). Generally speaking, these European networks have been grass-roots initiatives led, at least in the early stages, by enthusiastic individuals. This was congruent with the way in which the ERASMUS programme, before 1995, tended to favour a 'bottom-up' approach with applications being drafted and programmes managed by particularly entrepreneurial individuals or departments. This stood in an uneasy relationship with the more senior and longer-established bodies such as the CRE, mirroring the tension within universities between the individuals and departments wishing to take international initiatives and the top-level executives wishing to develop a particular strategic profile. A major study of international networking within universities in the early 1990s showed that the 'main drive to initiate' came not from institutional managers but 'from enthusiastic and committed staff', but that this rarely featured in promotions criteria nor were there mechanisms for the institution to learn from these individuals' experiences (McNay 1995). In introducing the practice of the 'institutional contract' for staff and student exchanges, the SOCRATES programme was designed to ensure a balance between 'top-down' strategy and 'bottom-up' creativity and motivation. Such attempts to institutionalise European partnerships create a risk of managerial sclerosis at a time when the pace of globalisation is elsewhere forcing organisations to become more flexible and responsive to change, particularly in respect of their international activities.

European integration has also had consequences for the international activities of professional groupings. As well as those associations which involve professional educationists, other professional institutions have also increasingly institutionalised their international activities – largely as a result of the EU's impact on their occupation. The immediate reasons for this institutionalisation of international relations vary. The Council of Occupational Therapists of the European Community gained in standing because of complaints from the profession that the Commission gave preference to lobbyists from disability organisations (Neale 1994). From the Commission's perspective, good relations with professional associations form a helpful counterbalance to the views and votes of the member states. Thus, after the lobbying against its interest in a new distance university, the Commission reportedly found in the EADTU a 'vehicle...to facilitate its major policies' such as greater student mobility, education/industry links and a European identity (Tait 1996, p.232).

At a more specific level, though, the Union's policies are often contradictory. Thus the emphasis on student mobility seems to run counter to its support for open distance learning and lifelong learning: for, almost by definition, distance learners and part-time students cannot participate in mobility programmes which demand a minimum stay of three months abroad. A similar inconsistency marks the use of time as the basis for the mutual recognition of qualifications (the first general Directive defined a higher education qualification as a qualification gained after at least three years' study) with the Commission's oft-repeated desire for flexibility and recognition of prior learning. The Commission's response to such criticisms is usually denial. Thus in the *Memorandum on Open Distance Learning* the Task Force on Human Resources argued that:

> At first sight this use of course duration [in the General Directives] seems to pose a problem for Open Distance Learning, where the mastery of a set of learning objectives is the criterion for completion and where credit for experiential learning can form part of the assessment. However, in actual fact the General Directive is compatible, without the need for amendment, with Open Distance Learning in that it makes provision for recognition between Member States not only of professional education and training of at least three years' duration at higher education level, but also of all other types of education and training which are recognised by the member state in which they are offered as being of an equivalent level and confer the same rights in pursuit of the regulated professional concerned. (CEC 1991b, p.13)

Denial is accompanied by an absence of mechanisms for building upon experience. While the Union is strong on financial verification, it is notoriously weak on reflexive evaluation.

One difficulty is the uneven extent to which the Commission itself functions as a learning organisation. Frequently the substance of policy appears to take second place, at best. As one Commission officer said, 'I felt that a great deal was learned in the old action programmes, but in a rather diffuse way. No one ever asked what was the *Acquis* in an overall way that could be carried over on a systematic basis' (Interview, November 1996). Yet the Union's officials and politicians clearly acquire particular skills and knowledge which help them to further their policies. This form of organisational learning is the product of the peculiar mixture of politics and administration, of legislature and executive, which characterises so much of the work of the Union's institutions. What matters so often is the construction of administrative, legal and procedural arrangements which will allow business to go ahead and, at key stages, to combine these with the creation of coalitions of opinion which will allow the passing of a new policy threshhold. This has functioned well in terms of keeping a complex business agenda moving, despite the difficulties of juggling the differing perspectives and interests of the Union's institutions, the member states and other players. It has also served to limit the influence of the Union as a supranational steering agency.

## Conclusions

The main aim of this chapter was to examine the results of Union programmes in three important areas. Because these areas, in turn, provided a basis for further EU proposals, they are particularly helpful in reaching a view of its overall influence in education and training. In fact, they provide limited basis for confidence in the Union's ability to develop mature policies for this field and they suggest some grounds for suspicion as to its motives. What is even more striking, though, is the extent to which the Union is itself one among many other globalising tendencies at work in contemporary societies. Education and training systems, like many other areas of social life, are both influenced by and play an active part in shaping these globalising tendencies.

Most current EU programmes are directed against two aspects of this globalisation. First, they seek to create a common sense of identity, of a shared European citizenship, among young people at a time when many young Europeans are as interested in what is happening in Los Angeles or Sydney as in Lisbon and Milan. Second, the programmes are designed to foster competitiveness by smoothing out friction within the European labour market at a time when it is culture and consumerism that have become international while employment as a whole remains stubbornly locked into regional and national boundaries (this argument is pursued in the next chapter). At national level, moreover, the challenges of globalisation lead individual member states to continue to compete, and not solely co-operate, with one another.

Yet while it may be true that national structures continue to exercise most influence over education and training, and that this situation is legally embedded in the Treaty on European Union, it is also clear that a growing number of institutions, individuals and activities now function within a European frame of reference. Many – perhaps most – teachers probably know little or nothing of the EU's policies and programmes; the radicalism of the Union's diagnosis is, nonetheless, widely cited by those who participate in public debate over policy issues and who usually draw a favourable contrast between the EU's analysis and the more conventional (and even anti-teacher) approaches of member states. Furthermore, although the EU's budget for education and training is comparatively small, it is particularly attractive to an institution or an entrepreneurial teacher at a time when mainstream funding sources are restricted. Of course, the European framework continues for most purposes to be subordinate to the national – not least because the latter is where the key decisions over resourcing and curricula are usually made. And, as this chapter has repeatedly demonstrated, we should not exaggerate the extent of the Union's influence. Despite its continued ability to operate beyond the strict limits of its competences, the Union remains a relatively minor player in most areas of education and training. Wider and more powerful tendencies towards globalisation have eclipsed its attempts to become a significant supranational force in the field. Yet for all these qualifications, the EU has had a real impact at institutional, regional and national level. More important, it seems set to become a force to be reckoned with in setting the agenda for the future.

Chapter Five

# Mobility, Qualifications and the Citizen's Europe

Although European policies for education and training developed rapidly from the mid-1980s, they rest upon a number of initiatives that appeared in the 1970s. Moreover, although there have been important changes of emphasis, they still rest upon the same underlying assumptions. In essence, the measures taken during the 1970s were intended to promote mobility of labour across the Union. Freedom for workers to move, according to the Commission, would contribute towards greater economic competitiveness and also reduce disparities between the different regions and member states. Free movement across borders would also be a tangible benefit for workers, helping make the common market a reality for the ordinary citizen. This underlying analysis, and the overarching goal of promoting mobility as a means of promoting competitiveness, continued to underpin the action programmes of the 1980s, which used student or trainee mobility as a mechanism to allow Europe's skilled and professional workers of the future to gain experience of studying and working abroad.

In fact, strengthening the single market for labour has, since the 1960s, become a major policy objective in its own right. Although it has lost some of its impetus since the energetic regulatory initiatives of the Delors Commission in the later 1980s, it also remains an important objective. The notion of 'an open European vocational training and vocational qualifications area' was listed among the common framework of objectives for the newly-created LEONARDO programme in 1994 (*OJ*, 29 December 1994). Improvements in labour mobility were among the main themes of the Union's Second Social Action Programme, which was to cover the period 1995–1997 (CEC 1995a). In 1996 Commissioner Cresson even argued that 'one of the causes of this European sickness that is intractable unemployment is the fragmentation of the European labour market, in complete contrast with the situation in the United States' (Cresson 1996b). A 1996 Green Paper spoke of the 'absurd' snags facing trainees and students wishing to study in another member state and proposed a series of measures designed to help create 'a real European area of qualifications' (CEC 1996d, p.2), while in the same year the President of the European Parliament asserted that 'There is still a lot for the Union to do in this respect' (Kops and Hänsch 1996, p.3). For over two decades, then, European labour mobility has remained an important goal for the Union.

Yet this was no recent concern. Freedom of movement was one of the founding principles of the Common Market. In drafting the Treaty of Rome the aim was set of achieving 'four freedoms': capital, goods, services and labour. This only became explicitly an educational matter with the establishment of the single market programme in the early 1980s. Under the Single European Act, the Treaty of Rome was amended so that the Union had clear powers to issue legislation requiring member states to recognise one another's qualifications. This change also effectively closed down the option of forcing member states to change their national qualifications systems so as to bring them more into line with one another (McMahon 1995).

As in other policy areas, the result has been a slow and uneven expansion of the EU's powers. This process of 'creeping competence' was, in turn, assisted by the Court's interpretation of the right to freedom of movement, which has consistently favoured a broad reading of the rights enjoyed by individuals under the Treaties and any subsequent legislation. While it remains an article of faith that labour mobility is an important factor in building Europe's economic competitiveness, increasingly, the right to mobility has also become an expression of belief in a 'Citizens' Europe' or a 'People's Europe', since it is 'one of the most tangible benefits of the Union for individuals in the different member states' and therefore has symbolic significance in addition to its economic importance (CEC 1995e, p.27). The importance of this issue was further underlined in May 1989 with the publication of the Commission's proposals for a Fundamental Charter of Workers' Social Rights (or the 'Social Charter', as it came to be known), which listed

freedom of movement as first among the twelve fundamental
rights of workers in the Union. Yet in this area competence has
expanded through legislation, duly enforced by the Court of Justice, as the Union has used the powers granted under the Single
European Act. Harmonisation – the process of constructing a
European system of qualifications – was rejected as an encroachment upon the rights of member states. Other more limited efforts
– including legislation covering specific named occupations and
proposals for co-operation between the member states – had been
tried; the results, while not entirely negligible, were too modest to
complement the more ambitious programme set out for the single
market.

## Comparing qualifications

Fostering labour mobility was of increasing importance for the EU
from the late 1960s. At that stage the Commission concentrated
largely on encouraging employers and member states to recognise
one another's qualifications. By the mid-1980s it was apparent that
simple encouragement had failed to create a more mobile labour
market, particularly among highly qualified employees, and this
experience, in turn, influenced the development of COMETT,
ERASMUS and the EU's other education and training action programmes. For although the vocational qualifications system in
each member state is designed to serve similar purposes, the
national systems for vocational education and training remain far
more diverse than do their equivalents at primary and secondary
level (Wolf 1995). Thus although many of the EU's policies for
labour mobility do not have any intrinsic educational dimension,
the qualifications issue raised a large number of questions about
the EU's rights in the educational area and also led the Commission
to confront other educational issues more directly.

In the first decade of the Common Market relatively little was
done to enable labour mobility. What action there was at this stage
was taken by the Court of Justice, and that was limited. With the
achievement of a common policy for agriculture, and significant
progress towards tariff reductions, the Commission turned its
attention to other issues such as regional policy and monetary
union. Employment policy developed initially as a complementary field of action designed to underpin measures of greater

intrinsic importance to the building of the European common market. In 1968 the Commission adopted a Regulation (EEC 1612/68) on the freedom of mobility within the EU which required member states to dismantle the most obvious legal barriers to labour movement. In 1971 the Commission briefly turned its attention to an important indirect barrier: adopting a further Regulation which required member states to assure equal entitlements to social insurance for migrant workers from other member states. The Commission took a further step towards enabling mobility of labour in 1976 when it launched an action programme for migrant workers and their families, aiming to tackle further discriminatory measures in the member states. By this stage, however, rising unemployment levels across the EU had slowed migration flows so dramatically that the issue was simply not a priority. Quite the reverse: to take any more ambitious measures and actively promote labour movement would have been to risk a perception that the Commission was threatening the jobs of British or German or French workers. The issue only regained its importance when the single market project happened to coincide with a partial economic recovery.

With the drive towards completion of the single European market, labour mobility again returned to the Commission's agenda. Once more the agenda was a multi-dimensional one, even extending in the late 1980s to family policy, stimulated by anxieties over the complex issue of family reunification among migrant workers (Tierlinck 1994). However, education and training issues were particularly prominent during this period. Conscious that actual migration rates were rather low between the member states, particularly after the recession of the late 1970s, the Commission sponsored research which attributed this, in large part, to uncertainty among employers and member states over foreign workers' certificates of academic achievement or vocational competence. At this stage, therefore, the main thrust of the Commission's efforts concerned the comparability of academic and vocational qualifications.

Initially, the Commission's approach to this problem had been somewhat piecemeal. In the 1970s the Commission started with a two-track policy: on the one hand, it sponsored research into the national qualifications frameworks of the member states with the aim of providing a comparative map of the different areas and levels covered by vocational qualifications in each member state. In addition, it issued a series of Directives covering specific occupations where it believed there had been or might be particular problems. These are dealt with in greater detail in the following section.

The decision to compare national qualifications systems was a medium-term measure. Harmonisation of vocational qualifications was ruled out at an early stage, though it is doubtful whether, in fact, it had ever been a serious option. On the other hand, comparability studies would clearly take time if they were to be sufficiently comprehensive and thorough to have any credibility. Following a Council decision of July 1985, CEDEFOP, the Centre Européenne pour la Développement de la Formation Professionelle (European Centre for the Development of Vocational Training), was charged with the task of comparing vocational qualifications (*OJ*, 31 July 1985).

CEDEFOP had been created in 1975 for the purpose of providing information and advice on training matters in Europe. Its governing structure included representatives of the Commission, the member states and the social partners (trade unions and employers), and its approach to the comparability exercise reflected its general commitment to social partnership. As a small organisation, with only 42 staff in 1984, CEDEFOP undertook only a limited number of direct and central services; most of its activity concerned the co-ordination of research contracts and facilitation of documentation and information exchange. Even by 1995, at the time of CEDEFOP's transfer from Berlin to Thessaloniki (as part of a wider trade-off within the Union, whereby the Council agreed to locate its new central bank in Frankfurt), it had a permanent staff of 76 (CEC 1996e). As late as 1984, CEDEFOP reported that it had agreed contracts with corresponding organisations in only six member states, limiting the capacity of both its bibliographic and dissemination services (CEDEFOP 1984). In fact, its coverage and credibility were slow to develop and the comparability exercise did little to restore its reputation, which was only repaired –slowly – following changes in the senior staff in the mid-1990s. Nevertheless, CEDEFOP continued to manage studies in such areas as 'The transparency of qualifications and certification of occupational experience' as well as convening research networks (including one of researchers concerned with the forecasting of trends in occupations and qualifications) and extending its role to support studies of the training and qualifications systems in central and eastern Europe. CEDEFOP's role in this area has, then, been that of a broker and clearing house for information, rather than that of an active developer of policy.

CEDEFOP started by establishing a series of sectoral working groups, with representatives from the relevant employers' associations and trade unions on each, along with experts specialising in the industry. Each working group had oversight of the mapping exercise in its own occupational area, which was based on an exhaustive analysis of the tasks involved in each occupation, and how these were recorded through the vocational qualifications system of each member state. Despite the fact that they benefited from CEDEFOP's earlier efforts in this area, the working groups experienced enormous difficulty. One trade union representative in the retail sectoral working group said:

> each member state had its own separate system and some didn't even have a system, and each qualification you looked at covered different things, and even when you thought you knew what one person's job was you could always find someone who had a different definition. (Interview, April 1994)

Unsurprisingly, it was a time-consuming process. The outcome was an enormous number of somewhat unwieldy comparative tables, duly published in the *Official Journal* (hardly an employer's first point of reference), and offering detailed, yet very approximate, guides to the different types and levels of qualification in an enormous range of occupational fields from agriculture and horticulture through motor vehicle repairs to construction.

The sheer scale of the lists was intimidating. Even so, the consensus was that the sectoral studies were insufficiently robust to provide a basis for comparison between occupational qualifications in the different member states. CEDEFOP rather naïvely expected that 'Publication by the EC Commission of the results of the comparative studies of CEDEFOP in the *Official Journal* would undoubtedly attract the interest of respective employees and those concerned with the issue at Community level from the perspective of 1992' (CEDEFOP 1987, p.26). Regardless of the number of 'respective employees' who scanned the pages of the *Official Journal*, CEDEFOP was already experiencing difficulties. Above all, the comparability studies ducked the question of quality. The retail sector representative said that 'there was simply no way that we were going to be allowed to say in public that one set of certificates was okay and another was rubbish, it just wasn't going to happen, whatever we thought and said behind closed doors' (Interview, September 1994).

In the end, the Commission effectively chose to bypass the comparability studies. By 1992 CEDEFOP's activities had established comparative descriptions for 209 occupations, from 16 of a potential 19 occupational sectors, including hotels and catering, automobile maintenance, building, woodworking, electrical engineering, agriculture, forestry, horticulture, fisheries, textiles and clothing (CEDEFOP 1994). Once a list was published in the *Official Journal*, it was left largely to member states to decide what use it could make of the information. So far as quality was concerned, CEDEFOP concluded that member states would have to accept the self-definitions of level and content that were approved by the national ministries of labour. The sheer scale of the task meant that progress was painfully slow. A 1993 evaluation concluded that although researchers and other specialists made use of the system, 'the direct use of the system by workers and employers...has been extremely low as yet'; indeed, almost half of the careers advisers in the European Employment Service did not know of the comparability studies (CEDEFOP 1994, pp.22–5). Nevertheless, CEDEFOP's mapping did produce a number of useful findings; more important, perhaps, was the fact that its halting rate of progress helped persuade the Commission that a more radical approach – albeit one short of harmonising the different national systems – was required.

## Mutual recognition

In attempting to achieve the single market for labour, the Commission turned to legislation rather than persuasion. In doing so it shifted attention from trying to provide information on national systems to insisting on mutual recognition of qualifications. Under the general heading of 'Freedom of Movement', the 1989 Social Charter stated that 'Every worker of the European Community shall have the right to freedom of movement throughout the territory of the Community, subject to restrictions justified on grounds of public order, public safety or public health'. In particular, it stated that 'The right to freedom of movement shall also imply...elimination of obstacles arising from the non-recognition of diplomas or equivalent occupational qualifications' (CEC 1989, p.7). By the time that the Social Charter was signed, though, this right was already enshrined in legislation.

A number of attempts were made in the 1970s to guarantee the recognition by member states and employers of one another's qualifications. In particular, the Commission issued a series of Specific Directives covering named occupations, following the guidelines laid down in a 1974 Council Resolution on the matter, which emphasised the need for flexibility and co-operation rather than the detailed listing of training requirements. Subsequently, Directives were issued covering such professions as nursing, midwifery, veterinary medicine, dentistry, pharmacy and architecture. In each case an advisory committee was established with national experts from each member state. Initially at least, the Commission and Council seem to have intended to achieve a degree of harmonisation of the training curricula – a fact which one judge of the Court of the First Instance described recently as having 'made deep inroads into the independence of national education policy' (Lenaerts 1994, pp.16–17). A proposed Directive covering engineers' diplomas was never adopted by the Council; indeed, the only specific Directive adopted after 1980 was that regulating pharmacy diplomas in 1985. Professional associations mostly regarded the prospect of harmonisation with dismay, leading to a vigorous if poorly-co-ordinated lobbying effort that was ultimately successful (Neale 1994).

Though the Specific Directives achieved some measure of acceptance, sizeable difficulties remained. First, this was a rather slow process. Once the movement towards the single market gathered pace it was clear that there was no prospect of passing Specific Directives at a comparable speed. Second, there were problems of definition: a nurse's or journalist's responsibilities might differ substantially between member states, so that an apparently similar terminology might disguise important practical differences (a continuing problem for many transnational partnerships, incidentally). CEDEFOP's task-analysis approach might have helped here, but many felt that it was moving rather too slowly. Third, the growing number of Specific Directives, accompanied sometimes by amendments or supplementary legislation, threatened to create a legal situation that would be Baroque in its complexity. Fourth, a number of national professional associations exploited loopholes in the legislation to block the acceptance of incomers holding qualifications from another member state. In the early 1980s a series of disputes came before the Court of Justice, covering occupations as varied as lawyers, nurses, doctors, dentists, journalists, travel agents, sports trainers, architects and civil engineers, some of which were covered by the Directives while others were not (McMahon 1995; Meehan 1993). Since the Court's decisions tended to clarify and support the rights of individuals under the Treaty to enjoy freedom of movement regardless of nationality, case law meant that the absence of specific Directives did not necessarily inhibit free movement – it simply led to the prospect of judicial complaints from aggrieved individuals. Finally, as noted, the Council of Ministers was no longer prepared to support proposals requiring harmonisation of training curricula.

At its June 1984 meeting the Council noted that the equivalence of university diplomas would help support the single market programme. In 1988 the Council approved two General Directives on vocational qualifications across the EU. The first General Directive, adopted in December 1988 and effective from January 1991, covered all higher education diplomas (or 'degrees', using the normal English-language term), which it defined as any qualification awarded by a 'competent authority' (chiefly universities) for all post-secondary education and training of at least three years' duration or an equivalent part-time, which shows that the holder is able to pursue a regulated profession in the member state. If the training has lasted for less than three years, then a host member state may refuse to recognise the diploma unless there is evidence that the person has practised the profession; in any such case there is an upper limit of four years on the length of practical experience that the host state may demand.

Effectively, the first General Directive meant that each member state had to accept that a university degree awarded in one member state must be treated as a university degree in all member states. Although the Directive allows host countries to require an aptitude test before a migrant professional is allowed to practise, the courts have repeatedly insisted that any such aptitude test must be genuinely justified by the requirements of the profession.

In some occupations, such as accountancy or law, some member states have insisted on an upgrading course of three years' duration (such conversion courses are also required by some member states for professionals moving from one region to another: thus British lawyers must undergo further training before practising in Northern Ireland, and vice versa). Nationals of other member states must also comply with the normal rules of the host state regulating the profession, though the Court has insisted – in relation to veterinarians in France, for example – that any such rules must be compatible with Union legislation on free movement (McMahon 1995).

The second General Directive dealt with vocational qualifications below degree level. Adopted in 1988 and coming into force in June 1991, the Directive on the recognition of vocational training covers vocational qualifications gained over training of two or three years' duration at post-secondary or secondary levels. It also encompasses a number of other training programmes rather vaguely defined as those not covered either by the first General Directive or by any specific Directive. Under its terms, member states must recognise certificates and diplomas awarded in other member states for those entering a given occupation. The difficulties here are substantial ones: the second General Directive is silent on craft-level skills, a complex area which the Commission decided to leave alone for the time being but which was probably rather more relevant to the realities of Europe's labour markets than either of the General Directives passed in 1988. CEDEFOP's listings may provide a useful guide to the terrain as it once existed; since then, many occupations have changed, some substantially, and new ones emerge on a routine basis. Once more, national governments or professional associations are empowered to require that candidates pass an aptitude test or undergo further training before practising their profession in another member state than the one in which they gained their original qualification. Justified by the Commission as a safeguard to consumers and employers, such measures are intended to ensure that incomers are competent to operate in an environment other than that in which they were trained.

Both General Directives have been resisted from time to time, most often by professional associations and sometimes by member states. Generally, the Court takes the view that where there is a dispute about entry to a profession in another member state, the burden of proof lies with the member state which is insisting upon further retraining. The Court of Justice has insisted, for example, on the right of estate agents qualified in Britain or Germany to practise their trade in Spain without undergoing a lengthy retraining. Where the Court has accepted the right of a member state to insist on evidence of competence in the official language of the state, such a policy must (a) not be disproportionate and (b) must not be discriminatory (McMahon 1990). The ECJ has taken the notion of an official national language to include those languages (e.g. Irish, Welsh or Catalan) that are not one of the official languages in which the EU conducts its business. In other words, from the Court's point of view there is a cultural dimension to the issue of labour mobility; in its view, the right to free movement in search of work does not override the desire of a member state to protect its cultural identity (McMahon 1990).

Particular problems to one side, the Commission has taken a number of steps designed to ensure that qualifications are recognised throughout the EU. By the late 1990s the Commission had issued legislation requiring mutual recognition by member states of all higher education diplomas and the more substantial vocational certificates or diplomas that were recognised in other member states. Legislation itself rested on the degree of confidence and mutual trust that exists at any given time between member states in relation to their higher education and professional training systems. Moreover, it was combined with other underpinning measures: for example, in the mid-1990s a staff of 250 advisers was appointed to help the European employment service (EURES) answer queries from employers and workers about vacancies and applicants across the Union. Much has been done since the mid-1980s to remove what the Union sees as artificial barriers to mobility. In fact, this is the one area of education and training policy where the Union has used the full gamut of decision making powers at its disposal; as well as action programmes and research, this area has also witnessed the use of Regulations and Directives which are legally binding on the member states. Has this persistent investment in policy development paid off? What have been the results in practice?

Actually, the effect of the mutual recognition Directives is at first sight rather puzzling. According to details published by the Commission, between 1991 and 1994 some 11,000 people throughout the EU applied successfully to have their diplomas or degrees recognised by another member state than their own – something which, at the time, the Commission's press service claimed as a triumph for the 1989 Directive. Of these, though, some 6000 – well over half – entered the UK (*Frontier-free Europe*, 4, 1996). So far, so peculiar. What was, in fact, happening, however, was not at all odd: the largest single number of entrants to posts in the UK under the Directive were 1674 graduates and diplomates from the Republic of Ireland, four-fifths of whom were schoolteachers (*Irish Times*, 22 February 1996). In other words, to a considerable extent the 1989 Directive had simply institutionalised, and the EU had recorded, a pattern of movement which already existed. Is this representative of the wider European labour market and what are the prospects for greater genuine movement in the future?

## Mobility and the European labour market

On the whole, it appears that there has been remarkably little cross-border traffic in human resources within the EU. In comparison with the USA, for example, Europeans seem rather reluctant to leave home in search of employment. Moreover, the vast majority of migrants inside Europe have been not those with craft or professional or managerial qualifications but those who have relatively low skills levels. In short, it would seem that the goal of increased labour mobility has not been achieved. Quite the reverse: the fall in demand for unqualified labour has been so powerful that internal migration inside the Union, far from rising since the 1970s, has actually fallen. This judgement may seem surprising but it is based on a range of evidence about movement within the single market.

First, the numbers of EU migrants within most of the member states have fallen since the mid-1970s (see Table 5.1, p.128). The reason is simple: the rise in unemployment from the early 1970s was associated with diminished opportunities for unskilled labour. At the same time, economic growth in Spain, Italy and, subsequently, Ireland has reduced the income differentials between richer and poorer nations within the EU so that the incentive to move is smaller; greater affluence has also led to smaller family sizes, reducing the overall supply of young migrants. The consequences

**Table 5.1: Number of employees from other EU member states, 1975 and 1988**

| Country | 1975[1] | 1988[2] |
|---|---|---|
| Belgium | 174,000 | 130,000 |
| Denmark | 14,000 | 13,000 |
| F.R. Germany | 849,000 | 484,000 |
| Greece | 5,000 | 7,000 |
| Spain | 31,000 | 28,000 |
| France | 1,045,000 | 569,000 |
| Ireland | 13,000 | 20,000 |
| UK | 347,000 | 345,000 |
| Luxembourg | 49,000 | 64,000 |
| Netherlands | 59,000 | 85,000 |
| Portugal | 7,000 | 10,000 |

1  No figures available for Italy; reporting date = 1980 for Greece, Portugal, Spain and 1985 for Ireland.
2  No figures available for Italy; reporting date = 1987 for Belgium, F.R. Germany, Greece, France and Ireland and 1983 for Spain.

*Source:*   Werner 1994, p.42.

were straightforward. In Germany, for instance, the number of employees from other member states who paid social security contributions – the most simple indicator of migration levels – actually fell between 1977 and 1989 from 730,000 to 497,500; in France the number dropped from over one million to 569,000 (Werner 1994).

Second, those who move appear to come from the traditional labour suppliers. The most mobile peoples by far appear to be the Irish, followed by the Portuguese (both nations are defined as Objective One regions within the Structural Funds). Over 13 per cent of all Irish citizens living in the EU in 1992 lived outside the Irish Republic, while over 8 per cent of Portuguese citizens in the EU lived outside Portugal. The Greeks and Luxembourgeois follow some way behind and the other nations dwell almost entirely in their home country. Moreover, migrants within the EU are still largely heading for traditional destinations, taking a well-trodden pathway to – they hope – better employment. Thus if we take the 536,000 Irish citizens living elsewhere in the EU in 1992, it turns out that almost 95 per cent of them live in the United Kingdom –

a pattern which has not changed noticeably since the early 1970s (or, for that matter, since the years of the Great Hunger). Of course, this does not stop Irish employment ministers from telling EU meetings that Ireland has the most mobile workers in the Union (for example, *Irish Times*, 23 November 1996). Similarly, Portuguese citizens are concentrated largely in France (which accounted for 78 per cent of Portugal's emigrants within the EU), while of 80,000 Danes living in other member states, 35 per cent were in Sweden – which was only to join the EU in 1995 (Eurostat 1995). This suggests that the EU's impact upon labour mobility has been strictly limited. It also suggests that it is the poorer countries – with the exception of Luxembourg – that have supplied most of the migrants.

So far, then, the single market has not created cross-border flows of labour on a grand scale. High unemployment levels in the richer nations have sharply reduced the traditionally high level of movement among the inexperienced or unskilled. Skilled and qualified labour, and more experienced labour, are generally less mobile than qualified labour, partly because those who are best qualified tend to find a relatively comfortable position at home so that the benefits of migration do not outweigh the risks and also because many of their skills are valued precisely because of their grasp of local and context-bound knowledge. Thus one study of personnel managers in British-owned multi-nationals suggested that those firms who were developing a European approach tended to rely less on British expatriates and more on locally-recruited managers (Walsh 1996). Those executives who do move across frontiers tend to be transients who are appointed for specific periods because of their knowledge of the firm, rather than to carry out general duties over time (Boyle *et al.* 1996). This well-established pattern calls into question the entire emphasis upon labour mobility within the EU. However, it could be argued – and sometimes is by EU officials – that the development of the single market for enterprises will bring greater labour mobility in its wake.

Is significantly greater labour mobility, particularly of the well-qualified, a realistic prospect? Clearly, the answer will depend upon the pace and direction of changes within a fast-evolving labour market. By the later 1990s there were signs that globalisation was creating some mobility within the higher strata of the labour market. A magazine survey of eleven of Germany's largest employers in 1995 suggested that most had specific plans to

internationalise their senior management; the car giant Mercedes-
Benz aimed to raise the number of foreigners to 10 per cent of all
directors and departmental heads by the year 2000; at the US-
owned GM-Opel the figure was already estimated at 15 per cent
(Hoffritz 1997). Such trends are, reportedly, stimulating a sharp
growth in the international work of executive search agencies as
companies try to recruit senior managers able to handle their
foreign operations (Boyle *et al.* 1996).

However, such historical evidence as exists suggests that national factors will continue to determine the direction and extent
of labour mobility for some years to come. Per Lundborg has
analysed mobility within the Nordic labour market, where barriers
were abandoned in 1954 with an agreement among the five Nordic
states that they would distribute shared information on vacancies
through the national and local labour offices. The major consequence was a sizeable movement of unskilled and semi-skilled
Finnish workers, largely into Sweden, throughout the 1960s and
1970s. The main reasons for this movement were the substantial
income differentials (wages and other benefits) between the two
countries, prospects of employment in Sweden and, after the first
years, the impact of chain migration. From the early 1980s the onset
of recession in Sweden reduced both the employment possibilities
and income differentials, leading to a sharp and sustained
downfall in immigration from Finland. Lundborg concluded
that migration within the Nordic nations was 'higher for the low
educated than for the well educated. Instead, people with a high
level of education have a higher propensity to migrate to non-
Nordic countries than do those with a lower level' (1995, pp.47–9).
In other words, the Nordic experience between 1954 and the
mid-1990s is very similar to that of the EU in the 1980s and early
1990s. It is also worth noting that the two General Directives on
mutual recognition apply in all the Nordic nations, Norway and
Iceland having agreed to abide by their provisions despite their
non-membership of the EU.

Has the Union simply got it wrong then? Certainly there is no
shortage of evidence to show that the Commission and Council,
and, above all perhaps, Delors, believed that the freedom to move
was a fundamental element of the single market. In its *Memorandum on Higher Education*, the Task Force on Human Resources
argued that 'The free movement of persons and the recognition of

qualifications for professional purposes create, in effect, a single labour market for the categories of persons concerned' (CEC 1991a, p.7). In fact, they did no such thing. The Union's policies on labour mobility have, I am suggesting, advanced some way ahead of the actual demand for flexible labour on a European level. Although there is some evidence of a more competitive environment in some very specialised labour markets, in general, the evolution of a European labour market appears to be some way off. Moreover, the internationalisation of these specialist labour market segments has not generally been specific to the European scene but has affected multi-national firms who operate globally (Hendry and Pettigrew 1992). Yet the Union's policy of removing barriers to mobility have been pressed through with some determination and they continue to influence wider policies towards education and training. Why has this happened?

In general, the European labour market remains heavily segmented along national lines. David Marsden's judgement in respect of the labour market for skilled workers in the EU was that 'The forces of convergence are strong, but so is the capacity of national systems to adapt to external pressures and yet retain certain distinctive features' (1993, p.3). Thus social work, for example, has strong religious associations in some countries while in others it is completely laicised; in some countries social workers function as advocates for clients, while in others they deliver a wide range of associated services; in some countries it is a graduate profession, in others there is a comparatively short period of specialist training; national legislation varies from loose enabling powers to close and prescriptive regulation. Little wonder, then, that there has been no agreement to date on the 'core' of tasks and competences of social work and that the impact of the single market on social workers' mobility has been 'extremely weak' (Cassard-le-Morvan *et al.* 1995). Moreover, the higher the level of specialist skill and knowledge required of employees in a particular market segment, the stronger the effects of national borders in inhibiting mobility. This reflects the wider pattern of economic organisation within the EU, which has changed less than anticipated in response to moves towards a single market (Kay 1991).

The organisation of the European economy also changed in different ways from those expected by the politicians. One result of the single market that was not predicted by the Delors Commission was a massive influx of capital deriving from outside the EU entirely. Much of this capital is American, though the Asian-Pacific region has also been an increasingly significant source and one that has been readily latched onto by journalists. The Republic of Ireland – one of the EU's success stories and a nation that is characteristically open to inward investors – offers a telling example. The proportion of the manufacturing workforce employed in firms whose ownership lay in other EU member states actually fell between 1973, when it was 24.5 per cent, and 1995, when it had reached under 17 per cent. Meanwhile, the number working in non-EU firms rose from 9 per cent of the manufacturing workforce in 1973 to 28 per cent in 1995 (*Irish Times*, 25 November 1996).

Perhaps present labour market trends will Europeanise the professional and managerial labour markets at some future stage? Certainly, some claim to discern a degree of convergence in managerial roles across the different European regions. Noting a tendency for some of the larger companies to groom managers for transnational careers, two recent commentators even go so far as to predict that a recognisably 'European' concept of management will emerge in the next ten or twenty years (Forster and Whipp 1995). The far more significant development for employment growth, though, is the expansion of the small- and medium-sized firms sector. If small and medium enterprises recruit and promote their employees in the future in the way they have usually done in the past, then the mutual recognition of foreign qualifications is likely to prove largely irrelevant. This is because smaller enterprises tend to rely heavily on personal knowledge of a candidate's abilities; indeed, in the case of very small firms, the largest source of recruits is the employer's own family. Certificates and diplomas, by contrast, are important in large, bureaucratic and impersonal organisations who rely not on local knowledge but on external labour markets. In practice, many larger employers tend to use diplomas as a way of screening out undesirables as a group rather than a positive means of recruiting the worker with the specified skills, trusting that anyone with a certain formal qualification will turn out to be trainable by the company (Field 1995b). One survey of European integration concluded that while there will be continued, if limited, demand for the unqualified migrant, 'the emergence of European labour markets for the intermediate and higher levels of qualification seems more problematic, except in so far as employers begin to extend their internal labour markets across national borders, in order to develop suitable management structures in the wake of takeovers and mergers' (Marsden 1994, p.19). Barring any specific legal or professional requirements for an employee to possess a particular qualification in order to practise in the member state concerned, the 'portability' or trans-parency of qualifications for managers moving around within their own company is not even a fringe issue.

Globalisation of employment has, then, made little progress – if we take the term to mean labour mobility beyond national bounda-ries. Europeans, particularly if they are highly-educated, remain reluctant to travel abroad in search of employment; a look at the labour market confirms that they are generally making a rational decision. Nevertheless, there is evidence of a partial globalisation of the labour market for the well-educated, though not always in the ways predicted. Three forms of job mobility seem to have developed within the EU. First, there are those who work for transnational corporations and whose careers involve some degree of cross-border movement. Frequently, this movement is short-term: there has been an explosion in the number of short business journeys within Europe over the past twenty years but the number of managers or professionals moving permanently abroad has been relatively small. Crucially, this development has arisen not from the EU's policies, or even from the creation of the single market, but as a contingent phenomenon arising from global changes in economic organisation and, accordingly, it is associated as much with firms under American or other non-European own-ership as with those based primarily within the EU (Forster and Whipp 1995). Second, there are those who are employed in what we might call the Eurocracy: not just civil servants but lobbyists, consultants, promoters, journalists, PR specialists and so on. This is a rather specialised labour market, if an influential one. Third, there are those whose employer and employment are both transnational but who work at a distance in their own country. Some of these workers are hired as consultants because they have local knowledge that is of value to the firm; the use of fixed-term, flexible contracts means that they are less costly in the short run (and perhaps the long run as well) than the traditional expatriate manager. How-ever, a more recent example is the workforce in telebusiness, which conducts its affairs across borders using communications technologies like the telephone or e-mail. Such workers can be based anywhere within the EU (including in the home) and access to local knowledge is often not a factor. According to Ireland's Minister of Enterprise and Employment, some 3000 people in the Republic were employed in the telebusiness sector in 1996 and he expected the number to rise to 6000 before the year 2000. Significantly, many Irish telebusiness workers were university graduates – not always because their academic knowledge is required in call centres but because they tend to possess language skills (*Irish Times*, 23 November 1996).

Yet even if economic restructuring were following the trans-European patterns of ownership predicted by the Commission, the labour market will not necessarily follow the same direction. Foreign-owned and transnational enterprises will be able to recruit most of their labour force within the local, regional and national labour markets where their operations are situated; for reasons of goodwill, as well as efficiency, they will also be aware of the benefits of local recruitment wherever possible. The economic gains from recruiting non-local labour will be highest where they combine the benefits of scale with low penalties arising from lack of local knowledge – and these conditions arise largely among the most unskilled forms of labour, engaged on repetitive and menial tasks, rather than among decision takers and knowledge workers. Incoming firms opening a new site may import some managerial and specialist staff with company-specific skills or in response to local shortages, but these are as likely to be brought in from a third country as from another EU member state. Empirical studies of inter-regional mobility confirm the importance of the firm's existing labour force as the chief resource for recruiting skilled mobile workers, many of whom move on a short-term basis only (Marsden 1993; Marsden 1994). Cross-border recruitment efforts by employers for university graduates seem to be increasing, but not dramatically (Everett and Morris 1993). Before the 1995 enlargement, it was estimated that, in total, only 2.5 million EU citizens worked in another member state than their own – equivalent to roughly 1.5 per cent of the working population (*Financial Times*, 13 April 1994).

By the mid-1990s the goal of promoting mobility had been overtaken by competitiveness as the prime objective of the EU's training and education policies. Nevertheless, it continued to play an important role in shaping policy makers' thinking on the Union's policies. Thus a Council Resolution in December 1994, on the 'quality and attractiveness of vocational education and training', noted that 'In the European internal market, having a skilled job increasingly means being able to communicate and cooperate across borders... Vocational training policy should play an important part in bringing about the freedom of movement and promoting the mobility of workers in the European internal market' (*OJ*, 30 December 1994, p.3). By this time the Union's own specialist advisers had published evidence which contradicted the central assumptions behind this approach. Nevertheless, the goal of a 'European area' for education, training and qualifications clearly continues to influence politicians' thinking and to legitimate policy and measures at the European level.

As yet, then, the EU's work on comparability and recognition of qualifications remains largely untested on any scale, particularly at the higher levels of specialist skills and knowledge. It has, nevertheless, been of considerable importance. It remains the one area of education and training policy where the Union has chosen, since the mid-1980s, to focus on legislation rather than action programmes, funding mechanisms or co-operation between states to achieve its goals. In so far as the Directives have been systematically supported by the Court of Justice, and the member states have ultimately accepted the legitimacy of its approach, the Union has, therefore, been largely successful in using legislation in this area. From the member states' perspective, the Court's development of the Union's competence under Article 7 of the Treaty of Rome could be seen as an erosion of national sovereignty. With the decision to adopt general legislation, the Union acted decisively and clearly to pursue the goal of fostering labour mobility by creating a 'common European area of qualifications'. It remains to be seen whether this development at the political level corresponds to the requirements of an increasingly turbulent and unpredictable labour market.

## Education and training qualifications – a policy gambit?

By the early 1990s Europe's politicians had lost much of their interest in labour mobility. In complete contrast with the USA, Europe's labour force stubbornly refused to move in search of employment. Those who did move were not the skilled workers and professions who had been the subject of so much policy attention; it was the unskilled and semi-skilled who moved, mostly migrating to destinations where they knew the language or had established contacts among fellow nationals. Was all the policy effort – the comparability studies, the mutual recognition Directives – simply wasted? Seen from the strict perspective of the labour market, the answer must be that very little was achieved.

Seen from the wider perspective of policy development within the Union, though, the mobility issue served a useful purpose, if largely a symbolic one. It demonstrated that the Union could act decisively, as it did when Delors chose to let the comparability studies fall into the background and tackle the issue through comprehensive regulation. It also allowed Delors to claim that the Union was pursuing the interests of workers every bit as vigorously as it pursued those of employees. Did this persuade any single individual to feel better about the single market than they would have done otherwise? Probably not, but this is largely beside the point. As part of the wider picture, the mobility provisions helped the Commission claim that the 'People's Europe' was not just an empty slogan (de Witte 1993). In a 1996 speech to French regional politicians, Commissioner Edith Cresson blamed low levels of public enthusiasm of European integration on the lack of progress in securing mobility:

> Capital and goods circulate freely in Europe. This fluidity is far from being achieved for the citizens. Thus one should not be surprised if a good number of Europeans appear perplexed or resentful in the face of a European construction in which they see, even if wrongly, a source of constraints rather than a force for progress. (1996a)

More specifically, the right to move freely from one state to another provided a symbol of the single market that might relate to ordinary citizens' lives and aspirations and now the Commission could claim that it had done something to make that right a reality. Having achieved that goal, the Commission increasingly turned its attention to other priorities.

Chapter Six

# Maintaining the European Model of Society

From their origins as adjuncts to the construction of an economic common market, education and training have evolved as an important policy area in their own right. However, many of the EU's policies involve some aspect of education or training and their number and influence has increased with the move towards the single market. For example, the abolition of internal trade barriers was accompanied by a retraining programme for Europe's customs officers (named MATTHAEUS, after the tax-collecting Apostle Matthew); with the deregulation of broadcasting, the Union established a programme to support the European television and film industries (MEDIA), which included support for improved management skills at the European level. Many of these initiatives are relatively modest, particularly compared with the area of social policy. This chapter starts by examining the broad social thinking which underpins EU policy in this area and then considers the role of the Structural Funds, and particularly the Social Fund, as important vehicles by means of which the Union pursues its social policies and outlines the importance of equality of opportunity, particularly between men and women. Finally, it looks at the way that the EU has promoted a dialogue between what it calls 'the social partners', by which it chiefly means employers and trade unions, as a means of developing its policies in fields such as vocational training and education.

## The European social model

Social policy is a relatively well-established field of interest for the EU, if at times a somewhat contentious one. It is particularly important for education and training, not simply because these are invariably influenced by wider frameworks of social policy thinking but because the Commission directly funds vocational training and, to some extent, education through the Structural Funds, and has done so now for some decades. While social policy is chronologically the first of the three areas considered here, it also represents a substantial financial commitment: the ESF alone accounted, in 1996, for 7146 million ECUs out of the total EU budget of 75,000 millions –just under 10 per cent of the whole (CEC 1996e). Since the mid-1980s the ESF has been given a central role in underpinning the Union's approach to European integration. Although economic goals still dominate the Union's policies and activities, social cohesion became, during the 1980s, an important secondary objective in its own right and has come to occupy a central part in the way that politicians have developed their thinking about Europe's future development.

With the rise of social policy within the Union's interests, there has also been a growing debate, since the 1970s, over the Union's preferred social model. This, in turn, has generated intense controversy between the Union and its member states, as well as between the member states themselves, reaching near-crisis in the debates around the Treaty on European Union. In 1992 the UK, with a preference for market solutions to social problems, managed to negotiate a partial 'opt-out' from the social chapter of the Treaty (this came to an end following the election of the Labour Government in 1997); the government of Denmark, by contrast, fearing that the social chapter would undermine its comparatively high levels of social support, insisted that the Union should do no more than indicate minimum standards. The Commission, meanwhile, sees itself as occupying the broad consensual middle ground that lies somewhere between these two extremes. However, there is no doubt that the Union's leading policy makers strongly favour an active social policy; for much of the 1980s and early 1990s this generated an aggressive programme of legislation, covering a wide range of individual and collective employment rights (Field 1995a). By the mid-1990s the pace of regulation had slowed, to be replaced by an emphasis upon negotiation and consultation involving the trade unions, employers' associations and, increasingly, the representatives of voluntary organisations and campaigning movements.

The Union's interest in social policy has, as in so many other areas, grown incrementally from rather humble origins. Legally speaking, it had no real role in this area. Article Two of the Treaty of Rome vaguely mentioned the improvement of living conditions as one of the new body's general objectives. However, it gave the Commission very few specific competences and most of its founders seem to have assumed that the improvement and harmonisation of living and working conditions, and of social protection more broadly, would flow on from the realisation of a common market (Berghman 1995). Initially, the EU's concern was largely with reducing regional inequalities; the European Social Fund and, later, the European Regional Development Fund were intended to support regional development strategies within member states with the aim of reducing inefficiencies and inequalities within the common market (Preston 1994).

While the ESF remained the main focus of social policy implementation, the Commission also moved ahead in a number of other areas. In one – advancing the position of women – its contribution was a significant one, and this is dealt with in the section which follows. In addition, the Commission, in 1975, developed a small five-year programme of pilot projects and studies around the topic of poverty. These ran until 1980 and were sufficiently influential to stimulate a further action programme in 1980. Subsequent action programmes on poverty continued into the 1990s. The poverty programmes brought together a number of prominent policy specialists from the member states and had a visibility in scholarly and policy circles out of all proportion to its budget. Limited largely to demonstration studies, and comparatively small scale, though, their longer-term significance lay largely in establishing the legitimacy of the European dimension in what was very much an arena of domestic policy.

Four factors in particular influenced the development of social policy in the mid-1980s. First, the move towards the single market raised the visibility of the non-economic barriers to free movement of goods, services, capital and – above all – people. Greater economic integration would create unmanageable political tensions within member states, especially those most adversely affected by what was known as 'social dumping' – that is, price reductions brought about by low social overhead costs rather than increased productivity. Explicit talk of social dumping disappeared after

1992, replaced by a general consensus in most member states that there should be a 'level playing field' in social affairs as well as in other matters.

Second, Europe's political leaders believed that if it was to succeed in its goals, the move towards a single market should command broad support among Europe's citizens. Yet the single market would, it was anticipated, lead directly to short-term job losses – most obviously among groups such as customs officers, whose jobs existed largely to defend Europe's borders, but also among those working in trades that had been protected from competition by artificial barriers (Preston 1994). Third, far from disappearing in the booms of the 1980s, large-scale unemployment came to be seen as a consequence of the new patterns of world trade. Such globalising influences as the GATT talks meant that economies with relatively low labour costs, and, especially, the innovative and rapidly industrialising nations of the Pacific Rim, posed a growing threat to the competitivity of the established capitalist nations. The collapse of communism in central and eastern Europe – while apparently removing a horrific military threat – also brought a host of new potential competitors, where low labour costs were mostly accompanied by high educational standards. In the face of such uncertainties, all of Europe's member states – even those where wages costs were lowest – had to reconsider the place of the welfare state. As governments proposed reductions in welfare spending, so the Union's political leaders saw an opportunity to emphasise the European dimension to social policy. This brings us to the fourth factor: as in so many other policy areas, an increasingly confident Commission under President Jacques Delors was pressing for extensions to its existing competences and actively mobilising expert opinion to speak publicly for a more comprehensive European dimension to social policy. These pressures were sufficient to ensure that social policy was an important, if hotly contested, aspect of the 1992 Treaty.

European interventions in social policy thus acquired an increasingly systematic character, and this was accompanied by a growing debate over the nature of the European social model. In turn, this debate has disseminated what, in many member states, is a new language for discussing social policy: terms such as social cohesion, social inclusion, marginalisation, social exclusion, all of which have been widely used in European policy circles in recent years, have become familiar to a much wider group of users. The language derives, however, from a set of beliefs about the nature of society that are acceptable to both the Christian Democrat and democratic socialist traditions; they have not appealed to the radical right or, in the past, to the Marxist left. One example is the concept of social exclusion, which was proposed in the 1980s by French researchers involved in the poverty action programme as an alternative to the tradition of empirical poverty studies favoured by their Anglo-Saxon colleagues (and perhaps rivals). Ideas of social exclusion arose within the framework of a rather conservative and Christian vision of society as a broad moral order with an obligation on élites to ensure that the dispossessed do not become detached from that order (Room 1995). The Commission itself in the early 1990s noted that 'social exclusion' did 'not yet have a precise meaning in all the Member States, but it does describe a real and increasing problem in all parts of the Community. Social exclusion refers to the multiple and changing factors resulting in people being excluded from the normal exchanges, practices and rights of modern society' (CEC 1993d, p.1). This usage continues to dominate the way in which social exclusion is discussed within the EU, where it has continued to appear in public discourse despite its unfamiliarity outside the circles of the Union's own policy makers and specialist advisers.

From the Commission's perspective, though, the very unfamiliarity of the term offers certain advantages. Policy makers from the member states do not face the term with the same baggage and reactions as if they were faced with language that sounded entirely familiar. Its adoption by the Directorate for social affairs, as well as by the relevant ministers and civil servants from social affairs ministries, reflects a reluctance to accept that poverty – in any traditional sense – can exist within a modern European society, at least in the richer nations. In Berghman's words, it offers a 'more adequate and less accusing expression' than poverty (1995, p.18). In practice, the Union's concept of exclusion also focuses strongly on exclusion from the labour market, rather than on exclusion as a general outcome of specific social and economic processes. This, I believe, reflects the Commission's tendency to use the term in arguments designed to legitimate its use of its rather limited powers in the social policy field. At any rate, a term which first appeared in a Union report in 1988 had, by the mid-1990s, become almost pervasively used in the social policy debate.

In entering the social policy field as a key player, the Commission has constantly sought to justify its presence by reference to the impact upon competitiveness. Against those who believe that high social welfare costs place an unacceptable burden on Europe's employers, the Commission has argued that social cohesion is entirely consistent with (and even underpins) a competitive capitalist economy. One explicit aim of the EU in developing its social policy goals during the 1980s was the improved competitiveness that could be gained by avoiding what was widely known as 'social dumping' – that is, relocation by employers from regions where the costs of employment were comparatively high to regions where the costs were lower (CEC 1988). By the 1990s the Commission was focusing more directly on social policy as a central complement to its policies on competitivity. As the 1994 White Paper argued:

> The objective in the coming period must be to preserve and develop the European social model as we move towards the 21st century, in order to give the people of Europe the unique blend of economic well-being, social cohesiveness and high overall quality of life which was achieved in the post-war period… This is essential because the efficiency of our societies as a whole conditions how competitive they may be and the growth they can deliver…the pursuit of high social standards should not be seen only as a cost but also as a key element in the competitive formula. (CEC 1994a, pp.7–10)

This approach has two chief consequences: first, the Commission tries to take social cohesion into account across the entire range of policy areas, albeit with varying degrees of commitment and success. Second, it is specifically seeking to develop a distinctively European approach to social policy with the aim of supporting cohesion while minimising the costs.

In addressing the impact on social cohesion across the gamut of policy fields, the Commission has found it easier to identify problems than solutions. Thus Commissioner Bangemann's report on the global information society (discussed further in Chapter Seven) identified the 'main risk' as the:

> creation of a two-tier society of have and have-nots, in which only a part of the population has access to the new technol-

ogy, is comfortable using it, and can fully enjoy its benefits. There is a danger that individuals will reject the new information culture and its instruments. (CEC 1994d, p.6)

Bangemann and his advisors concluded that the 'central role' in tackling this risk belonged to education, training and promotion, rather than to the field of IT policy for which Bangemann had responsibility. Rather more constructively, Commissioner Edith Cresson pressed hard for the Fourth Framework Programme of Research and Technology Development (also known as RTD4) not simply to test new technologies but also to examine their social utility – a decision that one of her senior officials has publicly contrasted with the USA's approach to research and technology (Riché-Magnier and Metthey 1995). Chief among the social aspects of RTD4 was the impact of the new technologies on education and training.

Typically, in interviews the Commission's civil servants contrasted the European social model with those of Japan and the USA – societies which combine high growth levels with very different social models from Europe's and which are also Europe's two main competitors. The social model of the United States, relying heavily upon individualistic values and responsibilities, is seen as highly unattractive because of its tendency towards social fragmentation and conflict; the Japanese social model, characterised by close-knit collectivism around family and company, is believed to stifle initiative and inhibit individual development.

At its best, the European model is described as a successful combination of social solidarity and cohesion with individual autonomy. Its downfall is its cost. In justifying the European dimension to its social policy, the Commission has argued that social spending must be radically redirected. Some commentators have even suggested that the Union's adoption of a concensual social model masks an underlying common tendency, most visible in the UK but present across western Europe, towards the reconstruction of social welfare. Thus Bernd-Otto Kuper of the German Association of Welfare Associations has suggested that the EU is essentially 'a trading alliance pursuing off-stage, as it were, a common social policy implemented not at Union level but directly in the member states'. Moreover, Kuper argues, the goal of that common social policy is the reduction of social benefits in the hope of reducing unemployment and enhancing competitiveness (1994, pp.129–31).

Certainly the Union has reflected the growing reluctance of member states to continue welfare spending at its current levels, arguing, however, that the solution lies, at least partly, at the European level. Rather than 'passive' strategies which tend to reinforce dependency and exclusion (welfare benefit payments in particular), the Commission has argued for a dramatic turn towards 'active' social policies which promote inclusion (such as vocational training and employment stimulation). The Commission believes (on evidence which has never been entirely clear) that in the long run, active social policies of this kind will be more efficient in increasing social inclusion and less costly than the current passive model. The Commission has also emphasised that as the major threats to the European social model spring from international forces, action must be taken at the European level.

Once more it is clear that education and training are intended to play a major role in this process. The 1994 White Paper, for example, called for the elimination of basic illiteracy by the year 2000, a higher status for initial vocational education and training, co-ordination of guidance and placement services and tax incentives for firms and individuals to invest in continuing lifelong training and development (CEC 1994a). It also supported proposals for a radical overhaul of ESF, with a stronger focus on increasing competitiveness and preventing unemployment by developing a systematic approach to continuing lifelong training (CEC 1994a). The central purpose of these changes was to ensure a move away from a 'passive' approach to social support (that is, providing help to people who have fallen into need) towards an 'active' approach which concentrates on making sure that people remain within the social and economic mainstream. In terms of the Union's programmes, this is usually expressed in slightly militaristic language as placing priority on 'combating social exclusion', rather than on the milder form 'promoting social inclusion'. Dr Fritz Rath of ECOSOC, who believes that the French banker and economist Michael Albert is mistaken in arguing that globalisation spells the death of the European social model, based his case for the further development of that social model by pointing to its strengths. These include, he argues, a high educational level and 'polyvalence of skills' – that is, adaptability (Rath 1996). What is clear is that the politicians place considerable importance on education and training in promoting social inclusion. In particular, a central role is given to continuing lifelong learning in helping adults to avoid falling victims of exclusion in the first place. Whether Europe's education and training systems can in fact live up to these high expectations is, of course, another matter.

## The reformed Structural Funds

In promoting social inclusion, the largest instrument at the Union's disposal remains the Structural Funds. The prospect of the single market led to fears among poorer regions that it would help concentrate wealth in the core economies – especially the so-called 'golden triangle' of Milan/Grenoble/Baden-Wurtemberg. As well as the 1988 reforms (discussed in Chapter One), the Commission embarked upon a further review of the Structural Funds in the period up to 1992. Having secured provision for a new Cohesion Fund within the Treaty on European Union, in the so-called 'Delors Two' package the Commission proposed a sizeable increase in spending on the Structural Funds, with the increase going towards the objective of increasing cohesion. Once again it was widely believed that this proposal reflected a desire to maintain enthusiasm for the new Treaty among the poorer nations. Although Delors Two was only partly accepted by the Edinburgh Council meeting in December 1992, the share of the Structural Funds in the EU's budget was set to rise from 29 per cent in 1992 to 36 per cent in 1999 (Matthews 1994), with much of the increase supporting the cohesion programme (specifically, this was to be achieved through support for environmental protection and trans-European transport networks).

In addition to changes in the budget and the new Cohesion Fund, the Commission also proposed revisions to the framework regulations that govern the Funds' operation (Preston 1994). Generally, the 1988 regulations were viewed by the Union's policy makers as having functioned fairly effectively. The largest change was the integration of the old third and fourth objectives, with some liberalisation of the conditions under which member states could provide training and guidance to the unemployed, and the introduction of a new Objective Four providing for assistance to workers being made redundant, or at risk of redundancy, as a result of industrial restructuring. The UK announced in 1993 that it would refuse to participate in the new Objective Four, claiming that it amounted to an unfair subsidy to employers and might bring unintended bankruptcies to any industry where it was implemented. The new regulations also allowed for investment in the health and education sectors in Objective One and Objective Two regions and simplified the decision making process slightly. Also, the Commission attempted to strengthen further the principle of 'additionality', under which member states are required to demonstrate an agreed commitment of their own resources before they may claim support from the Union – something which has so far typically proven very hard to verify (Barnett and Borooah 1995).

Finally, the Commission also restructured its Community Initiatives. The Community Initiatives are special programmes within the Structural Funds (see Chapter One). They are proposed by the Commission to support measures which will help solve problems that it identifies as having particular impact at European level. Responding to a proposal from the Commission for an increase in the resources available for the Community Initiatives, the Edinburgh Council limited their allocation to between 5 per cent and 10 per cent of the total structural budget. In order to achieve the goal of establishing closer contacts between citizens and the Union, the Commission announced that the Initiatives would have three clear distinguishing features:

- they would support cross-border and inter-regional co-operation and networks
- they would be based on a bottom-up approach
- they would generate a high local profile for the EU. (CEC 1994b)

The Commission also proposed a reduction in the number of Initiatives, with a corresponding increase in the size of each (CEC 1993a). Essentially, it planned to group the Initiatives into two broad clusters: one set was to tackle the problems of unemployment for disadvantaged groups and individuals, largely through human resource development activities (encompassing NOW, HORIZON and a new programme for young and unqualified job-seekers, YOUTHSTART, to which was joined, in 1996, a new initiative, INTEGRA, largely aimed at supporting victims of racism) and the other concerned with enabling the workforce to adapt to technological and organisational changes in industry. Overall, the Initiatives would aim to meet five broad objectives:

- cross-border, transnational and inter-regional co-operation and networks
- rural development
- outermost regions (that is, the non-European territories of the EU)
- employment and the development of human resources
- the management of industrial change.

The agreed budget, at 13.45 billion ECUs for 1994–1999, amounted to some 9 per cent of the total allocation for the Structural Funds; within this, the Commission held 1.6 billion ECUs in reserve so that it could propose other initiatives during the programme period.

The 1994–1999 programme was neither an entirely new departure nor a simple revision of existing activities. In terms of the principles of sovereignty that it embodied, the 1994 programme maintained the *status quo*, whereby the Commission was able directly to allocate resources to centrally agreed priorities, thus providing it – as ESF and ERDF did not – with an important means of dialogue and negotiation with non-governmental players at local, regional and national level. In terms of coverage, they extended slightly, but not radically, the scope of the Union's activities – encompassing urban policy, for example. Organisationally, the 1994 programme embodied a response to earlier criticisms against the Community Initiatives on the grounds that they were too small, too *ad hoc* and too invisible. They therefore represent an important means by which the Commission can put its human resources policies to work at national, regional and local level, giving it a presence within the education and training system which is widely, if unevenly, visible to actors on the ground.

## Equal opportunities

Elizabeth Meehan (1993) has argued convincingly that, for a number of years, sex equality effectively was the 'cornerstone of Community social policy'. Interest in women's opportunities has, like so many other goals, been largely driven by economic concerns. Sex equality was one of the more significant social issues during the negotiations that led to the foundation of the common market in 1957. Article 119 of the Treaty of Rome required a commitment from member states to ensure equal pay for equal work. Little was done to follow this through until the late 1960s. Since then sex equality policies have developed rapidly in their extent and started to influence a range of other policy areas, including education and vocational training. Although the implementation of these measures was vigorously criticised by feminists (including representatives of women working for the Commission), the changes were nonetheless striking. Indeed, by the early 1990s it was plausibly argued that sex equality had effectively become the 'cornerstone of Community social policy' (Meehan 1993, p.68).

This shift can be traced through the rapid extension of Union legislation. Between 1975 and 1992 the EU complemented Article 119 with six Directives (which take precedence over national law) and three Recommendations (which are not themselves binding) on equality issues. Although much of the legislation was concerned with such questions as social security entitlements and continuity of employment for pregnant working mothers, the Commission defined 'pay' as encompassing the right to equal access to vocational training. It did this in the 1976 Directive on the Implementation of the Principle of Equal Treatment for Men and Women, which covered access to employment, promotion and working conditions as well as access to vocational training. This represented a substantial reworking of the Commission's competences under Article 119, which was strictly concerned with pay and was originally understood to mean wage rates. In a number of judgements against member states and employers, the European Court of Justice consistently backed the Commission in its expanded definition of equal pay (Field 1995a). In particular, it supported infringement proceedings brought by the Commission against member states that had not incorporated the expanded definition into national legislation. In Ireland, for example, although both government and employers' organisations lobbied intensively for exemption from the 1975 Equal Pay Directive, the end result was that it was integrated, as were other equal treatment Directives, into national legislation (Mangan 1993). Legislation has become less common since the ratification of the 1992 Treaty, partly because member states are less willing to place new legal constraints upon employers and the Commission and Council have tended to promote equality through Recommendations (on sexual harassment or parental leave, for example) and through its own Action Programme for Equal Opportunities between Men and Women. Following commitments made in the White Paper on Social Policy, the Commission has also developed equality monitoring in the operation of the Structural Funds and a number of other activities, including the selection and recruitment of its own staff.

The Commission's Action Programmes on equal opportunity demonstrate a growing, but strictly limited, desire to develop policies in this area. Its initial steps were extremely hesitant. The first Action Programme, launched in 1982, placed responsibility for most non-legal measures with the member states. The second appeared in 1985, a time when much of the Commission's energy was consumed with completing the internal market, and was held back by a reluctance to burden industry, particularly small- and medium-sized undertakings. The Commission included widening access to vocational training in the new technologies among its goals (Springer 1993). Introduced after the debates over the Social Charter, the Third Action Programme (1991–1995) was aimed chiefly at ensuring compliance with existing legislation (e.g. through awareness-raising activities); by stimulating employment and entrepreneurship (e.g. through the Commission's Local Employment Initiatives scheme for women, which was started in 1984) and aims to provide support and training for new women entrepreneurs; and by encouraging wider access to training (through measures such as IRIS, the Commission-funded network of centres offering specialist women-only training schemes created in 1988).

Even the fourth Action Programme (1996–2000) is somewhat modest. Its most ambitious element is an attempt to promote the Commission's aim of achieving more balanced participation between men and women in decision making (a phrase that encompasses managerial positions in the public service and in companies as well as a higher profile for women in politics and public life more generally) combined with the collection and publication of information on women's situation in the member states. As most forms of positive action – and particularly quotas – were deemed by the ECJ in 1995 to overstep the limits outlined in the 1976 Directive (C-450/93, Kalanke v. Freie Hansestadt Bremen), the Commission, in 1996, brought forward proposals for a new Directive on women's access to employment, vocational training and promotion (CEC 1996m). However, perhaps surprisingly, education and training measures continue to form a minimal element of the fourth Action Programme. Steps forward in this area have been hesitant, then, with the Action Programmes helping maintain the visibility of gender equality issues but making a very limited contribution to their resolution.

By far the most significant concrete achievements appear to have been those realised within the framework of the Structural Funds. Most specifically, the Commission funds a programme of training, guidance and work placement (NOW, or New Opportunities for Women) within the Community Initiative on Employment with the aim of improving women's access to employment through training and development in management and high-technology skills. However, NOW has relatively limited funds. At 370 million ECU for the period 1995–1999, it admittedly enjoyed over six times the amount allocated to the fourth Action Programme on Equal Opportunities but the NOW allocation accounts for a mere 2.75 per cent of the total allocation for the Community Initiatives. IRIS, the network of women's training initiatives, is much more modestly funded still.

Finally, there remains the question of how far EU policy on equality has influenced its wider policies and programmes for education and vocational training. In a Recommendation of 24 November 1987 the Council called on member states to ensure equal access for women to vocational training, particularly in growing occupations and in fields where women have been traditionally under-represented (*OJ*, 4 December 1987). The right to access to vocational training for all workers, throughout their working life, was also specified in the 1989 Social Charter. The EU also claims to promote equality through its own education policies and action programmes. However, one authoritative evaluation of women's position in current EU programmes concluded that while there were many instances of good practice, the overall approach to equal opportunities was 'haphazard' (Rees 1995). There is also some evidence that women are proportionately under-represented in the education mobility programmes – perhaps not surprisingly, given that they continue to have other responsibilities, such as childcare, which constrain their mobility. In attempting to set standards across its training and education programmes and policies, then, the Commission is still far from achieving consistency and coherence.

In some ways, the story of equality issues in vocational education and training seems a sorry one of missed opportunities. It is impossible to avoid the conclusion that the Union's leaders wish to be *seen* to respond positively to women's demands for improved access to education, training and employment but that this is rarely matched by action. For example, it is typical of the EU's interventions in this field that the 1987 Recommendation is dominated by wishful thinking; many of the jobs where women are under-represented are in steady decline (particularly in manufacturing) while many of the fastest-growing occupations are low-wage and part-time and are already attracting a predominantly female workforce without any visible effort by the EU. Similarly, it is a goal of LEONARDO to help promote 'effective equality of access to continuing training for women' (*OJ*, 4 March 1994), but how this was to happen remains unclear.

On the other hand, it is also clear that the EU's policies on equal opportunities have become increasingly significant over time. Institutionally, the EU has created an equal opportunities unit within DGV and has appointed an Advisory Committee on Equal Opportunities, whose membership includes employers, trade unionists, and specialists. DGV has committed itself publicly to ensuring that there is adequate consultation on all proposals affecting women and there is a growing lobby for women's interests, as well as a growing number of highly effective networks of European women (such as the European Women Entrepreneurs grouping). Women working within the European institutions have also become increasingly well-organised, to the point where the Parliament threatened to remove Commissioner Flynn from his equal opportunities responsibilities as a response to what many perceived as his obstructionism. Flynn has since made a point of speaking up in public on behalf of women's issues, particularly in his home country (part of the Parliament's criticism involved Flynn's alleged intervention against a woman candidate during a presidential election). The Court of Justice has favoured a broad interpretation of women's rights. Above all, women on the Commission's staff have acted with increasing self-confidence as an interest group and lobby as well as drafters and agents for policies decided elsewhere (Springer 1993). It remains to be seen whether these forces, taken together, provide an effective counterbalance to the member states, who are increasingly concerned with the achievement of a more competitive business environment and are reluctant to give priority to social justice issues. Development of policy for women's equality, therefore, continues to be highly contentious, difficult and complex. If concrete achievement to date is limited, though, the visibility of the issues is comparatively high and the existence of European networks and lobbies for women ensure that the issues of sex equality remain on the policy agenda.

## Social dialogue and the European social model

Ideas of a European social model also influenced the way in which the Union reached its decisions over education and training policy. Although it is the Union's own institutions which make policy, invariably with an eye on the responses of member states, the Union has opted to develop its policies through consultation with a range of external interests, the most important of whom are those interest groups described in its documentation as 'the social partners'. The concept of social partnership has a number of different dimensions within the EU. First, it characterises a broad approach to society, which is typically expressed through the political world-views of both Christian democracy and social democracy and which believes that things work best when there is a broad understanding and co-operation between the various parties making up society. Second, in many European societies the major social and economic decisions are channelled through a range of institutions that are tripartite in structure, allowing for the views of government, employers and workers to be debated and considered before decisions are reached. Institutions representing workers and employees were, therefore, given access to a range of consultative bodies and, in some cases, they even acquired an executive role (thus trade unions and employers' associations frequently provide publicly-funded training in such areas as health and safety, for example). In general, these institutions were regarded not as simple interest groups but as the organised expressions of the great forces – labour and capital – which together make up a capitalist society.

Both dimensions are present in the EU's approach to social partnership, though in recent years the concept has been widened to include new partners whose interests are not necessarily represented in the tripartite approach. For many years, though, the Union considered that the key social partners were employers' associations and trade unions. In each case the Union operated through joint meetings with the European umbrella associations known as the 'peak organisations'. Thus the employers' associations were recognised for the private sector through UNICE, the Union des Industries du Communauté Européen, and for the public sector through CEEP, the Centre Européen des Entreprises Publiques. The trade unions were involved primarily through the European Trades Union Confederation (ETUC).

Until the 1980s the Union did little to put the idea of social partnership to work. In general, the employers' organisations – and particularly UNICE – were reluctant to commit themselves to a level of discussion which might seem to endorse the idea of a European level of collective bargaining. Anyway, UNICE, like most of the national associations which it represented, was not empowered to make decisions in its own right. By contrast, the trade union organisations made much of their desire to move towards a European level of policy debate. However, in reality, their powers were limited, not least by the extremely low levels of union membership in France, Spain and some other nations and the wide variation in union functions across the member states more generally. Moreover, the trade union movement was ideologically and institutionally riven in Spain, France and Italy and remained so until the collapse of Soviet communism in 1989/90. Even after the majority of trade unions decided to join the ETUC, the difficulties of representing such a diverse movement at European level were considerable (Jensen, Madsen and Due 1995).

The high point of social partnership during the 1980s came with the move towards the single market. Before 1985, attempts to establish a dialogue between the social partners had been largely unsuccessful. They did generate a small number of standing committees, including the Standing Committee on Employment (which discussed training and other human resources issues in the context of unemployment), and these may have generated a degree of trust between the individuals involved. However, their purely symbolic functions also fostered cynicism, within the trade union movement and among individual employers who were active in their national associations, about the likely effectiveness of dialogue at the European level. On assuming the presidency in 1985, Jacques Delors invited UNICE and the ETUC to a series of round table discussions at the Vale Duchesse chateau near Brussels. While ETUC and UNICE failed to reach any significant measure of agreement during the Val Duchesse meetings, they established themselves firmly as the two peak organisations representing the social partners at European level. The Val Duchesse discussions also ensured that vocational training was one of the issues which any future social dialogue would cover, reaching a broad agreement in March 1987 on training, motivation and consultation. By this time the Commission had also commissioned a CEDEFOP study of the 'role of the social partners in initial and continuing vocational training', leading to a series of published reports covering the situation in each member state, as well as two studies on the possible role of the social partners at Community level (CEDEFOP 1987). A further set of studies, this time of the social partners' role in continuing vocational training, was commissioned under the FORCE training action programme (Blanpain, Engels and Pellegrini 1993).

Perhaps most important of all, however, were the provisions of the Treaty on European Union. Article Three of the Treaty required the Commission to submit all social policy proposals to the European peak organisations before agreeing on any action; Section Four of the Protocol on Social Policy provided for agreements between the social partners, provided that they were backed by a qualified majority in the Council, to be implemented through a Council Decision. This power has rarely been exercised. However, in the course of a 1996 interview on vocational training, the President of the European Parliament suggested that one way out of the impasse would be to involve the social partners at European level. Social dialogue is becoming a valuable alternative to the traditional solution of legislation, which is increasingly inefficient, particularly in the social area (Kops and Hänsch 1996).

By the mid-1990s, then, the concept and practice of social dialogue were reasonably well-established in the Union's training policies. Admittedly, the CEDEFOP studies had concluded that 'The participation of the two sides of industry in the structuring of vocational training has by no means been adequately institutionalised in all areas; there also appears to be room for further improvement at Community level' (CEDEFOP 1987, p.25). Put more bluntly, trade unions in several countries played little or no part in the determination of training priorities and provision, whether because they had little interest in training matters or because employers and government had kept trade union involvement to a minimum. In some other member states, such as Germany and France, trade unions took a more active role in training decisions and it was this model that the Commission hoped to adopt at the level of the Union. Predictably, this was resisted by the UK and other member states and by the employers' associations. If this blocked the process of 'institutionalisation' anticipated by CEDEFOP, the Union did create greater scope for social dialogue within its own training action programmes.

By the late 1980s Delors was actively promoting the concept and practice of social dialogue as a means of building popular support for integration. As an area where the Union had its own budgets, and had clear competences of its own, vocational training was a particularly fruitful area for developing the Union's policies in dialogue. For Delors, the single market had to be seen to benefit workers and consumers as well as business. Following consultations with member states, employers and unions, the Commission unveiled what it called the 'Community Charter of Fundamental Social Rights of Workers', which was eventually adopted by the European Council in Strasbourg in December 1989 by eleven member states. The twelfth was the United Kingdom, whose Prime Minister described the 'Social Charter' in her memoirs as 'quite simply a socialist charter' which was designed to preserve jobs in the richer member states by raising labour costs in the poorer ones (Thatcher 1993).

For the UK government, the very idea of an institutionalised social dialogue – certainly in the form offered by the Commission – was unacceptable. In 1988 Margaret Thatcher asked the UK civil service to identify ways in which 'the Commission was pushing forward the frontiers of its competence into new areas – culture, education, health and social security'. The use of 'advisory committees whose membership was neither appointed by, nor answerable to, member states and which tended therefore to reach *communautaire* decisions' was high on the list of culprits (Thatcher 1993). In its formal response to the Commission's 1992 proposals for vocational training, the UK government emphasised heavily the principle of subsidiarity, arguing that with the exception of unemployed people, training decisions were best left to employers and individuals in an unconstrained market; above all there should be no 'imposition of unnecessary and unacceptable burdens on employers' (UK Government 1992, ss. 3.6, 4.1, 4.2).

The Social Charter was, though, less of a landmark than either its supporters or critics assumed at the time. Most of its 30 paragraphs either restated the present legal position of employees under existing Union law, described current entitlements in the member states or summarised the views of Europe's political leaders as reflected in Council resolutions. The first three paragraphs, for example, simply summarised the legal position on freedom of movement, while the paragraph on social protection merely described existing welfare provision across the member states. Paragraph 15, covering vocational training, also said little that was new or particularly controversial:

> Every worker of the European Community must be able to have access to vocational training and to benefit therefrom throughout his working life. In the conditions governing access to such training there may be no discrimination on grounds of nationality.

> The competent public authorities, undertakings or the two sides of industry, each within their own sphere of competence, should set up continuing and permanent training systems enabling every person to undergo retraining more especially through leave for training purposes, to improve his skills or to acquire new skills, particularly in the light of technical developments. (CEC 1989, p.3)

What was new was the reframing of these rather general statements of provision in the language of 'rights'. Elizabeth Meehan has argued convincingly that this was not the Commission's primary intention; rather, European politicians were thinking 'not in terms of establishing entitlements but in terms of removing anomalies and increasing the Community's legitimacy' (1993, p.60). Moreover, among the wealthier member states at least, there was widespread concern over the prospects of 'social dumping': that is, the practice by employers of using the internal market to transfer operations from comparatively expensive environments to those nations and regions where the standards (and costs) of labour protection were lowest. Training, according to Delors, was an effective means of ensuring that 'European integration is brought about not by social dumping but by helping others catch up' (Delors 1988, p.3). In so far as any subsequent action was expected, this was largely a matter for the member states and the social partners themselves; the results, such as they were, came to be published in a series of annual supplements to the DGV magazine *Social Europe*.

If nothing else, as Meehan points out, the language of entitlement certainly helped raise expectations on the trade unions' side and created anxiety among employers' representatives. However, its application to vocational training in particular helped keep the question of social dialogue on the agenda while the Union debated its future policies. Vocational training offered a means of achieving a degree of institutionalisation of the social dialogue within the EU's own policy processes and programmes. A number of tripartite structures already existed, albeit largely consultative in function; the ESF Committee and the Advisory Committee on Vocational Training both include equal numbers of employers' and workers' representatives, as does ECOSOC. During the debate over the future of the Union's education and training programmes, the principle of social dialogue was formally adopted by the Council. In a 1993 Recommendation on access to continuing vocational training, the Council called for member states to encourage the 'information and consultation of employees' representatives or, in the absence of such representatives, the employees themselves on the development and implementation of the training plans and programmes of the undertakings concerned' (*OJ*, 23 July 1993, p.39). In a more wide-ranging Resolution agreed earlier in the same month, the Council urged that the aims and contents of training programmes are decided in partnership with relevant bodies which may include the social partners, in accordance with national systems and traditions. It called on member states to update skills and qualifications by 'developing co-operation between the national and local authorities, employers and unions, enterprises and others, in accordance with national practice' and asked the Commission to bear this in mind when drafting the LEONARDO proposals (*OJ*, 8 July 1993).

By 1994 the new LEONARDO programme specifically included the social partners at national and Union level among those eligible to participate, though with the now familiar caution respecting national legislation and practice (CEC 1995b). Moreover, the Council

Decision establishing LEONARDO required the Commission to involve the social partners in the work of the LEONARDO Committee; for although the Committee itself consisted solely of representatives from the member states (each of whom was to appoint two members), under Article 7 the Commission was able, when consulting the committee on the implementation of the Decision, to appoint an equal number of representatives from the 'peak bodies' to act as observers (*OJ*, 29 December 1994). Subsequently, trade union organisations and employers' associations were strongly represented among the projects approved under LEONARDO when it came into effect in 1995. This was the case at Union level; one of the first projects approved was a proposal from UNICE and ETUC for the development of training modules on the European social dialogue with the aim of promoting the skills and attitudes required to improve the social dialogue. This was as true in the UK, despite its opt-outs from the Social Charter and the Social Chapter of the 1992 Treaty, as anywhere else in the Union.

By this time, though, the concept of social partnership had itself undergone revision. It had always been criticised by those who, like the Conservative government in the UK, regarded it as little more than a typical case of trade union protectionism by socialist political leaders who were anxious to protect their electoral base. A number of feminist critics suggested that the Union's model of social partnership simply reinforced existing patterns of patriarchal power, resting as it did on a largely male constituency of managers and trade union officers. A much larger number of politicians and business leaders, less ideologically driven than the UK government, shared its fears that the institutionalisation of the social dialogue was harming Europe's competitiveness. A group of Anglo-German businessmen, convened by Chancellor Kohl and Prime Minister Major, reported in 1994 that the social dialogue was producing Directives which were 'inconsistent with the growth of flexible working' (*Financial Times*, 12 April 1995). This argument was turned on its head by one of the expert advisory committees that Mrs Thatcher had so sharply criticised as a vehicle for *communautaire* dogma, the working group on work organisation, which argued in 1995 that 'flexibility...frequently requires less strict and definitive regulations and more social dialogue and negotiated solutions. The major problem here is to ensure the equality of the social partners at all levels' (Working Group on Work Organisation

1995, p.32). By this time the Commission had already decided to widen its concept and practice of social dialogue to include the so-called 'third sector' of non-governmental organisations (NGOs).

NGOs had long played a vital role in other inter-governmental bodies such as the United Nations as well as in a number of member states in consulting on policy and, in some cases, taking part in implementation. As a result of the 'bottom-up' approach which was supposed to characterise the Community Initiatives, some of the programmes did indeed involve something akin to a community development model of partnership between local agencies; in particular, the LEADER initiative for rural economic development placed a strong emphasis on community involvement and partnership, a feature that was subsequently strengthened in the second phase of LEADER from 1994 (Black and Conway 1995; Larkin 1993). This approach was, in turn, absorbed into the Union's Special Support Programme for Peace and Reconciliation in Northern Ireland, launched in the wake of the paramilitary cease-fires in early 1995. Quite unusually, the Commission insisted that funding under the Support Programme should be allocated by a number of 'intermediary bodies', which could include government departments but would not be limited to them and would include several NGOs; like LEADER, the programme strongly favoured partnerships and community involvement (Wulf-Mathies 1995).

By the mid-1990s this type of approach was becoming institutionalised. The Commission's social policy White Paper envisaged the creation of a forum which would bring together the representatives of 'civil society'. In its first meeting in March 1996 the European Social Policy Forum brought together representatives of the social partners, local and national authorities, Commission and NGOs from across the Union to discuss such issues as employment, equal opportunities and the future of working life. A similar policy also emerged more clearly in other areas: the 1996 framework for the NOW programme (equal opportunities for women) emphasised that priority was given to actions which actively involved 'the Social Partners and women's organisations...at all levels' (*OJ*, 10 July 1996, p.14).

Social dialogue has also been built increasingly into the EU's regional policy institutions. EU cohesion policy is, as has repeatedly been emphasised, strongly influenced by regional considerations (see also, Preston 1994). Although the details of the EU's regional policies need not concern us here, they also have influenced the development of education and training policy since human resources have generally been regarded as a central dimension in regional economic success. Moreover, the European Union's regional measures are increasingly acquiring a political dimension in addition to their economic aspect, seen most clearly in the establishment of the Committee of the Regions in 1994 (CoR). This new body, set up by the Treaty of Maastricht in recognition of the role of local authorities in the member states, had already come into conflict with both the Parliament and ECOSOC by 1996. One UK city councillor who was a founder member of CoR explained that:

> in some countries, for example Germany, Belgium and Spain, the CoR members are more senior politicians than those representing their country as MEPs. I'd say that this creates a resentment that goes some way towards explaining why the European Parliament reduced the budget requested for the CoR. (Interview, April 1995)

Consultation of the CoR is mandatory on five community policies: education, public health, the trans-European networks (transport, telecommunications and energy) and economic and social cohesion. One of its eight sub-committees is responsible for Education and Training while others were created to handle the People's Europe and Social Affairs and Health.

By promoting social dialogue, the Commission is pursuing a social model which is congruent with the dominant political philosophies of social democracy and Christian democracy. Delors, Flynn and Santer have all argued that a strong model of social solidarity is, in turn, the best way to strengthen Europe's competitiveness (CEC 1994a; CEC 1994c; Delors 1988). If there is little evidence, to date, to confirm this strategic faith, there is not much to show that the opt-outs have significantly advantaged the UK economy over that of other member states. This may simply be because the opt-outs were intended more for domestic political consumption than as a serious act of defiance. Previous experience suggested that the UK opt-out would be largely ineffective as a means of avoiding Union legislation (Curwen 1995a); and the UK has generally had to live with the wider social policy framework as manifested through the objectives of the Union's action pro-grammes. In other words, it is just not possible to say with any confidence whether the European social model will ultimately harm or favour Europe's economic competitiveness. What we can say is that the increasing demands for flexibility which arise from a fluid and uncertain economic environment have started to erode the existing boundaries between providers of education and training and to create pressures for increasing collaboration and partnership between the different stakeholders. The EU's policy of promoting social partnership as a guiding principle in delivering education and training can best be seen as an example of a wider trend within the advanced economies to favour collabo-rative networking and shared resources in the face of intensifying global competition (Green 1995).

It could be argued, though, that the concept of a common European social model is not particularly helpful. Historically, it makes little sense to conflate the very different welfare systems of, say, Italy, Denmark and Spain as though they do indeed represent a shared underlying structure which is threatened by globalisa-tion. It is true that the debate over globalisation in Germany is surrounded by anxieties over the impact of eastern Europe and the 'dragon economies' of the Pacific Rim upon the traditionally high levels of employment and its associated benefits for individuals and for social stability. A similar anxiety exists within France, the other nation which constitutes a 'core' member of the EU. Thus the 'social model' which the Union's politicians like to present as a common pattern across the Union is, in fact, the social model of some countries only – and a model, at that, which is being subjected to increasing pressures even within Germany, France, Sweden and Denmark as the impact of global competition has eroded the politicians' willingness to maintain social spending levels.

Yet competitiveness was not the only factor in the politicians' minds when they created the social dialogue. Delors claimed that the main aim of the Val Duchesse process was the creation of 'a European autonomy and a European personality' so that 'both management and workers can play a whole-hearted part in Euro-pean integration' (Delors 1988, p.3). This type of public statement needs to be treated with all the caution we usually reserve for politicians' pronouncements, but it is consistent with the broad strategy that Delors followed. Yet there is also something in

Mrs Thatcher's description of the institutions that the Commission creates to pursue the social dialogue at European level. Quite understandably, each grouping uses the space created by the Commission in order to advance its collective interests –including those interests that may receive a less than sympathetic hearing at national or regional level. It is common enough for critics to claim that NGOs, trade unions or employers' associations have been manipulated by 'corporatist' structures within the framework of the nation state or within other inter-governmental bodies such as UNESCO. There is little doubt that the convening of European meetings of NGOs, unions, employers and others is equally a part of a wider process of seeking legitimation for European integration. In so far as this has opened up the fields of education and training policy to debate at the European level, it has helped promote the European dimension.

## Conclusion

Social policy concerns have helped shape the Union's policies for education and training in specific ways. In particular, they have shifted attention towards lifelong learning as a means of achieving two important social policy goals: in the short term, it can play a compensatory or remedial role in helping individuals overcome the consequences of social exclusion; in the longer term, it can build social cohesion by enhancing competitiveness and ensuring a flexible, adaptable and productive workforce. By contrast, the EU has had relatively little to say about education and training in respect of other social policy goals (the quality of life of the expanding population of elderly Europeans, to take one example). Employability has been the keystone of Europe's social policy interest in education and training, reinforcing the strategic importance of lifelong learning to the Union.

Lifelong learning is, for the EU's social policy initiators, not simply about the continuing education and training of adults, important though that may be in reinforcing social cohesion. Increasingly, the EU's social policy preoccupations have come to embrace not merely vocational training but the entire education system. Hence the priority given within education and training policy to the goal of combating exclusion, identified in the 1995 White Paper on education and training as third among the five general objectives proposed for this area (CEC 1995e, pp.62–5). In the event, only one of the specific measures under this objective was accepted by the member states; a small-scale European voluntary service for young people was funded within the existing budget (chiefly under the Youth for Europe programme) but the proposal to support 'second chance' schools in 'problem areas' under SOCRATES and LEONARDO proved much more contentious. National sovereignty over both social policy and education has limited the extent to which social policy concerns have been able to influence EU policy over education and training, other than confirming the general tendency for the Union to expand the range and radicalism of its potential agenda. Nevertheless, social policy concerns have had some influence – as is demonstrated, above all, by the Union's experiences on equality of opportunity, where small, but nonetheless real, gains have been made throughout the 1980s and 1990s (Rees 1996; Waddington 1996).

Chapter Seven

# Fostering Innovation and Competitiveness in the Information Society

Since its inception, EU policies have been primarily concerned with economic issues. Educational and vocational training policies, like social and regional policy, the language of citizenship and other policy interests, were originally developed and viewed as legitimate because of their potential contribution to building the common market. The very *raison d'être* of the EU was that it would help its separate member states to achieve faster growth, and hence greater prosperity and more peaceable relationships, than they would if they had to compete against one another. Is this still as true today? Has the new European settlement overtaken the early agenda? Or are the imperatives of capitalist growth still driving the Union's development? I think that, despite the important changes of the 1980s and 1990s, the EU is still chiefly about the business of supporting economic growth. If anything, the requirements of post-industrial restructuring have reinforced rather than diluted this preoccupation. Should it fail to achieve this task, the politics of European integration will lose its attraction for its member states and applicants alike. It follows that the Union's policies for education and training are shaped, to a large extent, by the primacy of growth among its objectives.

If the Union does not 'add value' by its activities, then there is no plausible case for action at the European level. For all the member states, the preferred form of added value is a contribution towards the competitiveness of the European economies. This does not, of course, mean that other goals are unimportant. Apart from anything else, as this book has repeatedly argued, the EU is certainly not a monolithic entity. Despite its centralising tendencies and an absence of democratic (as opposed to judicial) checks and balances on the Council and Commission, the Union remains, in many ways, a loose federation of independent nations who pursue their own policy objectives within its institutions. For their part, the Union's own institutions have their own agendas, interests and constituencies which, at times, may be in competition with one another; moreover, they actively seek to work with players at ground level within the member states who, when required, become external allies whose support can be played-off against the member states or against other Union institutions. As a comparatively new and open collection of institutions, moreover, the Union has been served by a number of politicians who are particularly attracted by the idea of innovation or motivated by ideals of international unity. Jacques Delors is the most obvious example in recent times, but he was far from unique in his desire to make a mark on Europe's development.

In these circumstances we might expect a high degree of spill-over between different policy areas, as the Union's leaders search for new ways of pursuing their original goals. Nevertheless, economic growth remains a strong priority and this can be clearly seen in the way that the EU's education and training policies have developed. What has happened, and this is a change associated with the period between around 1990 and 1996, is that human resources issues occupy an increasingly central place in the Union's overall strategy for development. A recent example is the importance given to education and training in the EU's response to the changes being wrought by the new information technologies. Rather than simply re-focusing the education and training action programmes to embrace the new technologies more effectively, as might have been the case in the early 1990s, the EU is now seeking to bring these elements together across a range of different programme areas. In turn, this process has prompted a qualitative change in the way that some of Europe's leading politicians think about education and training with the growing interest, since the late 1980s, in the idea of Europe as a 'learning society'. In a world of constant change and uncertainty, this idea is tied to a particular public stance. As the Commission President told the employers' federation, UNICE, in 1995: 'Instead of congealed knowledge, acquired at a given moment, stands a capacity for acting and reacting in a mutating environment' (Santer 1995b). As has been seen, these concepts surfaced more publicly in the 1995 White Paper on education and training (discussed in Chapter Three). However, their origins lie in the Union's growing preoccupation with the competitive threats which now face Europe's economies in a complex and turbulent global marketplace.

## Competitiveness and human resources policy

Western Europe is, by world standards, a very rich region indeed. Even its poorest nations – Greece, Spain or Portugal – belong unambiguously within advanced, post-industrial capitalism. Its wealthiest nations are able to export manufactured goods and services across the world. What, we might reasonably wonder, is the problem? At one level, the answer is simple: it is the economic, social and political costs of unemployment. After nearly three decades of full employment, the western European economies generated persistently high levels of unemployment from the early to mid-1970s onwards; increasingly, the unemployed inexorably became the long-term unemployed. Unemployment was the single issue which prompted the June 1993 Council at Copenhagen to call for a Commission White Paper on competitiveness, growth and employment. One 1996 report noted that 'in many countries', the introduction of new information and communications technologies was 'widening traditional zones of job-insecurity to include the middle classes' (Information Society Forum 1996, p.19). By contrast, such nations as Japan and the USA are seen as more successful economically and give rise to more stable employment because their economies are more competitive. Behind the concern with competitiveness and growth lies a recognition that Europe's social settlement since 1945 rested primarily upon the twin pillars of social insurance against risk and stability or growth in individual affluence, both of which relied, in turn, upon steadily increasing growth. For most of Europe's politicians, a failure to maintain at least one pillar poses unacceptable risks to the social fabric.

In his study of the 'creeping' extension of the Union's competences, Mark Pollack (1994) argues convincingly that the issue of competitiveness was fundamental to the passing of the Single European Act. For years the member states had generally used the Council to block or oppose the Commission's proposals for further harmonisation; why, asks Pollack, did they accept the Delors

Commission's proposals for an accelerated programme of single market completion with its clear consequences in terms of regulation and extension of competence? His answer is that the deep recession which commenced in 1980 led to a perceived crisis of competitiveness against Japan, the USA and, increasingly, the newly-industrialising countries of the Asian-Pacific region. In itself, the single market programme meant that the Union would be 'concentrating on its role as a huge market, with all the opportunities that would bring to our industries' (Thatcher 1993, p.556). It was accompanied by a series of ambitious research and development programmes following on from the ESPRIT programme (see below for further details), a vigorous programme of regulatory harmonisation and a clear deadline. It also, as Pollack noted, created powerful pressures for 'spill-over' of the Union's interests and, therefore, its competences into new areas. In the intensively competitive world-marketplace of the 1990s, it would be surprising if issues of competitiveness, innovation and growth did not play a similar role in the Commission's strategy development. Thus in one 1996 speech Commissioner Cresson said that:

> I was struck, on taking up my duties in Brussels, by the European paradox which was revealed by a collection of studies conducted by as well as outside the Commission. Europe is still maintaining its scientific excellence, though it is necessary to be vigilant in this respect since constant budget restrictions threaten to weaken its position – but this excellence is not sufficiently translated into industrial and commercial terms. Europe does not innovate enough, and anyhow it innovates less than the United States or Japan. (Cresson 1996b)

Such concerns, centrally focused as they are on the quality and capacities of Europe's human resources, have fuelled the debate over education and training, fostering a substantial spill-over effect as failures of competitiveness are blamed on the workforce's inability to apply innovations sufficiently productively.

In its 1994 White Paper on competitiveness, largely drafted under the direct supervision of its then President, Jacques Delors, the Commission sketched a stark diagnosis of Europe's competitive weaknesses. Despite continued growth and restructuring during the period between 1986 and 1992 – that is, the substantial completion of the single market –'the rest of the world has changed even faster'. The White Paper identified a number of new external factors (or 'changes in the décor', in Delors' phrasing):

- the emergence of new competitors incorporating the latest techniques
- the potential for economic growth following the end of communism, which, as yet, the Union had not been able to harness
- the aging of the population and transformation of family structures
- the far-reaching changes wrought by the 'new industrial revolution'
- the shift towards a knowledge-based economy, where 'the possession and transmission of information is becoming crucial to success'
- the interdependence of global markets as an inescapable fact of economic and financial life. (CEC 1994c, p.11)

The Commission painted an even more dramatic picture of crisis and threat in its Green Paper on Innovation, which identified a significant gap between the achievements of Europe in patenting and applying new products, services and processes and those of its major competitors (CEC 1995c). In all these cases the Commission concluded that the present arrangements of education and training constituted a barrier to Europe's competitiveness.

How has education and training policy come to occupy this central and critical position? First, according to the Commission, education and training play an important part in increasing competitiveness at a general level. It is not simply that individuals require new skills if they are to remain employable. In today's conditions, the Commission has come to regard lifelong learning as a public good. As the Delors' White Paper put it: 'In a society based far more on the production, transfer and sharing of knowledge than on trade in goods, access to theoretical and practical knowledge must necessarily play a major role' (CEC 1994c, p.133). However, the White Paper also argued that this required changes in the education and training systems of the member states, such as a stronger emphasis upon 'basic skills' (including learning 'how to learn throughout one's life'), more practically-oriented training and closer co-operation between education and business. Above all, it argued that:

> All measures must therefore necessarily be based on the **concept of developing, generalising and systematising lifelong learning and continuing training**. This means that education and training systems must be reworked in order to take account of the need – which is already growing and is set to grow even more in the future – for the **permanent recomposition and redevelopment of knowledge and know-how**. (CEC 1994c, p.136; emphasis in original)

A similar emphasis emerged in the Commission's 1996 action plan on Innovation, which linked lifelong learning and enterprise education to the development of a dynamic culture of innovation (CEC 1996f).

## Human resources and the EU's policies for research and development

The challenges of science and technology to Europe's growth were recognised at an early stage of the Union's development. Until its amendment under the Single European Act, nothing in the Treaty of Rome explicitly permitted the promotion of research and development, leaving the Union to operate solely on the basis of unanimous decisions of the Council. This meant that the Union's role developed only slowly, and largely on the basis of co-operation rather than regulation. Margaret Sharp (1993) has argued convincingly that the turning point came in the late 1970s when the European Union became a net importer of information technology, partly as a consequence of concerted government intervention in the Japanese IT sector. This development, following the sharp decline in the 1970s of such staple industries as textiles, shipbuilding, steel, coal-mining and motor vehicle manufacturing, prompted the Council to agree, in 1982, to launch the ESPRIT programme – the European Strategic Programme for Research in Information Technology. As was often the case when proposing action in a new area where the Union lacked legal competence, the Commission's original proposal was for a pilot programme. However, following the Single European Act, ESPRIT became a model for the EU's overall programmes of research and technology development (RTD) which have had a considerable impact – indirect as well as direct – upon aspects of education and training.

In promoting RTD the Union was strictly limited to supporting the 'pre-competitive' stage. Certainly, the member states were reluctant to approve support for applied research, partly because they saw this as a matter best left to each nation (most of whom regarded applied research as the responsibility of employers and other end-users) and partly because it smacked of a direct subsidy to private enterprise. The EU's RTD role was to help develop new knowledge and technologies; it was for the end-users and member states to put them into operation. Initially, the Union's emphasis upon supporting pre-competitive RTD meant that ESPRIT, which was primarily concerned with developing technologies in microelectronics, advanced information processing and software engineering, had no direct impact upon education and training. Similarly, the first and second framework programmes for RTD, developed following the Single European Act and running between 1987 and 1991, were not initially concerned with the ways in which the technologies or research were applied. By the time that the third framework programme for RTD was developed, with a lifespan of 1990–1994, human resources issues had assumed a rather higher profile. Some 9 per cent of the framework programme budget was given over to promoting mobility and training for researchers (the Human Capital and Mobility programme). Running alongside but separately from the framework programme, the Union, in 1987, also developed a programme for development and application of learning technologies – DELTA (an acronym derived from Developing European Learning through Technological Advance). By requiring all projects to disseminate their findings to end-users, the third framework programme also encouraged closer contact between the research community and companies (including their training departments).

According to the Commission's director of telecommunications policy, the DELTA programme arose in response to the competitive challenges of direct broadcasting satellites. With DELTA, the Union 'intended to provide stimulus and develop expertise in a field in which Europe will have to invest a large measure of effort if it is not to forego in the very near future its edge in industrial and scientific expertise' (Schuringa 1988, p.6). Launched in 1988 as a two-year exploratory programme of studies of advanced learning technologies, in 1991 the DELTA programme was absorbed into the third Framework Programme with a budget to 1994 of 54.5 million ECUs. Some 23 projects were subsequently approved, exploring the educational potential of such telematics applications as CD-ROM, videodisk, electronic mail and conferencing via ISDN, and satellite broadcasting (CEC 1993e). According to its evaluators, the programme confirmed the technical feasibility and the educational value of the new telematics systems; but the extent of a European market, fragmented as it was by linguistic diversity and national educational arrangements, remained doubtful (Collis, Parisi and Ligurio 1996; Lloyd 1993).

With the fourth framework programme (from 1995 to 1998), the Union extended its RTD interests to encompass investigations into social and economic issues. Within the wider RTD area, research specifically into education and training research was for the first time identified as a priority area for support, albeit a relatively minor one. Along with the evaluation of science and technology and social exclusion and inclusion, education and training formed one of three themes within the Targeted Socio-Economic Research (TSER) programme, itself a relatively small element within the fourth framework programme which was dwarfed by the larger programmes such as biotechnology, telematics applications, communications technologies and transport. TSER, in total, accounted for roughly one per cent of the EU's total RTD budget for 1995–1998. However, this is not the whole story: most of the areas previously covered by DELTA now fell within the Telematics Applications Programme (TAP), where, in fact, rather more support was available for education and training research than under TSER (see Table 7.1). Indeed, the average EU grant to education and training research within TAP was over three times the average given in TSER: 1,521,000 ECUs in the average TAP project, compared with 428,000 ECUs in TSER. Even allowing for the element devoted to equipment and laboratory space under TAP, this is still a sizeable difference. Finally, the human capital and mobility programme continued under FP4, as did the requirement for project dissemination. In other words, as with the EU's policies overall, to understand the impact upon education and training we have to look beyond the field of research specifically into education and training alone.

**Table 7.1: Education and Training Programmes within the EU's Fourth Framework Programme for Research and Technology Development**

| Programme | Number of education and training research projects approved in 1995 | EU contribution to education and training projects |
|---|---|---|
| Telematics applications programme | 29 | 44,119,470 ECU |
| Targeted Socio-Economic Research Programme | 11 | 4,706,500 ECU |

*Source:* CEC 1996b.

Predictably, education and training research funded under TAP is concerned with applying the new communications and information technologies. Most of the projects approved in response to the 1994 calls for proposals were concerned with the production, piloting and demonstration of new learning materials. Examples include CL4K (Cyberspace Learning for Kids), a UK-led consortium of 22 partners who aimed to offer on-line facilities to support peer-learning, provide a vehicle for teachers and stimulate parental involvement; DOMITEL, a Dutch-led group of six aiming to develop and demonstrate the potential of interactive cable TV to support home-based learning; and COAST (Courseware Authoring for Scientific Training), a French-led partnership of nine organisations aiming to provide multi-media simulations to replace high-cost lab practicals in science teaching. Two of the TAP projects are specifically concerned to work with the publishing industry: KAMP (Knowledge Assurance in Multi-media Publishing) was to develop advanced multi-media training sessions to this specialised sector of the industry, while POLLEN (Publishers on Information Highways) brought together European publishers of interactive educational materials and trainers to design mass-audience multi-media educational materials in the sciences.

Organisationally, the TAP research projects tended to be based in universities or foundations. Very few were co-ordinated by employers or other end-users such as professional associations (most of the companies who co-ordinated the projects approved in 1995 were consultancies specialising in training and/or training research). This is not to say that employers and other end-users were absent from the projects, as a number of consortia included employer partners and all of the projects were geared towards outcomes which had value for specified markets of end-users. Rather, it is to say that the RTD projects were mostly academically led. The largest single number – five of the 29 – were co-ordinated by UK institutions, generally (and misleadingly, on this and similar evidence) thought of as a reluctant member of the Union. What is more striking, though, is the significant role played by two of the smaller and poorer member states: three of the projects were led by institutions based in Greece and and three by institutions in Ireland (none, though, was co-ordinated by a Portuguese institution). By definition, all had to involve transnational partners; over half were comparatively small, with up to ten partners but four, though, had more than 20 partners (the largest being the 24-member COINS consortium for multi-media education and training led by the Galway-based Irish language authority, Udaras na Gaeltachta).

**Table 7.2: Organisational features of education and training research projects supported in the 1995 call in the Technology Applications Programme**

| Co-ordinator – nationality | | Type of co-ordinating institution | | Number of partners | |
|---|---|---|---|---|---|
| United Kingdom | 5 | Higher education institute | 11 | 20–25 | 6 |
| Germany | 4 | Foundation | 8 | 16–20 | 1 |
| Netherlands | 4 | Company | 6 | 11–15 | 5 |
| France | 3 | Government agency | 2 | 6–10 | 11 |
| Greece | 3 | Voluntary/professional body | 2 | 1–5 | 4 |
| Ireland | 3 | | | | |
| Spain | 3 | | | | |
| Belgium | 1 | | | | |
| Italy | 1 | | | | |
| Sweden | 1 | | | | |
| Switzerland | 1 | | | | |

*Source*: CEC 1996a

In addition, ten education and training projects were approved in the TSER programme (Table 7.3). Almost all were based on networks of academic researchers and co-ordinated by higher education institutions. There appeared to be a slight, but noticeable, bias towards the study of education rather than vocational training. As already noted, the TSER partnerships, on average, enjoyed less than a third of the funding available to TAP consortia. Yet if the education and training projects within TSER were inevitably fewer and smaller in scale than those supported in TAP, they did enjoy a certain symbolic importance.

## Education and training in the information society

As earlier sections have shown, the EU has a well-established interest in the new information and communication technologies which it pursued through such programmes as ESPRIT and STAR. However, as two of Mme Cresson's senior officials commented in 1995, 'These initiatives were always immediate, with no strategic global vision' (Riché-Magnier and Metthey 1995, p.418). In 1994 the Commission attempted to develop a more long-term approach, launching a debate about Europe and what it called the 'global information society' (CEC 1994d) and subsequently presenting a Green Paper called *Living and Working in the Information Society: people first* (CEC 1996h). In picking up the language of the 'information society', the Union was deliberately drawing on journalistic hype and specifically on American media comment.

Fear of American technological superiority – and hence economic hegemony – has never been far from the surface in the EU. This particular turning point for the EU reportedly came when Bill Clinton made the 'information superhighway' an election issue in 1992, following it up after his election with an attempt to assume leadership within the G7 group of nations on the issue. Indeed, according to Marielle Riché-Magnier and Jack Metthey (1995), the net effect of the hype was to entrench the supremacy of the USA in the new technologies; the Clinton initiatives thus 'acted as a release mechanism' on the Union, forcing the Commission to tackle the American competitive challenge with some vigour. Delors' White Paper, which spoke of a 'new industrial revolution' which was being led by the USA, urged the creation of a 'common information area' within the EU and proposed that the Council

**Table 7.3: Education and Training Research within the targeted Socio-Economic Research Programme, 1995**

| Theme of project | Co-ordinator | Partners | EU grant |
|---|---|---|---|
| Improving science education – research on different forms of labwork | Université de Paris XI, France | 7 | 650,000 Ecu |
| Early literacy teaching and learning in four national contexts | University of Brighton, UK | 4 | 14,996 Ecu |
| Comparative analysis of the effectiveness of labour market training for the long-term unemployed | Universiteite Twente, Netherlands | 7 | 810,000 Ecu |
| Evaluation and self-evaluation of universities in Europe | Université de Paris X, France | 11 | 796,000 Ecu |
| Teletutoring and reflective competencies in secondary and vocational teacher training | Universiteit Utrecht, Netherlands | 4 | 99,504 Ecu |
| Design of policies for new job skill needs and low-skilled workers | London School of Economics, UK | 6 | 661,000 Ecu |
| Developing models of the learning organisation in clusters of small and medium enterprises | Fondazione Istituto Guglielmo Tagliacarne, Italy | 7 | 400,000 Ecu |
| European Network for Educational Research on Assessment, Effectiveness and Innovation | Universiteite Twente, Netherlands | 19 | 300,000 Ecu |
| The potential of open and distance learning and advanced learning technologies for improving access | Tavistock Institute, UK | 8 | 450,000 Ecu |
| European Child Care and Pre-school Study | Freie Universität Berlin, Germany | 5 | 525,000 Ecu |

*Source*: CEC 1996b

convene what became the High-Level Group on the Information Society, assembled by Commissionner Martin Bangemann and including representatives of industry and academia as well as European politicians (CEC 1994c).

The main result was the creation, within DGXIII, of the Information Society Project, an attempt to promote the integration of global information tools and processes into education, training, business, government, health and leisure. The Information Society Project, although co-ordinated by DGXIII, cuts across a number of policy areas, including media, employment, sustainable development and education and training.

In its report, the Bangemann Group stressed Europe's position as laggard behind Japan and the USA. Generally speaking, the High-Level Group took the view that as in the USA, the marketplace was the best means of producing the necessary changes (reflecting perhaps a long-held view among policy makers and industrial leaders that governments, including the EU, had done rather badly at 'picking winners' in the past). However, in order to achieve 'critical mass' across Europe, the Group identified a number of 'demonstration applications' which it believed the Union should support in order to show the potential benefits of the information society. A number of these touched implicitly on education or training issues – the creation of 'city information highways', for example, was designed to provide access to telelearning as well as teleshopping, teleworking and information services, all of which would appeal to ordinary citizens as well as businesses and public sector agencies (CEC 1994d). More substantially, though, one demonstration application concerned 'Distance Learning – Lifelong Learning for a Changing Society'. The aim of this application was to provide 'courseware, training and tuition services tailored for SMEs, large companies and public administrations'. The major challenge, according to the Bangemann Group, lay in the need to 'train the trainers and extend computer literacy among the teaching profession' (CEC 1994d, p.25).

Taking this ambitious agenda forward was a complex matter. Budgetary constraints and the reluctance of member states to accept a substantial erosion of their sovereignty in this area limited the Commission's freedom for action. In its 1996 Green Paper on the information society, the Commission again presented a far-reaching analysis which focused, in particular, on employment issues. Once more, the Commission adopted a discourse of crisis and change: 'The information society represents the most fundamental change in our time, with enormous opportunities for society as a whole but with risks for individuals and regions' (CEC 1996h, p.28). Not only Europe's competitiveness but also its social cohesion, according to the Green Paper, depended upon the new approaches to knowledge and working life that the new information technologies required. In particular, 'What Europe needs is a substantial overhaul of education and training'. In the short term, 'the urgent need is to arrest the growing skill obsolescence of the adult working population through a proactive approach to industrial adaptation and change'. However, the long-term aim should be 'for Europe to develop a new architecture of lifelong education and training, involving all parts of education and training systems, including schools, and designed and delivered in more appropriate ways' (CEC 1996h, p.18). The Green Paper singled out four particular developments which were required in the information society:

(a) the best foundations of knowledge and skills

(b) a shift from teaching to learning, including a new emphasis on self-directed learning using the new technologies

(c) an emphasis upon learning by doing, particularly within the workplace

(d) retraining and upgrading employees' skills, rather than deskilling and discouraging them through unemployment (CEC 1996h, pp.18–19).

Once more, then, the Commission presented proposals for a radical reshaping of the education and training system.

As on other occasions, though, the Commission combined an iconoclastic analysis with a bashful agenda. Of all the Commission's radical analyses of social and economic change, the Green Paper on the information society was remarkable for its lack of detail on practical policy. In a section inviting dialogue, the Commission spoke in general terms of the 'key role' of the Structural Fund, and particularly their Objective 4 and the ADAPT Initiative, in developing the information society (CEC 1996h). In the concluding section on the way ahead, however, the Green Paper addressed itself in the loosest and most general sense to suggestions for 'public policies', without specifying which body might formulate and implement these policies (CEC 1996h). As so often when it had faced policy traffic jams in the past, the Commission turned to its external networks to help build up the pressure on the Union to act.

In an attempt to create a forceful agenda for the Project, the Commission appointed an Information Society Forum. Half of the 128 members were appointed by member states and half by the Commission, representing employers, educators, publishers, specialists, trade unions, and broadcasters. Its first report was drafted by six working groups, one of which (chaired by the Principal of Newark and Sherwood College in Nottinghamshire) was charged with making recommendations on education, training and learning in the information society. Yet education and training also emerged as priorities right across the Forum's report. Indeed, the first of the six 'propositions' which summarise the report dealt with education and training in language that should now be extremely familiar to those who have followed the development of the Union's interest in this field:

> The pace of change is becoming so fast that people can only adapt if the Information Society becomes the 'Lifelong Learning Society'. In order to build and maintain competitive economic advantages, skills and talents must be constantly reshaped to meet the changing needs of the work place, wherever that is. These skills and talents will also have broader opportunities for expression because the Learning Society will offer unprecedented possibilities for personal development and fulfilment. (Information Society Forum 1996, p.2).

Other 'propositions' called for an inclusive approach, a broad-based improvement in the quality of life for 'ordinary people', an open and democratic style, greater effort in public awareness-raising and – more speculatively – a 'Second Renaissance' of creative scientific and cultural development (Information Society Forum 1996).

In the underlying analysis the Forum pointed to what it saw as important barriers to change. Particularly at secondary and primary levels, the Forum was concerned by the reluctance of teachers and institutions to make what it believed were the necessary changes, the shortages of hardware and software in education and training and the delays in some member states in introducing deregulation of telecommunications (Information Society Forum

1996; on deregulation see Curwen 1995b). Importantly, while appealing for more rapid deregulation, the Forum also challenged the Commission's belief in the effectiveness of market forces as the main driver in the information society (Information Society Forum 1996). Finally, the Forum emphasised the need to promote 'the "Learning Company", whose computer-literate members and employees will be using their electronic access to knowledge and information to update their skills' (Information Society Forum 1996, p.24). Despite differences of emphasis, then, the conclusion was similar to that already presented in the Union's own Green Paper on the information society.

In taking forward its ideas on the information society, the Commission has paid particular attention to education and training. One specific activity concerned support for the development of a European educational multi-media software industry. This was an issue that had been raised at the Standing Conference of European Ministers of Education held at Istanbul in 1989 under the auspices of the Council of Europe – at the conference, politicians and senior civil servants heard that even in the large north American market, the educational software market was small when compared with either the commercial software market or the print-based textbook market and that the linkage between software and hardware, which reduced the market still further, was limited to cross-national transfer and shortening the lifetime of software products, concluding that this was 'an area where European co-operation could make a significant difference' (Eraut 1991). Specific areas for co-operation identified at the Istanbul meeting included standardisation, copyright solutions, organised co-production, sharing of expertise and common purchasing arrangements.

The north American comparison proved crucial in stimulating the EU into action. In her speech at the SOCRATES launch, Commissioner Edith Cresson stressed, in words largely drawn from the White Paper on teaching and learning, the perceived threat from American manufacturers:

> competition from the USA is particularly forceful in multimedia in general and in educational multimedia in particular. The weakness of Europe does not lie in inadequate creativity, quite the contrary. But the European innovators and industries face serious obstacles from the very

great fragmentation of the market which results from the
cultural and linguistic diversity of Europe… We must therefore think of the means which will enable the conception of
products which are more suited not only to dissemination in
Europe but also worldwide. (Cresson 1995)

Once more, the response was to appoint a working group – the Task
Force on Educational Multi-media Software – which brought together
specialists, the industry and politicians. Numerically, however, it was
overwhelmingly dominated by the Commission's own officials –
including Cresson's own senior adviser, Marielle Riché-Magnier.

In its wide-ranging report, the Task Force provided a sketch of
the current software industry and an outline of its educational
potential (CEC 1996k). Contrasting Europe's fragmented markets
with the United States, with its 'huge internal market which is
culturally and legally more homogeneous', the Task Force concluded that Europe's main weakness was 'the absence of major
software producers' able to benefit from economies of scale (CEC
1996k, pp.10–11). In response, the Task Force proposed a number
of measures – most of which were subsequently adopted by the
Commission but operationalised and funded within existing Union programmes (RTD4, SOCRATES, LEONARDO, MEDIA II,
INFO 2000 and the Structural Funds).

Broadly, the Task Force report was welcomed within the
Commission. The Council argued, predictably, that most of the
recommendations should be directed towards the member states.
However, it also urged the Commission to 'identify and encourage
support activities which could be developed on a European level'.
In particular, it called for all parties to 'encourage a solid partnership between educational establishments and the suppliers of
hardware, software and services with a view to creating a big
market in multimedia applications and services truly adapted to
teaching needs' (*OJ*, 6 July 1996, pp.8–11). Subsequently, the Commission decided to promote four priorities:

- linking up electronic networks of schools at the Union
  level, with a particular focus on providing infrastructural
  support for schools in disadvantaged regions under the
  Structural Funds
- encouraging broadcasters, educators and software
  manufacturers to create educational materials with
  contents of European interest

- training teachers and trainers in the use of the new technologies, including the use of 'active' pedagogies
- raising awareness about the educational opportunities of multi-media through an interactive platform on the Internet. (CEC 1996n)

Its aims, in addition to promoting employment 'in an increasingly knowledge-based society', were to 'help bring different cultures together, strengthen the European identity and reinforce European integration' (CEC 1996n, p.18).

The Information Society Project provides a stern test of the Union's ability to press its priorities across a number of departmental boundaries. It remains to be seen whether this attempt at a concerted lateral policy thrust will be successful, and this is particularly clear in the case of the education and training aspects of the Information Society Project. Strictly speaking, DGXIII has no direct business in the education and training field, yet the Bangemann project clearly identified education and training as an important contributor to the future information society. While this is a logical position in itself, it requires the Commission to intervene in an area where – as Chapter Three has described – the Union's statutory competences are strictly subordinated to the sovereignty of the member states. Yet there are few signs that this legal limitation inhibited the involvement of the Information Society Project Office (ISPO) with the education and training system in the member states. Rather, the establishment of ISPO enabled DGXIII to adopt incentive measures that are designed to provide a direct pathway between the Commission and the most active providers in the field, using the funding available under existing programmes.

At one level, ISPO's education and training policy simply consists of providing incentives to enable providers to integrate global information tools and processes into their teaching. Superficially, this is a minimalist approach which relies entirely on voluntary participation in co-operation; its success depends entirely on the extent to which member states and providers decide of their own free will to participate in the co-operation programme. At most, this looks simply to be a form of 'co-operative federalism' (Lenaerts 1994). Yet the Commission has also tended to use this process to engage in a dialogue with the programme partners about the implications of its action programme, the results of which can then be used to counterbalance the views of member states and justify the decision to intervene at the European level. Thus one official in DGIII reported, in 1996, that among a number of 'key issues emerging in this debate' was the need for an education plan at local, national and European levels in order to 'offer a coherent educational system in our global society'. In language very similar to that found in the education and training field, he reported that 'The European Union will help where it can, by highlighting shared experiences and best practice across borders, and by linking schools across borders' (Folkmanis 1996, p.3). ISPO was following a well-trodden path, engaging with external networks of specialists and professionals in the hope of achieving sufficient momentum to justify further Union activity.

Once again, though, there was an uneasy balance between iconoclasm and continuity. One of the most visible of the projects supported under the Information Society banner was the Web for Schools project, funded as part of the ESPRIT programme in 1996 with the aim of training some 600 teachers in 150 schools across Europe in the use of the World-Wide Web as a mechanism for creating new teaching materials. Without denying the practical value of this exercise, it hardly marked a radical stride towards the informational society of continuous lifelong learning or a break with the established educational system with its transmission of 'congealed' knowledge. Although the initiative was designed in the hope of encouraging group learning and active teaching, these aspirations proved hard to enforce. Rather than transformation, the Web for Schools initiative represented a means of bringing information technology into the existing educational system; many, of course, would see it as none the worse for that.

## Discussion

The EU's concern with competitiveness and the new technologies, and its increasing fears over Europe's innovation deficit, at first appear to be simply one more example of its well-known tendency to focus on the economic question and seek a technological answer (Szerszynski, Lash and Wynne 1996). There is much truth in this account: certainly the energy with which the Union has pursued the advanced learning technologies far outstripped the demonstrated demand from potential users (Lloyd 1993). In addition, particularly in the politicians' expressed anxiety over Europe's faltering capacity for innovation and enterprise, we can see what should by now be a familiar combination of a discourse of crisis with the presentation of modest and reasonable proposals for action. Finally, in pursuing its agenda the Union was able to call upon a far wider range of resources to underpin its innovative ideas than were available in the constrained field of education and training policy alone. In practice, it took these ideas furthest in the application of telematics to education and training delivery.

By the late 1990s, then, the Union had acquired considerable experience in the development of telematics-based approaches to education and training. This experience was not uniformly positive, of course. Problems identified by the late 1980s included not simply the obvious linguistic problems: in respect of relatively compact units of learning they also encompassed substantial differences of vocabulary, semantic differences, varied teaching styles and lack of standard interfaces and, when it came to the adaptation of an entire course, then course designers faced enormous variations of content, instructional delivery and institutional organisation (Collis, Parisi and Ligurio 1996). While it lay well within the capacity of the evolving computer industry itself to solve the technical problems, the cultural, educational and organisational challenges were more substantial and less readily solved by the market-place. This created a potential obstacle to innovation and dissemination of the advanced learning technologies – an obstacle that the Union saw itself as ideally placed to tackle, and this was reflected in the Commission's proposal for the fifth Framework Programme for Research and Technology Development to address educational issues substantively in two of its six themes (CEC 1997b).

But how would the Union's activities rise to the substantial challenges that it had itself identified? The Union's concern with competitiveness, innovation and the information society helped generate ever more radical thinking about education and training. Although the demands of capitalist restructuring have reinforced the Union's primarily economic identity, they are also helping to break down the boundaries that in the modern nation state have separated the economic from other policy areas. Take the role of IRDAC, ERT or UNICE – all of which are business-led organisations – in calling for the Union to assume the leadership of the march towards the learning society. Politically, of course, this has been highly convenient for the European policy makers, allowing them to convene advisory networks which produced reports that were even more radical still than the Union's existing analysis, followed repeatedly by calls for a reorientation of education and training towards the promotion of continuous lifelong learning. Yet the ambition of the Union's analysis far outstripped its capacity to formulate and implement policy, leading to something of a credibility gap between its public promise and its perceived ability to deliver. This should not be overstated. Although the Parliament and external networks sometimes expressed the view that the Commission was raising expectations then failing to meet them, no sign had emerged by the late 1990s of an alternative agenda or of any grouping which was willing and able to pursue a more radical agenda than that endorsed by the Union. Conversely, there remained others who doubted whether even Europe's perceived crisis of innovation was sufficient to justify an extended role for the Union in education and training. The fact was that the Union had already extended its role beyond the limits of the Treaty and had done so by mobilising resources within its RTD and Structural programmes. By the late 1990s the resulting pressure on existing policy boundaries appeared to be at a critical stage.

Chapter Eight

# Human Potential, Globalisation and Europe's Future

This book has focused on two chief developments that characterise the development of education and training policy within the EU. The first is the way in which human resource issues have moved steadily closer to the centre of the process of European integration. The second is the extent to which, by the late 1990s, the Union had embraced a radical, reforming approach to the existing education and training system in Europe. However, we have also repeatedly seen that while steps have been taken to pursue this radical policy within the framework created by the Treaties, they have in the end been somewhat limited. Given that the Treaty on European Union, in particular, clearly identifies education and training as matters of national sovereignty, it is not surprising if there has been a gap – rather a wide one, however – between analysis and rhetoric on the one hand and policy and programmes on the other. Yet we can see bridges, albeit often rather slender ones, which are constructed not from the narrow timbers of the Union's competences in education and training but from the broader planks available within other policy areas where its competences are stronger.

In pursuing its wider aims for education and training the Union remains wedded to a technocratic and growth-oriented agenda (Sultana 1995; Szerszynski, Lash and Wynne 1996). Some commentators have suggested that what may be required, both for reasons of ecological stability and human identity, is less enhanced competitiveness rather than a general deceleration of economic growth in Europe (Altvater, Mahnkopf and Scheub 1996), but this view is not one that I have encountered in any official Union document, whether intended for internal or external consumption, nor in interviews with the Commission's officers. To complain that the

EU has some interesting ideas but mistakenly places them in the context of an overwhelmingly vocational agenda is to miss the point: the Union has come to place such a high priority upon human resources issues precisely because of their potential contribution to Europe's competitiveness.

How has this situation come about? And how likely is it to create a new educational settlement? Certainly, the present settlement is characterised by a substantial degree of fragility. For one thing, the EU is a relative newcomer to the field of education policy and, to a lesser extent, the same is true of training policy. At times, moreover, it is hard to remember just how hesitant were the Union's early steps into this secret garden. In 1986 the Commission even withdrew the proposed ERASMUS programme to prevent it being neutered by the Council; at that stage it was by no means certain that the EU would develop more than a handful of small scale initiatives in this area. Yet if the present balance is a delicate one, there is no precedent in the EU's history of competences being returned to the member states and there are plenty of examples – including a number in this book – of the Union pressing beyond the strict limits of its powers and managing to hold on to the ground it has gained.

## Education and the policy process

How has the Union come to place such great stress upon education and training? It is important not to exaggerate the EU's interest in this area, which continues to account for a relatively small element of its expenditure and, indeed, its time. Nevertheless, there is no doubting that education and training have come to be seen by the politicians as an important means of enabling the Union to achieve its most central goals; in some ways it has even come to be a goal in its own right.

Human resources issues have reached their present standing largely as a by-product of the perceived crisis of competitiveness. In this the EU is hardly unique. Several member states have also turned towards ideas of a learning society in response to the perceived failings of the national economy and, like the EU, they have found it difficult to identify plausible strategic policies which will systematically promote lifelong learning without raising public spending (Coffield 1996). One UK civil servant outlined the background to the development of public policy favouring lifelong learning:

> The reason that life-time learning in Britain has a degree of government commitment is that we were able to link it to competitiveness. That linkage has been very important. That's not to deny the importance of social cohesion. That is a problem which is recognised and the arguments are not buried, especially with the 16–19-year-olds, but the driving force has been an economic one and that's what's driven the political parties to pay attention. (Interview, October 1996)

Increased global competition in manufacturing and services, the application of new information and communications technologies at global level and the accelerating pace of innovation are widely cited as the underlying causes of this concern among policy makers with Europe's competitiveness. Delors mobilised such concerns very effectively in support of the single market process – a process which he also widened out to embrace a range of social, political and even cultural policy areas which he saw as underpinning and complementing the process of economic integration.

In his White Paper on competitiveness and growth, Delors provided precisely the linkage between education and training and economic recovery that was described above by the British civil servant. But the Delors White Paper also represented a significant moment in the development of the EU's thinking on human resources issues. As well as a general linkage, the White Paper specifically committed the Union to promoting lifelong learning. This idea had been aired previously, though in somewhat general terms, and the 1991 *Memorandum on Higher Education in the European Community* had even suggested that governments should switch resources away from the initial stages and towards continuing education and training (CEC 1991a). By 1994 the promotion of a learning society had become a more focused objective; essentially, Edith Cresson's 1995 White Paper on education and training simply tried to provide clothing for this central idea. Similarly, the idea of the information society, identified in the Delors White Paper and developed by the Commission subsequently, also became closely associated with the move towards lifelong learning and the learning society (Riché-Magnier and Metthey 1995).

If the genesis of this ambitious agenda can be explained by politicians' responses to the perceived crisis in Europe's competitiveness, a more complete answer requires attention to the processes of power and influence within the EU. These have received close attention from political scientists since the 1960s and, particularly, since the mid-80s. In an attempt to explain the remarkable momentum behind the general drive to European integration, a number of political scientists have drawn on the ideas of neo-functionalism. In Paul Teague's helpful summary:

> Neo-functionalism sets out to explain the process whereby political actors in separate national settings are persuaded to shift their traditional loyalties, expectations and activities from a well-established political formation towards a new constitutional order. A key proposition of this literature is that once different national political and economic elites decide to deepen co-operation between themselves, even in fairly prescribed policy areas, they will find that the scope or boundaries of the integration agenda are expanding quickly... After a time it is not only the political and administrative elites who are engaged in the integration process, but citizens too. (Teague 1996, pp.560–1)

Integration benefits from unintended spill-overs from one policy area into another as agreements between the member states invariably have unintended consequences in other policy areas. Thus, in the case of education and training, it would seem that the spill-over effect has been quite considerable.

Yet there are problems in using this approach to explain the EU's evolving interest in education and training. One difficulty, noted by Teague (1996), is the possibility not just of spill-over from one policy area to others but of 'spill-back' as citizens reject aspects of the integration process. Public hostility to the single currency, evident in a number of member states since the ratification of the Treaty on European Union, is an example cited by Teague of the unintended weakening of political support to the EU among its citizens. So far there has been little evidence of public antagonism to the EU on grounds of its education and training policies, but a Eurobarometer survey conducted as part of the European Year of Lifelong Learning showed that in several member states – notably, including Germany and Austria – there was strong public opposition to the idea of greater EU involvement in education and training (Eurobarometer 1996). Spill-over in education and training policy may, then, already be approaching its limits.

Another weakness in the neo-functionalist account is the emphasis it places on unintended consequences. My own strong impression is that the EU's politicians are very much aware of the value of creating sympathetic networks, not of abstract citizens but of those whom they regard as potential opinion-formers who then give impetus for an extension of the Union's current policies and activities. For example, the creation of task forces and working groups on specific problem areas, and the appointment of expert advisers to select successful proposals, are presented by the Commission as a matter of public accountability and effectiveness. Yet they also serve the equally important function of providing a bridge between the EU and its citizens. Here is Edith Cresson, praising the work of a task force on research policy:

> It seems to me imperative to make research accessible and accepted by the citizens. That means, particularly for the European Union, placing their preoccupations and aspirations at the heart of the decisions and directions of research policy. It equally means asserting the links between research and industry, seeking as an end goal less pure technological performance than the creation of work and the satisfaction of citizens' needs. (1996b)

Institutions as remote as the EU's can only speak with their citizens through intermediaries – no central apparatus, however ambitious, can hope for a direct dialogue with 320,000 schools across fifteen nations! But as the example of the Study Group on Education and Training demonstrates, those who end up acting as intermediaries tend to take the importance of further European action as given. Certainly, I know of no task force or working group which has suggested that the EU should cede some of its powers. Moreover, the EU itself appoints its own advisers. In the field of science policy, for example, officials of the Deutsche Forschungsgesellschaft have been openly critical of the way that the Union asks specialist associations to draw up lists from which it then selects members of advisory bodies and whose advice the Commission then filters selectively (Schüller 1995).

The existence of powerful policy lobbies is also at odds with the neo-functionalist analysis, which rests on a simplistic division between élites (or insiders) and citizens (or outsiders). Pressure groups have certainly helped influence the details of EU policy while tending to favour a degree of Europeanisation at the general level. Among the most powerful interest groups seeking to influence the EU's education and training policy are the Conférence des Recteurs d'Europe (representing individual universities and the umbrella national associations of university rectors) and the European Round Table of Industrialists (whose membership includes some of the EU's largest companies). CRE and ERT have each worked on specific policy areas of interest to their own constituencies, and not always successfully (CRE, hoping to exclude national employment ministries from any say on university matters, failed to persuade the Commission to reverse its policy of dividing the previous COMETT programme between SOCRATES and LEONARDO). Moreover, ERT and CRE co-operated for a number of years in an attempt to persuade the EU to favour lifelong learning and continuing training and, indeed, to back its proposals for a learning society ( Cochinaux and de Woot 1995; Otala 1992).

How such processes work out at grassroots level is another matter. Despite the efforts of the politicians to build coalitions with experts and institutions, the potential for unplanned spill-back is real. The information officer for a large voluntary organisation, who at the time was responsible for a very sizeable budget under one of the Community Initiatives, described the process of obtaining support for an early-years' programme as rather convoluted:

> We found that they weren't really interested in the nought-to-threes but they would fund training, so we put in a proposal that fitted all their criteria. We were very insistent that it should be a community-led project, and Europe wasn't. They wouldn't trust us. We had to go through a lot of hoops. (Interview, November 1996)

Yet, in this particular case, direct communications between the project sponsors and the Commission had included personal contact with Monika Wolf-Mathies, the Commissioner. The end result was a purely fiscal relationship in which the local player had exploited opportunities to work around rather than within the formal programme criteria. In short, the coalition between Commission and local players was seen, from this voluntary organisation's perspective at least, as being highly instrumental and fixed-term in nature.

We can conclude, then, that there has been considerable policy spill-over in the field of education and training but that this does not fully explain the EU's growing attention to human resources issues. Perhaps it is not surprising that neo-functionalism cannot be applied simplistically to a policy area which is so tightly ring-fenced by the member states (Pollack 1994). The constraints of the Treaty, combined with the growing interest in human resources issues among the Union's leaders, suggest that there is consider-able potential for conflict between the EU and the member states in the future. Yet the EU's existing influence in education and training does not suggest that this sphere is particularly open to international policy initiatives.

Does any of this suggest a change in the balance of power between state and civil society, with the Commission helping to shift influence towards the citizen? This type of argument is fre-quently found among those who favour a 'Europe of the Regions' or a 'Citizens' Europe', but the evidence is somewhat inconclusive at best. One study of the administration of the European Regional Development Fund in Germany and the UK in the 1980s concluded that national governments remained 'critical intermediaries be-tween subnational groups and the Community' (Anderson 1991, p.431). However, the evidence suggests that some sub-national groups have started to develop effective transnational coalitions and alliances and, given the Commission's interest in finding counterbalances to the power of the other EU institutions, this may be helping destabilise existing relationships and balances of power in favour of the better-organised professions and regional authori-ties. By implication, the less influential interest groups will miss out. Further, this process appears to be accompanied by the loss of power and status by some established bodies within the EU, such as ECOSOC or the ETUC. In facing destabilisation and reorientation, the Union's institutions are themselves experienc-ing the globalising tendencies which the EU both expresses and seeks to contain.

## The radicalisation of policy

In one sense it is quite easy to explain how the Union's education and training policies come to be so radical. It is precisely because its policies are marginal that the EU is able to declare the emperor's clothing a fake and demand that stronger fabrics are adopted to withstand the hurricanes of globalisation. Were Mrs Thatcher to cast her beady eyes upon such policy documents as the White Paper or the 1997 report of the Union's Study Group, she would surely denounce the idea of an education and training policy being dreamt up by the producers rather than the consumers. There is, as usual, something in this explanation – certainly the Commission's policy advisers were drawn mainly from the world of academic life and their work is best regarded more as the output of a think-tank than as blueprints for policy. In that sense, when we compare the Union's policy statements with those of member states or the German *Länder* we are simply not comparing like with like.

Nevertheless, the Union has to live in the real world. As Chapter Four amply demonstrated, it has to negotiate its policies not only with the other Union institutions and the member states but also with those who represent the larger vested interests in the education and training systems – professional associations, the headteachers, the university rectors, the research community, the business lobbies and so on. With relatively few exceptions, the vested interests tend to favour the *status quo*. Those exceptions, interestingly enough, include some of the employers' representatives and – on certain issues – the university rectors, who have co-operated on a series of reports which recommend precisely those measures which appear to be so radical when included in the official policy papers of the EU: active pedagogic approaches, a massive investment in technology-mediated teaching and movement towards a learning society (Cochinaux and de Woot 1995; Otala 1992). Why is it that the leaders of third-level education, the representatives of some of Europe's larger employers and the Union have come to these iconoclastic conclusions?

In a word, the answer appears to be: globalisation. Consistently, EU policy makers have compared the old continent's economic performance with that of competitor nations and regions (above all, Japan and the USA but, increasingly, also the Pacific Rim and central/eastern Europe). Equally consistently, the findings have been depressing. A joint report on European education from the Employers' Round Table and the University Rectors' Association drew conclusions which are commonplace in European policy papers:

Globalisation means that many jobs that do not add much value are exported to poorer and cheaper countries. We have to provide our workers with the skills to compete at the upper end of the market. The only way for rich countries to stay rich in the long term is to have people who are more productive. (Cochinaux and de Woot 1995, p.22)

Or, as a magazine headline had it, I think rather more effectively, 'Die Jobs wandern aus' (The Jobs are Emigrating: *Der Spiegel*, 10 September 1995). The mobility of finance capital, the growth of transnational business organisations and the expanding world trade in goods and services mean that nation states cannot rely on established mechanisms to regulate the economy. As Vincent Cable puts it:

Globalisation is largely private sector driven. It represents, therefore, a shift in the locus of decision-making not only from the nation-state to transnational actors but also from national governments to the private sector. For this reason, economic liberalization and globalization have often gone hand in hand. (Cable 1995, p.37)

In Cable's view, this leads to the growth of political movements which try to protect and enhance the remaining areas of national discretion or which promote some form of cultural identity or which combine the two (Cable 1995). This implies a growing tension between the EU and its member states over education and training policy, which is, characteristically, both a matter of national sovereignty and a means of expressing and reproducing national, confessional and linguistic identities.

The complex relationship between globalisation, the economy and culture is powerfully expressed in current developments in education and training. Education, and the university system above all, is one of the more powerful globalising tendencies in late modern society. This is, in part, because academic knowledge and organisation tend to be internationally oriented and, in part, because third-level education tends to represent a form of experience which is not rooted in local and habitual forms of knowing. Further, this book has already shown the extent to which young people, especially students, are deliberately disembedding their life-world from the local through international travel and the consumption and creation of quasi-cosmopolitan cultures. Economically and politically, individual institutions may see increasing advantages from positioning themselves publicly as a transnational operator. The changing role of the UK's Open University is, perhaps, an extreme example but it still illustrates this general trend (this section is based largely on Tait 1994). Conceived as a purely UK operation, the OU has, since the early 1970s, offered courses abroad – initially for British servicemen based overseas, and subsequently (and, for political reasons, somewhat quietly) in the Republic of Ireland. In 1980 the OU started to support UK civil servants working for the EU; by 1991 it had some 740 students in the area around the Union's three seats of office. From 1991 the OU decided strategically to recruit more widely in Europe (including Switzerland and Slovenia as well as the EU member states), though it continued to focus primarily upon British expatriates and other English-speaking immigrants. Alan Tait notes that while this process of internationalisation had, by 1994, generally left the curriculum untouched, there were some signs of a willingness to hire local staff who could revise course materials for local consumers. The OU is, though, only one of a number of distance learning institutions with international ambitions and it is increasingly competing with face-to-face universities who are extending their international operations through distance learning (Morrison 1995; Simpson 1996).

At one important level, then, globalising tendencies represent an important cultural challenge, or at least one in which cultural and financial matters are closely intertwined. Again, the example of distance learning comes to mind. Like the broadcasting organisations and the software industry to whom they are often closely linked, the distance learning industry is dominated by non-European players. Courseware from the USA is widely available in British and Irish schools and is often used to familiarise pupils elsewhere with the English language; although the American content is sometimes resented by young Europeans and the accents can be incomprehensible even in Britain and Ireland, some have chosen to re-engineer the software for local consumption rather than seek a locally-created product (Underwood and Brown 1997). From the Union's perspective, such developments have led to concern over the threat to a distinctive sense of a common European citizenship with its accompanying shared identity. Much of this concern has focused on broadcasting and multi-media software. In 1988, for example, the EU's director of telecommunications policy spoke about the 'danger of what could be called cultural pollution' arising from satellite broadcasting (Schuringa 1988). Hence the constant concern over the protection of airtime for material produced within the EU. The Union's interest in educational multi-media software, which is seen as the key to cultural domination of technology-mediated learning, arises from similar fears of cultural pollution. It has to be said that on the whole, teachers and young people do not share this concern and have few difficulties in enjoying products and services from non-European sources.

The European Union's response to these pressures attempts to balance conservation with transformation, through the attempt to create a European cultural identity as the basis for a shared citizenship. Its education programmes clearly express this view with their emphasis on the European cultural patrimony (the term directly imported by the Union from the French 'patrimoine') and a common citizenship. How helpful is it to speak of a common European citizenship not simply in the legal sense (Closa 1992) but as a felt sense of shared identity? The very names of the Union's action programmes evoke an imagined common past and anticipate an imagined common future. Perhaps the least well-known of these – Jan Amos Kosmensky, or Comenius – is also the most indicative. An educational theorist who believed profoundly in the virtues of an active pedagogy of direct observation and experiment, Comenius was also a devout Christian who believed that the teacher should always offer firm guidance (Murphy 1995). Less appealingly from some European perspectives, he was also a Bohemian and Protestant at a time when Europe was torn apart by vicious, lengthy conflicts over religion and nationalism; many Europeans, perhaps a majority, would cheerfully have burnt him. This is partly a problem of selective memory: as the historian Eric Hobsbawm notes, European fascism was also profoundly internationalist, seeing Germany as the core and guarantee of a future European order and appealing to the heritage of Charlemagne. Hobsbawm is stating the obvious when he notes that this was 'a phase in the development of the European idea on which historians of the post-war European Community do not much like to dwell' (1994, p.136). Yet obvious or not, it reminds us that 'the European idea' has a variety of precedents. After his conviction at Nuremberg, Albert Speer was fond of recalling that his father (certainly no Nazi) was a liberal who supported

Richard Coudenhove-Kalergi's Pan-European movement which was based on free-market economics and the belief that nationality was defined by identity rather than race (Sereny 1995). Today's debates about Europe's cultural identity have their roots in these earlier forms of rejection of division and conflict in the old continent. Beyond this simple negative reaction, 'the European idea' has assumed a variety of, sometimes contradictory, shapes and it is likely to continue to do so.

To what extent do ideas of a common European identity strike a chord among today's Europeans? A survey conducted among students at the European University Institute in 1987 showed that a large majority – 85 per cent – saw themselves as 'Europeans' and 65 per cent believed that Europeans shared a common identity (Wilterdink 1993). This would seem to indicate that among some Europeans at least (albeit a rather selective group in this instance), a common identity is emerging. Yet it is equally probable that some aspects of this common identity are being articulated as a response not so much to the positive potential represented by the Union but as a negative reaction to strictly *local* conditions. For example, Nationalists in Northern Ireland are generally more favourable towards the EU than are Unionists, a pattern explicable more in terms of national allegiances within the islands of Ireland and Britain than as an expression of positive enthusiasm for European integration (Smith and Corrigan 1995).

A profound tension exists within education between the national and international roles and identities of education and training (Allardt 1994), even though globalising tendencies are generally well-established. In reaching a judgement about the EU's influence, we should recollect that since all the member states are facing similar problems, some of their responses unavoidably cover much the same policy ground. One such area is core skills, where the Union is a relative latecomer. Similar debates have been under way in different member states for a number of years, with increasing effort to integrate core competencies or key skills into the curriculum. Another area where the Union was ahead of the field concerns the portability of qualifications. One researcher has deduced from the chronology that the UK's competency-based system of national vocational qualifications is derived from the CEDEFOP comparability exercise (Hargreaves 1995). In so far as both approaches attempted to foster transparency and comparability, there are certainly common elements. But whereas the CEDEFOP studies were based on groupings of existing qualifications, the UK system demands that the qualifications reflect defined national standards (Field 1995b). While there have been occasional attempts by the National Council for Vocational Qualifications to sell its standards and approach to other nations, the main foreign model for the UK system was not CEDEFOP but the much earlier influence of the programmed instruction movement – which began in the USA and was rapidly adopted during the 1960s and 1970s in Britain (Field 1996). Within the UK a group of scholars has drawn attention to the profound tension between increasing national regulation of the curriculum on the one hand and attempts to accommodate the global economy on the other (Avis *et al.* 1996).

In the context of globalisation, where is the EU heading? Does the Union remain at heart a common market, concerned, above all else, with promoting economic growth and prosperity while hoping to restrain the major European powers from declaring war on one another? To a large extent, these do appear to provide the underlying rationale for the Union's existence. It does seem that the member states are most willing to pool sovereignty when they are persuaded that their competitiveness in the global market-place will be enhanced by co-operating and co-ordinating their efforts. Other challenges – most obviously, environmental degradation and pollution – may also be international in nature but they rarely inspire the same willingness to give up national powers as does the threat of ferocious competition in the market-place (Szerszynski, Lash and Wynne 1996). The pursuit of other, less materialist aspirations – social cohesion or citizenship, for instance – must usually be justified by reference to their role in enhancing Europe's competitiveness.

While this is unlikely to pose any particular difficulty in the field of vocational training, which has always been closely linked with the economy, it does present problems for the development of education policy. Harnessing education to competitiveness may appear attractive to governments facing a future of uncertainty and turbulence in the global market-place, yet the rigidities which such approaches require of education themselves introduce new tensions and instabilities. Even in the field of vocational training, an unthinking emphasis upon specific and static competences is likely to prove functionally counterproductive. In emphasising the requirements of a learning society, the Union has broken with any narrow, constrictive linkage between education and competitiveness; yet for all the interest in citizenship and social cohesion, the policy documents of the 1990s are absolutely clear on the central role of education and training in enhancing European competitiveness. In seeking to promote the learning society the EU has effectively accepted that the process of change and restructuring in the world economy has become permanent, even that economic and technological cycles are becoming ever shorter. Rather than enabling individuals to acquire the knowledge and values required for living in a stable society, while discovering and developing their identity and potential as members of that society, the aim of the learning society is constant reinvention of the self and one's capabilities: in Giddens' words, 'The self is seen as a reflexive project, for which the individual is responsible' (Giddens 1991, p.75). Globalisation poses a profound challenge to the humanistic values which have come to dominate educational thinking and practice in western Europe.

## Europeanisation – a challenge for the future?

In a period when most of us believe that barely anything in human affairs can be predicted, it is certain that leaving the education and training system unchanged is not in prospect. We could draw up an almost endless list of pressures which are forcing change upon the system: enhanced global competition, changing cultures and values, technological innovation, the aging of western populations, the growing environmental challenge, and so it goes on. In these circumstances the forces of transformation appear to be irreversible and unavoidable. Even if we wish to see education and training as potential forces for stability, performing the role of conserving existing values and standards in a fast-changing world itself implies change as the system adapts to the availability of new competing sources of information and ideas in almost every European household.

In adopting the language and goals of the learning society, the EU is presenting an agenda which has radical implications not merely for adult lifelong learning (though those are demanding enough) but also for the organisation and emphasis of the entire process whereby we invest in and develop our 'grey capital'. The Union's conception of a learning society rests on an equally radical critique of the existing education and training system. As two of Mme Cresson's senior advisers put it: 'Teaching still rests on schemas inherited from the industrial period: it engenders "standardised" and congealed skills, sanctioned by diplomas that are acquired once and for all' (Riché-Magnier and Metthey 1995, p.420).

A similar critique was articulated by a Commission official in outlining the medium-term agenda for reform:

> Schools as we know them today are the organisational corollaries of mass industrial society, in which the majority of people will somehow get through. The structures of schooling are predicated upon a very powerful division of labour and upon a society in which knowledge changes very slowly, so that it is assumed that those who are older and more knowledgeable and experienced pass on what they know to those who are younger, less experienced and less knowledgeable, and they need to do that only once. We have to change those structures and processes, we simply have to do it, especially for those who fail at the moment, but in the end for everyone. (Interview, November 1996)

This outlook draws on the argument for recurrent education as promoted in the early 1970s by the OECD, who went further than most reformers in urging a switch of resources away from the 'front end' (i.e. schools) and towards recurrent learning throughout life (OECD 1973). It also contains elements drawn from the deschooling movement, as well as more recent debates in France, Germany and the UK over key skills. Yet it remains stronger on critique than on positive affirmation.

At this stage the precise direction of reform becomes rather fuzzy and imprecise. Nevertheless, there have been signs of a policy rethink in a number of areas, including the growing emphasis on learning within organisations (particularly the workplace), technology-mediated teaching and learning, recognising learning acquired from a variety of sources (including experience) and the use of active and interactive pedagogies among young people as providing the basis for learning how to learn throughout life. An interest in active pedagogies permeated the White Paper on education and training, as well as the earlier pilot action of European

School Partnerships and the subsequent COMENIUS programme, and is found throughout the report of the Study Group on education and training (CEC 1995e; CEC 1996c; CEC 1997a). This interest is supported at the highest level in the Commission: Madame Cresson, in a speech elaborating her proposals for a 'second chance school', took the opportunity of emphasising the 'use of active pedagogies, as informal as possible, facilitating understanding rather than passive learning, developing group work skills' (Cresson 1996b). Yet this interest in creativity and an active orientation towards learning is set not in the context of a critical and reflexive citizenship but of the vocationalising of the educational agenda – a process which is found across the member states and in nations such as Australia, New Zealand and the USA, where affluent electorates feel themselves threatened by competition from Japan and the Pacific Rim. In so far as the EU is pursuing educational strategies which mirror and advance those of the member states, it is essentially facilitating a convergence of policy making in response to the challenges of globalisation.

We are now in a position to draw this analysis towards some final reflections on the future. This book has shown that the growing centrality of education and training within the Union's policy agenda is tied to two other factors: the first is the tightly perceived linkage between human resources and economic competitiveness, which has been aired publicly through a discourse of crisis and anxiety and the second is the Union's capacity to gain entry to a terrain where its legal competences are clearly restricted. The outcome is a trio of what seem to be rather unstable balances: that between radical diagnosis and conservative prescription within the field of education and training policy, that between the EU's restricted competences and its capacity to pursue human resources goals within areas where its competences are wider – such as research and technology development or social policy – and that between the Union's ability to build alliances and raise expectations among professional educational and training constituencies and its weak ability to deliver effective change. Is this balance so unstable that it cannot survive? I believe that it is and that the likely outcome is a slow but steady expansion of the EU's *de facto* competence over this area followed, at some stage, by challenges and conflict from the member states. If the analysis pursued here is accurate, then the outcomes of this contest are open; to think otherwise is to assume that policy making in the EU is a relatively simple and one-dimensional process. Those who wish to ignore the EU can be reasonably certain that they will suffer no significant penalities. Those who prefer to influence Europe's future agenda can hope for some success, though the results will almost certainly be rather different from those they imagine. As this book has shown, despite the depth of the Union's 'democratic deficit' there are simply too many actors facing too many disorienting and unanticipated challenges for any conflict over competences to have a clear and predictable outcome. Particularly in a field so deeply affected by, and so deeply involved in, creating globalising tendencies as education and training, Europe's future is as yet open and undecided.

# Chronology

| | |
|---|---|
| 1957 | Treaty of Rome |
| 1973 | *For a Community Policy on Education* ('Janne Report') |
| 1973, January | Responsibility for education placed under DG12 |
| 1974, June | Resolution of the Ministers of Education on co-operation in the field of education |
| 1976, February | Community Action Programme in the field of education |
| | Establishment of Education Committee |
| 1981 | Education and training policy brought under DG5 |
| 1985 | Commission White Paper on completion of the internal market |
| | ECJ decision in case of Gravier |
| 1986 | Decision 86/365 creating COMETT (Co-operation between universities and enterprises in the field of technology training) |
| 1987, June | Decision 87/327 creating ERASMUS (European Community action scheme for the mobility of European students) |
| 1988 | Council Resolution on the European dimension in education |
| | European Court of Justice decision on ERASMUS |
| | European Court of Justice decision on case of Humbel |
| | YES (Youth for Europe Programme) |
| 1989, July | Lingua Programme |
| | European Court of Justice decision on COMETT |
| | Directive 89/48 on the recognition of higher education diplomas |
| 1990, May | Decision 90/233 establishing TEMPUS (Trans-European mobility scheme for university studies) |
| 1992 | Treaty on European Union |
| | Directive 92/51 on the recognition of vocational diplomas |
| 1994, December | Decision 94/819 establishing LEONARDO DA VINCI (Action Programme on vocational training) |
| 1995, March | Decision 819/95 establishing SOCRATES (Action Programme on education) |
| 1995, December | Publication of Commission White Paper *Teaching and Learning: towards the learning society* |
| 1997 | Report of the Commission's Study Group on Education and Training |

# Glossary

| | |
|---|---|
| CEDEFOP | Centre Européen pour la Développement de la Formation Professionelle (European Centre for the Development of Vocational Training) |
| CEEP | Centre Européen pour l'Entreprise Publique (European Centre for Public Enterprise) |
| COMETT | European Community Programme in Education and Training for Technology |
| CoR | Committee of the Regions |
| CRE | Conférence des Recteurs d'Europe |
| DELTA | Development of learning technology applications/ Developing European Learning through Technological Advance |
| DG | Directorate-General |
| EADTU | European Association of Distance Teaching Universities |
| ECJ | European Court of Justice |
| ECOSOC | Economic and Social Committee |
| ECTS | European Community Credit Transfer Scheme |
| ECU | European Currency Unit |
| ERASMUS | European Action Scheme for the Mobility of University Students |
| ERDF | European Regional Development Fund |
| ESF | European Social Funds |
| ESPRIT | European Strategic Programme for Research in Information Technology |
| EUI | European University Institute |
| EURES | European Employment Service |
| FORCE | Formation Continue en Europe |
| FP4 | Fourth Framework Programme for Research and Technology Development |
| GATT | General Agreement on Tariffs and Trade |
| IGC | Inter-governmental conference |
| IRDAC | Industrial Research and Development Advisory Committee |
| ISPO | Information Society Project Office |
| LEADER | Liaisons entre actions de développement de l'economie rurale |
| MEP | Member of the European Parliament |
| NGO | Non-Governmental Organisation |
| OECD | Organisation for Economic Co-operation and Development |
| OJ | *Official Journal of the European Communities* |
| PHARE | Pologne, Hongrie Aide à la Réconstruction |
| RTD | Research and Technology Development |
| SEM | Single European Market |
| SME | Small- or medium-sized enterprise |
| TEMPUS | Trans-European Mobility Programme for University Studies |
| UNICE | Union des Industries du Communauté Européen |
| YES | Youth for Europe Scheme |

# References

Adams, C.S. (1993) *The Impact of the European Community on Higher Education in Ireland*. 18th Annual Meeting of the Association for the Study of Higher Education, Pittsburgh, 4–7 November 1993.

Adick, C. (1992) *Die Universalisierung der modernen Schule. Eine theoretische Problemskizze zur Erklärung der Weltweiten Verbreitung der modernen Schule in den letzten 200 Jahren mit Fallstudien aus Westafrika*. Paderborn: Schöning.

Allardt, E. (1994) 'Internationalisation as a promise and a problem.' *Life and Education in Finland* 3/94, 1–10.

Altvater, E., Mahnkopf, B. and Scheub, U. (1996) 'Da hilft nur noch Entschleunigung.' *Die Tageszeitung*, 4 September 1996, 18–9.

Anderson, J.J. (1991) 'Skeptical reflections on a Europe of the regions: Britain, Germany and the ERDF.' *Journal of Public Policy* 10, 4, 417–447.

Avis, J., Bloomer, M., Esland, G., Leeson, D. and Hodkinson, P. (1996) *Knowledge and Nationhood: Education, Politics and Work*. London: Cassell.

Barnett, R.R. and Borooah, V. (1995) 'The additionality (or otherwise) of European Community Structural Funds.' In S. Hardy (ed) *An Enlarged Europe: Regions or Competition?* London: Jessica Kingsley Publishers.

Baumert, J., Benkmann, R., Fuchs, J., Hopf, D., Köhler, H., Krais, B., Krappmann, L., Leschinsky, A., Naumann, J., Roeder, P.M. and Trommer, L. (1994) *Das Bildungswesen in der Bundesrepublik Deutschland: Strukturen und Entwicklungen im Überblick*. Reinbek bei Hamburg: Rowohlt.

Beck, U. (1992) *Risk Society*. London: Sage.

Berghman, J. (1995) 'Social exclusion in Europe: policy context and analytical framework.' In G. Room (ed) *Beyond the Threshold: The Measurement and Analysis of Social Exclusion*. Bristol: Policy Press.

Bernard, C. (1992) 'The Maastricht agreement and education: one step forward, two steps back.' *Education and the Law* 4, 3, 123–34.

Black, S. and Conway, E. (1995) 'Community-led rural development policies in the Highlands and Islands: the European Community's LEADER programme.' *Local Economy* 10, 3, 229–45.

Blanpain, R., Engels, C. and Pellegrini, C. (eds) (1993) *Contractual Policies Concerning Continuing Vocational Training in the European Community Member States*. Leuven: Peeters Press.

Boer, P.D. (1993) 'Europe to 1914: the making of an idea.' In K. Wilson and J. van der Dussen (eds) *The History of the Idea of Europe*. London: Routledge.

Boyle, M., Findlay, A., Lelievre, E. and Paddison, R. (1996) 'World cities and the limits to global control: a case study of executive search firms in Europe's leading cities.' *International Journal of Urban and Regional Research* 20, 3, 498–517.

Brine, J. (1995) 'Educational and vocational policy and construction of the European Union.' *International Studies in Sociology of Education* 5, 2, 145–61.

Buczynski, M. (1993) 'European awareness.' In J. Edwards and K. Fogelman (eds) *Developing Citizenship in the Curriculum*. London: David Fulton.

Cable, V. (1995) 'The diminished nation-state: a study in the loss of economic power.' *Daedalus* 124, 2, 25–53.

Cassard-le-Morvan, M., Jeudy, C., Hayes, P. and Teerling, P. (1995) 'Formation en travail social: vers une européanisation dans le cadre communautaire.' *Vie Sociale* 4, 95–103.

CEDEFOP (1984) *Annual Report 1984.* Berlin: European Centre for the Development of Vocational Training.

CEDEFOP (1987) *Annual Report 1987.* Berlin: European Centre for the Development of Vocational Training.

CEDEFOP (1994) *Use of the System of Comparability of Vocational Training Qualifications by Employers and Workers.* Berlin: European Centre for the Development of Vocational Training.

Closa, C. (1992) 'The concept of citizenship in the treaty on European union.' *Common Market Law Review 29*, 1137–69.

Cochinaux, P. and de Woot, P. (1995) *Moving Towards a Learning Society.* Geneva/Brussels: Conseil des Recteurs d'Europe/European Round Table of Industrialists.

Coffield, F. (1996) *A Tale of Three Little Pigs: Building the Learning Society with Straw.* European Union Conference on Research on Lifelong Learning: implications for policy and practice, Newcastle, 25–27 November.

Collis, M., Parisi, D. and Ligurio, M. (1996) 'Adaptation of courses for trans-European telelearning.' *Journal of Computer Assisted Learning 12*, 1, 47–62.

Commission of the European Communities (1985a) 'A people's Europe: reports from the *ad hoc* committee.' *European Community Bulletin*, Supplement 7/85.

Commission of the European Communities (1985b) *The Completion of the Internal Market.* Luxembourg: Office for Official Publications.

Commission of the European Communities (1988) 'The social dimension of the internal market: interim report.' *Social Europe*, 1/88.

Commission of the European Communities (1989) *The Community Charter of Fundamental Social Rights of Workers.* Luxembourg: Office for Official Publications.

Commission of the European Communities (1991a) *Memorandum on Higher Education in the European Community.* Brussels: Task Force on Human Resources, Education, Training, Youth.

Commission of the European Communities (1991b) *Memorandum on Open Distance Learning in the European Community.* Brussels: Task Force on Human Resources, Education, Training, Youth.

Commission of the European Communities (1992a) *Treaty on European Union.* Luxembourg: Office for Official Publications.

Commission of the European Communities (1992b) *Commission Memorandum on Vocational Training in the European Community in the 1990s.* Brussels: Task Force on Human Resources, Education, Training, Youth.

Commission of the European Communities (1992c) *Communication from the Commission to the Council and the European Parliament Concerning European Higher Education-Industry Cooperation: Advanced Training for Competitive Advantage.* Brussels: European Commission.

Commission of the European Communities (1993a) *Green Paper on the Future of Community Initiatives under the Structural Funds.* Luxembourg: Office for Official Publications.

Commission of the European Communities (1993b) *Green Paper on the European Dimension of Education.* Luxembourg: Office for Official Publications.

Commission of the European Communities (1993c) *EC Education and Training Programmes, 1986–1992: Results and Achievements: An Overview*. Luxembourg: Office for Official Publications.

Commission of the European Communities (1993d) *Background Report: Social Exclusion – Poverty and Other Social Problems in the European Community*. London: European Commission.

Commission of the European Communities (1993e) *Research and Technology Development of Telematic Systems for Flexible and Distance Learning: DELTA 1993*. Brussels: DGXIII.

Commission of the European Communities (1994a) *European Social Policy: A Way Forward for the Union*. Luxembourg: Office for Official Publications.

Commission of the European Communities (1994b) *Guide to the Community Initiatives 1994–99*. Luxembourg: Office for Official Publications of the European Union.

Commission of the European Communities (1994c) *Growth, Competitiveness, Employment: The Challenges and Ways Forward into the 21st Century*. Luxembourg: Office for Official Publications.

Commission of the European Communities (1994d) *Europe and the Global Information Society: Recommendations to the European Council*. Luxembourg: Office for Official Publications.

Commission of the European Communities (1995a) *The Medium Term Social Action Programme, 1995–2000*. Luxembourg: Office for Official Publications.

Commission of the European Communities (1995b) *LEONARDO DA VINCI: Promoters Guide 1995*. Brussels: DGXXII.

Commission of the European Communities (1995c) *Green Paper on Innovation*. Luxembourg: Office for Official Publications.

Commission of the European Communities (1995d) *General Report of the Activities of the European Union 1994*. Luxembourg: Office for Official Publications.

Commission of the European Communities (1995e) *Teaching and Learning: Towards the Learning Society*. Brussels: DGV.

Commission of the European Communities (1996a) *Telematics Applications Programme: Education and Training Sector*. Brussels: DGXIII.

Commission of the European Communities (1996b) *Socio-Economic Activities Undertaken Within the Specific Programmes of the 4th Framework Programme During 1995*. Brussels: DGXII.

Commission of the European Communities (1996c) *Results of the Pilot Action of the European School Partnerships, 1992–94*. Luxembourg: Office for Official Publications.

Commission of the European Communities (1996d) *Education, Training and Research: Eliminating Obstacles to Transnational Mobility*. Luxembourg: Office for Official Publications.

Commission of the European Communities (1996e) *General Report on the Activities of the European Union 1995*. Luxembourg: Office for Official Publications.

Commission of the European Communities (1996f) *First Action Plan for Innovation in Europe*. Luxembourg: Office for Official Publications.

Commission of the European Communities (1996h) *Living and Working in the Information Society: People First*. Luxembourg: Office for Official Publications.

Commission of the European Communities (1996j) *Report on Evaluation of TEMPUS Programme*. Luxembourg: Office for Official Publications.

Commission of the European Communities (1996k) *Educational Multimedia: First Elements of Reflection*. Brussels: DGXIII.

Commission of the European Communities (1996l) *For a Europe of Civic and Social Rights: Report by the comité des sages*. Brussels: DGV.

Commission of the European Communities (1996m) *Commission Proposal for a Council Directive amending Directive 76/207/EEC on the Implementation of Equal Treatment for Men and Women*. Brussels: European Commission.

Commission of the European Communities (1996n) *Communication from the Commission: Learning in the Information Society: Action Plan for a European Education Initiative (1996–1998)*. Brussels: European Commission.

Commission of the European Communities (1997a) *Study Group on Education and Training Report: Accomplishing Europe through Education and Training*. Luxembourg: Office for Official Publications.

Commission of the European Communities (1997b) *Towards the Fifth Framework Programme: Scientific and Technological Objectives*. Luxembourg: Office for Official Publications.

Convery, A., Evans, M., Green, S., Macaro, E. and Mellor, J. (1997) *Pupils' Perceptions of Europe: Identity and Education*. London: Cassell.

Corradi, S. (1988) *ERASMUS e COMETT: Educazione degli adulti e formazione universitaria transculturale*. Roma: Bulzoni.

Cresson, E. (1995) *Intervention sur le programme SOCRATES, Bruxelles, le 9 novembre 1995*. Brussels: EUROPA News.

Cresson, E. (1996a) *Speech at the 9th European Conference of the European Continuing Education Network, 29 March 1996*. Brussels; EUROPA News.

Cresson, E. (1996b) *Intervention devant les élus de la Région des Pays de la Loire, le 27 Juin 1996*. Brussels: EUROPA News.

Curwen, P. (1995a) 'The acquired rights directive: the European Union renders ineffective the UK's "opt-out".' *European Business Journal* 7, 1, 37–44.

Curwen, P. (1995b) 'Telecommunications policy in the European Union: developing the information superhighway.' *Journal of Common Market Studies* 33, 3, 331–60.

Delors, J. (1988) 'The social dialogue.' *Vocational Training* 2, 3.

Deutscher Volkshochschul-Verband (1996) *Lehren und Lernen – Auf dem Weg zur kognitiven Gesellschaft: Stellungnahme des Deutschen Volkshochschul-Verbandes zum Weissbuch der Europäischen Kommission*. Bonn: DVV.

Dineen, D. (1992) 'Europeanisation of Irish universities.' *Higher Education* 24, 391–411.

Egede, H. (1994) 'Stops out on choice.' *Times Higher Education Supplement*, 4 February 1994, 9.

Eraut, M. (ed) (1991) *Education and the Information Society*. London/Paris: Cassell/Council of Europe.

Eurobarometer (1996) *Attitudes to Education and Training*. Brussels: European Commission.

Eurostat (1995) *Yearbook '95: A Statistical Eye on Europe, 1983–1993*. Luxembourg: Office for Official Publications.

Everett, M. and Morris, C. (1993) *The Recruitment of UK Graduates to Work in Continental Europe*. Brighton: Institute of Manpower Studies.

Farrington, J. (1994) 'Keeping the balance.' *Le Magazine* 3, 4–5.

Field, J. (1994) *Educational and Vocational Training Policy*. London: Longmans/Spicers European Union Policy Briefings.

Field, J. (1995a) *Employment Policy*. London: Cartermill International.

Field, J. (1995b) 'Reality testing in the workplace: are NVQs "employment-led"?' In
P. Hodkinson and M. Issitt (eds) *The Challenge of Competence: Professionalism
Through Vocational Education and Training*. London: Cassell.

Field, J. (1996) 'Learning for work: vocational education and training.' In R.
Fieldhouse (ed) *A History of Modern British Adult Education*. Leicester: National
Institute of Adult Continuing Education.

Field, J. (1997) 'Continuing education and the European dimension: a survey of
British professionals' attitudes.' *Journal of Further and Higher Education 21*, 1,
19–32.

Folkmanis, A.J. (1996) 'Bringing education into the information society.' *Information
Society News 6*, 1–3.

Forster, N. and Whipp, R. (1995) 'Future of European human resource management:
a contingent approach.' *European Management Journal 13*, 4, 434–42.

Giddens, A. (1991) *Modernity and Self-Identity*. Cambridge: Polity Press.

Giddens, A. (1994) *Beyond Left and Right: The Future of Radical Politics*. Cambridge:
Polity Press.

Gordon, J. and Jallade, P.-J. (1996) '"Spontaneous" student mobility in the European
Union: a statistical survey.' *European Journal of Education 31*, 2, 133–51.

Grant, W. (1993) 'Transnational companies and environmental policy-making: the
trend of globalisation.' In J.D. Liefferink, P.D. Lowe and A.P.J. Moll (eds)
*European Integration and Environmental Policy*. London: Belhaven.

Green, A. (1995) 'The European challenge to British vocational education and
training.' In P. Hodkinson and M. Issitt (eds) *The Challenge of Competence:
Professionalism Through Vocational Education and Training*. London: Cassell.

Gribbon, A. (1994) 'Idealism or a marriage of convenience? An examination of
internal relationships in international exchange programmes.' *Higher Education
Management 6*, 1, 23–31.

Hargreaves, G. (1995) 'The influence of the European communities on the
emergence of competence-based models of vocational training in England and
Wales.' *British Journal of Education and Work 8*, 2, 28–40.

Hendry, C. and Pettigrew, A. (1992) *The Processes of Internationalisation and the
Implications for Human Resource Management and Human Resource Development*.
Coventry: Centre for Corporate Strategy and Chance, Warwick Business School.

Her Majesty's Inspectors (1991) *The Responsiveness of Further Education to the Single
European Market*. London: Department of Education and Science.

Higher Education Statistics Agency (1996) *Students in Higher Education Institutions*.
Cheltenham: HESA.

Hobsbawm, E. (1994) *Age of Extremes: The Short Twentieth Century, 1914–1991*.
London: Michael Joseph.

Hoffritz, J. (1997) 'Immer auf den Punkt.' *Wirtschaftswoche*, 16 January 1997, no. 4,
64–5.

Houwers, J. (1994) 'International exchange and programmes and their effects on
institutional planning and management: the administrative perspective.' *Higher
Education Management 6*, 1, 7–23.

Hrbek, R. (1994) 'Die Rolle der Subsidiarität in der Europäische Union.' In R. Hrbek
(ed) *Europäische Bildungspolitik und die Anfordungen des Subsidiaritätsprinzips*.
Baden-Baden: Nomos.

Hughes, J. and Paterson, K. (1994) 'Primary geography and the European dimension.' In B. Marsden and J. Hughes (eds) *Primary School Geography.* London: David Fulton.

Information Society Forum (1996) *Networks for People and their Communities: First Annual Report to the European Commission from the Information Society Forum.* Luxembourg: CORDIS Focus, Supplement 10.

IRDAC (1991) *Skills Shortages in Europe.* Brussels: Industrial Research and Development Advisory Committee of the Commission of the European Communities.

IRDAC (1994) *Quality and Relevance.* Brussels: Industrial Research and Development Advisory Committee of the Commission of the European Communities.

Janne, H. (1973) 'For a community policy in education.' *Bulletin of the European Communities, Supplement 10/73.*

Jensen, C.S., Madsen, J.S. and Due, J. (1995) 'A rôle for a pan-European trade union movement?' *Industrial Relations Journal 26,* 1, 4–18.

Kassim, H. (1996) 'Policy networks, networks and European policy making: a sceptical view.' *West European Politics 17,* 4, 15–27.

Kay, J.A. (1991) 'Myths and realities of the European market.' In J. Anderson and M. Ricci (eds) *Society and Social Science: A Reader.* Milton Keynes: Open University Press.

Kops, S. and Hänsch, K. (1996) 'The internal market needs a European market for skill certification.' *Cedefop Info,* 2/1996, 1–3.

Kozek, T. (1994) 'Wandlungen der internationalen Ausbildungshilfe für Polen.' In QUEM-report 16, *Transformation durch Qualifikation: Weiterbildung im Übergang zur Marktwirtschaft.* Berlin: QUEM.

Kreher, A. (1996) 'Forschungsforum zeit zwanzig Jahren.' *Eumagazin 10,* 28–9.

Kuper, B.-O. (1994) 'The green and white papers of the European Union: the apparent goal of reduced social benefits.' *Journal of European Social Policy 4,* 2, 129–37.

Larkin, C. (1993) 'Non-governmental organisations – their role in European policy.' In *Partners or Adversaries? The Voluntary Sector's Developing Relations with Government.* Belfast: Northern Ireland Council for Voluntary Action.

Leitner, E. (1993) 'Developments in European community politics of higher education: observations from outside.' In C. Gellert (ed) *Higher Education in Europe.* London: Jessica Kingsley Publishers.

Lenaerts, K. (1994) 'Education in European community law after Maastricht.' *Common Market Law Review 31,* 7–41.

Lesniak, I. and Le Billon, V. (1996) 'À quoi sont servi les milliards de l'Europe pour l'Est?' *L'Expansion,* 24 October 1996, no. 535, 122–4.

Lloyd, C. (1993) 'European community policy and the market.' *Journal of Computer Assisted Learning 9,* 3, 86–91.

Lundborg, P. (1995) 'Experiences from the integrated Nordic labour market.' *Vocational Training 4,* 46–51.

McCallum, S. (1995) 'The European university – a structural challenge.' *International Higher Education 1,* 34–9.

McGrew, A. (1992) 'A global society?' In S. Hall, D. Held and T. McGrew (eds) *Modernity and its Futures.* Cambridge: Polity Press.

McMahon, B.M.E. (1990) 'Case Law: Case 379/87, Groener v. Minister for Education and the City of Dublin Vocational Education Committee.' *Common Market Law Review 27*, 129–39.

McMahon, J. (1995) *Education and Culture in European Community Law.* London: Athlone Press.

McNay, I. (1995) 'Universities going international: choices, cautions and conditions.' In P. Blok (ed) *Policy and Policy Implementation in Internationalisation of Higher Education.* Amsterdam: European Association for International Education.

Mangan, I. (1993) 'The influence of EC membership on Irish social policy and social services.' In S.Ó. Cinnéide (ed) *Social Europe: EC Social Policy and Ireland.* Dublin: Institute of European Affairs.

Marsden, D. (1993) 'Skills and the single European market.' *Skills Focus 2*, 1–3.

Marsden, D. (1994) 'The integration of European labour markets.' In D. Marsden (ed) *European Integration and the European Labour Market*, Supplement 1/94 to Social Europe.

Matthews, A. (1994) *Managing the EU Structural Funds in Ireland.* Cork: Cork University Press.

Meehan, E. (1993) *Citizenship and the European Community.* London: Sage.

Ministère des Affaires Étrangères (1995) *La France dans le Monde.* Paris: Ministère des Affaires Étrangères.

Morrison, T.R. (1995) 'Global transformation and the search for a new educational design.' *International Journal of Lifelong Education 14*, 3, 188–213.

Mulcahy, D.G. (1992) 'Promoting the European dimension in Irish education.' *Irish Educational Studies 11*, 179–90.

Murphy, D. (1995) *Comenius: A Critical Reassessment of his Life and Work.* Dublin: Irish Academic Press.

Neale, P. (1994) 'Expert interest groups and the European Commission: professional influence on EC legislation.' *International Journal of Sociology and Social Policy 14*, 6/7, 1–24.

NICC (1992) *Thinking European: Ideas for Integrating a European Dimension into the Curriculum.* Belfast: Northern Ireland Curriculum Council.

*Official Journal of the European Communities.* Commission of the European Communities, Brussels.

Organisation for Economic Co-operation and Development (1973) *Recurrent Education: A Strategy for Lifelong Learning.* OECD, Paris.

Otala, L. (1992) *European Approaches to Lifelong Learning.* Geneva/Brussels: Council of European Rectors/European Round Table of Industrialists.

Papandreou, V. (1992) 'Foreword/Préface.' In ERASMUS Bureau (ed) *Directory of Higher Education Institutions in the European Community.* London: Kogan Page.

Paterson, L. (1994) *The Autonomy of Modern Scotland.* Edinburgh: Edinburgh University Press.

Paterson, W.E. (1994) 'Britain and the European Union revisited: some unanswered questions.' *Scottish Affairs 9*, 1–12.

Paterson, W.E. (1996) 'Beyond semi-sovereignty: the New Germany in the New Europe.' *German Politics 5*, 2, 167–84.

Pollack, M.A. (1994) 'Creeping competence: the expanding agenda of the European Community.' *Journal of Public Policy 14*, 2, 95–145.

Preston, J (1994) *Regional Policy.* London: Longman/Spicers European Policy Briefings.

Rath, F. (1996) 'Globalisierungsprozess und gesellschaftlicher Wandel.' *Eumagazin, 1,* 2, 18–19.

Rees, T. (1995) *Women and the EC Training Programmes.* Bristol: School for Advanced Urban Studies.

Rees, T. (1996) 'Women and the European Commission's training programmes.' *Adults Learning 8,* 2, 35–7.

Reynolds, D. (1995) 'Why are the Asians so good at learning?' *Demos Quarterly 6,* 35–6.

Riché-Magnier, M. and Metthey, J. (1995) 'Société de l'information: "new deal" libéral ou nouveau modèle de societé?' *Revue du marché commun et de l'union européenne 390,* 417–22.

Room, G. (1995) 'Poverty and social exclusion: the new European agenda for policy and research.' In G. Room (ed) *Beyond the Threshold: The Measurement and Analysis of Social Exclusion.* Bristol: Policy Press.

Rüttgers, J. (1996) Europäische Forschungspolitik: Rede an der Universität Leiden, 22 February 1996.

Ryba, R. (1992) 'Toward a European dimension in education: intention and reality in European Community policy and practice.' *Comparative Education Review 36,* 1, 10–24.

Santer, J. (1995a) *Address to the Confederation of British Industry, London, 16 May 1995.* Brussels: EUROPA News.

Santer, J. (1995b) *Discours de M. Santer à la conférence de l'UNICE, Madrid, 5 December 1995.* Brussels: EUROPA News.

Schüller, J. (1995) 'Aktuelle Tendenzen in der EU-Forschungs- und Bildungspolitik.' *Beiträge zur Hochschulforschung 3,* 219–34.

Schuringa, T. (1988) 'Audi-visual and television technology: towards a Community policy.' *Vocational Training,* 1/1988, 3–6.

Scott, P. (1995) *The Meanings of Mass Higher Education.* Buckingham: Open University Press.

Sereny, G. (1995) *Albert Speer: His Battle with Truth.* London: Macmillan.

Sharp, M. (1993) 'The community and new technologies.' In J. Lodge (ed) *The European Community and the Challenge of the Future.* London: Pinter.

Simpson, E.G. (1996) 'The issue of transnational certification.' *Georgia Center Quarterly 12,* 1, 6–7.

Smith, M.L. and Corrigan, J. (1995) 'Relations with Europe.' In R. Breen, P. Devine and G. Robinson (eds) *Social Attitudes in Northern Ireland: The Fourth Report 1994–1995.* Belfast: Appletree Press.

Springer, B. (1993) *The Social Dimension of 1992.* New York: Greenwood.

Sultana, R.G. (1995) 'A uniting Europe, a dividing education? Euro-centrism and the curriculum.' *International Studies in Sociology of Education 5,* 2, 115–44.

Szerszynski, B., Lash, S. and Wynne, B. (1996) 'Ecology, realism and the social sciences.' In S. Lash, B. Szerszynski and B. Wynne (eds) *Risk, Environment and Modernity: Towards a New Ecology.* London: Sage.

Tait, A. (1994) 'From a domestic to an international organisation: the Open University, the United Kingdom, and Europe.' *Higher Education in Europe 19,* 2, 82–93.

Tait, A. (1996) 'Open and distance learning policy in the European Union, 1985–1995.' *Higher Education Policy 9,* 3, 221–38.

Teague, P. (1996) 'The European Union and the Irish peace process.' *Journal of Common Market Studies 34*, 4, 549–70.

Teichler, U. and Maiworm, F. (1994) *Transition to Work: The Experiences of Former ERASMUS Students*. London: Jessica Kingsley Publishers.

Teichler, U. (1996a) 'Student mobility in the framework of ERASMUS: findings of an evaluation study.' *European Journal of Education 31*, 2, 153–79.

Teichler, U. (1996b) 'The British involvement in European higher education programmes: findings of evaluation studies on ERASMUS, human capital and mobility and TEMPUS.' In *The Thirtieth Anniversary Series*. London: Society for Research in Higher Education.

Thatcher, M. (1993) *The Downing Street Years*. London: HarperCollins.

Thurow, L. (1994) 'New game, new rules, new strategies.' *Journal of the Royal Society of Arts 142*, 5454, 50–3.

Tierlinck, M. (1994) 'The European Union and the family.' *Social Europe*, 1/94, 9–12.

Turner, B.S. (1990) 'Outline of a theory of citizenship.' *Sociology 24*, 2, 189–217.

Underwood, J. and Brown, J. (eds) (1997) *Integrated Learning Systems: Potential into Practice*. London: Heinemann.

United Kingdom Government (1992) *UK Response to Commission Memoranda on Vocational Training in the European Community in the 1990s and Open Distance Learning in the European Community*. Sheffield: Employment Department.

Urwin, D.W. (1995) *The Community of Europe: A History of European Integration since 1945*. London: Longman.

Venturelli, S. (1993) 'The imagined transnational public sphere in the European Community's broadcast philosophy: implications for democracy.' *European Journal of Communication 8*, 4, 491–518.

Waddington, S. (1996) 'The European white paper and women's education and training.' *Adults Learning 8*, 2, 33–4.

Walsh, J. (1996) 'Multinational management strategy and human resource decision making in the single European market.' *Journal of Management Studies 33*, 5, 633–48.

Watson, K. (1996) 'Banking on key reforms for educational development: a critique of the world bank review.' *Mediterranean Journal of Educational Studies 1*, 1, 43–61.

Werner, H. (1994) 'Economic change, the labour market and migration in the single European market.' In D. Marsden (ed) *European Integration and the European Labour Market*, Supplement 1/94 to Social Europe.

Wilson, L. (1993) 'TEMPUS as an instrument of reform.' *European Journal of Education 28*, 4, 429–36.

Wilterdink, N. (1993) 'The European ideal: an examination of European and national identity.' *Archives européennes de sociologie 34*, 119–36.

Witte, B. de (1993) 'Higher education and the contribution of the European Community.' In C. Gellert (ed) *Higher Education in Europe*. London: Jessica Kingsley Publishers.

Wolf, A. (1995) 'Vocational qualifications in Europe: the emergence of common assessment themes.' In L. Bash and A. Green (eds) *World Yearbook of Education 1995: Youth, Education and Work*. London: Kogan Page.

Working Group on Work Organisation (1995) 'Flexibility and work organisation.' *Social Europe*, Supplement 1/95.

Wulf-Mathies, M. (1995) 'Committee of the regions – milestone or millstone.' *European Information Service*, 159, May, 11–13.

# Subject Index

# Author Index